The Iron Hostage

A forthright and true account of the first
British civilian kidnapped and held hostage in
Iraq

Gary Teeley

THIS BOOK IS DEDICATED TO

MY MUM PATRICIA, FOREVER MY SUPPORTER.

CONTENTS

Acknowledgments

1	Prologue	Pg 1
2	Masirah Island	Pg 3
3	Down To Business	Pg 5
4	Jordan Here We Come	Pg 10
5	Arriving In Iraq	Pg 14
6	Location Number 1 – Nasiriyah Bound	Pg 21
7	Up And Running	Pg 28
8	Learning Curves	Pg 35
9	Time To Say Goodbye	Pg 44
10	On My Way Home	Pg 48
11	Back To Qatar	Pg 50
12	Back To Iraq	Pg 53
13	Working Life Without Paul	Pg 63
14	Utter Mayhem	Pg 68
15	Location Number 2 – Settling In	Pg 80
16	The Battle	Pg 88
17	Back To Reality	Pg 93
18	On The Move for My Birthday	Pg 102
19	Just Kill Me	Pg 104
20	Location Number 3 – Birthday Gift	Pg 115

21   Location Number 4 – Video Time   Pg 123

22   Location Number 5 – Fly Fury   Pg 127

23   Location Number 6 – What A Mess   Pg 151

24   So Close to Freedom   Pg 159

25   Freedom Is Calling   Pg 174

26   Arriving At Shaibah Base Basra   Pg 186

27   A New Life   Pg 199

28   Come On You Irons   Pg 204

29   Life Is Good   Pg 211

ACKNOWLEDGMENTS

This book could not have been written without the following people that were in but also came into my life in one way or another. I thank each and every one of them from the bottom of my heart… I would not be here without you and for that I will be eternally grateful.

My Mum
Mr. A
Mr. H
Jassim Al Misnad
The British Military
The Local Sheikhs of Nasiriyah
Sylvie Law
Alan Pardew, Angela & West Ham Football Club
And to all those that never gave up on me

1 PROLOGUE

APRIL 8, 2004

Mr. H walked over to me, he sat down near me with a glass of sulaimani lit up a fag and just sat there. What is his fucking problem? Why won't he talk to me for fucks sake? Eventually he turned to me, took hold of my hand and said in the normal broken English, "Mr. Gerry will not go home now but inshallah tomorrow I think but we have a big problem."

I closed my eyes, bit my top lip and dropped my shoulders, I fucking knew it wouldn't be today and so did he, so why oh fucking why can he not just fucking tell me, why is he lying to me, tell me the fucking truth!

He carried on, "Mr. Gerry you know Ali Baba men who take your ring and other things, they are looking for you, many of them are searching for you."

I replied, "Why are they looking for me now, you have me now and I think you are the same group of people yes?"

He came back, "Mr. Gerry these men are very bad men, things have changed and we have to move you, if they find you this is a big problem for you and me, so let's go now, we have to move fast."

I wanted to know more, "Mr. H, how many men are looking for me and if they find me, they will kill me? What will happen you have to tell me now?"

Mr. H looked me bolt right in the eyes, "Gerry, if they find you, they will kill you or sell you to more bad men, we have to go another place, they will come and search my brother's house, I'm sure. Gerry there are many now in Nasiriyah looking for you, maybe around three hundred men, they will look day and night to get you, this is very serious my friend."

I was up on my feet and was allowed to have my white polo shirt on, with jeans and trainers, I would be back to my normal dress.

My heart started to pound big time, just as I thought this was all coming to an end and now, I'm getting involved in deep political shit, someone wants to kill me or trade me to some sad fucker who wants to parade me on television in his cowardly fashion or maybe they will want to behead me on video! My body heat was turned up within seconds, I'm fucking shit scared, I can't get out of this mess and I can't take no more, I am not going home, I can feel it, nowhere to turn!

2 MASIRAH ISLAND

In the Summer of 2002, I found myself on Masirah Island, which is a small Island just off the East coast of Oman, 100 kilometres northeast of the Oman – Yemen border. The main business on the island was a military base which was the home to the Omani and American Air Forces. Abdullah was a long-term Omani friend of mine who I originally met in Dubai. Abdullah asked me if I would be willing to do some work for him.

What I thought was going to be a straightforward design for a laundry on the island, turned out to have some adventurous twists and not as simple as first thought but this is the Middle East, anything is possible.

I worked on the project with a French friend of mine, Yannick. Yannick worked for a laundry equipment supplier out of Dubai, so we worked together on the Island for three weeks. He was so easy to work with, he did not speak a lot, and he was a quiet character but I used to bring the worst out of him, we used to have a great laugh.

After the installation and staff training it was back to Dubai but for now my mind drifts back to the lovely Masirah Island. How could I have considered rejecting the offer from Abdullah, such an amazing island, peaceful and tranquil. Masirah Island is 649km2, has a population of approximately 12,000 people and we did not have much to do except work, eat, drink and enjoy the amazing beaches with my turtle friends, what a great sight and experience. They would come ashore by what looked like the hundreds and all that was in their minds was to lay their eggs.

Abdullah worked for Oman Municipality, he was the top man at the municipality and he had his fingers in all sorts of pies. The laundry was built

3

to serve the military contracts he had, best of luck to him, a great man he is. Abdullah knew I liked my football, so he asked me to get involved with the school football team.

"Why not?" I said. So, in the early evening when the sun went down, I would be playing on a dusty surface, not the flattest of surfaces but the kids did not care to much and after all it was not every day of the week that an Englishman was in town and willing to play football with them. The kids all knew my name and they wanted me to be on the A Team. The parents would come and watch all the fun roll out before them. Special times for sure.

Little Omar became very fond of having me around and his young Dad told me so and always thanked me for spending time with the kids, he knew it was special for him and he was clever to get the most attention from me. As usual, wherever I went I took that famous claret and blue shirt of West Ham with me and young Omar from day one seemed to have his sights set on the shirt and it was just a matter of time. Just before I left, the last time we played, I did not wear it and he asked me why I did not have it on. When the game finished, I went to my bag and gave him a nicely wrapped parcel, it had been washed and folded for him. When he opened it, his eyes lit up and began to jump up and down, shouting out the name on the shirt, "Di Canio, Di Canio!" A West Ham fan on Masirah Island, what was the world coming to?

Not sure if little Omar was going to thank me in 2003 after the relegation, but for that day he paraded that shirt until the sun went down, sharing his excitement with his Dad. Nice memories. An island full of friendly people, no frills living and happy with the tonic of the deep blue sea around them. Thank you Abdullah for having me, what a time we had.

3 DOWN TO BUSINESS

After being in Dubai since 2001, then arriving in Qatar in the August of 2003 it was going to be interesting with work to be found and a new life ahead.

I had met Paul Johnson in the November of 2002 and Paul was working for Qatar International Trading.

Qatar International Trading (QIT) was a well-known group in Qatar and had many divisions but the focus and strength was dealing with the American forces, based on two different camps, Al Udeid and Al Sailiya. Having already performed a turnkey project on behalf of QIT in Qatar, a purpose-built facility for laundry services for the US forces, it would not be too long until the next project came along.

A couple of weeks went by, I was sitting in Paul's House weighing up my options to which company to join in Qatar. Paul came back to the house at lunchtime bringing with him a bargain bucket from KFC, so we started to get that down our neck.

Paul turned to me and said, "You know I told you that QIT has offices in Iraq now, one in Baghdad and the other in Nasiriyah?" I just nodded as I was tucking in to a hot and spicy portion of wing. Paul continued, "Well they have just received a solicitation to tender for laundry services and Jassim has just printed them off, apparently they are in my office for you and me to look over." As I swallowed that spicy chunk, I coughed slightly and said, "Like who has asked me to look at them? I will take a look if Jassim does this correctly, is he paying?"

Right on cue Paul came back in one of his typical Californian moments, partially chewing a wasp and said, "Yeah ok ok, God damn it, sure I will put you in front of Jassim Gary, damn fucking Brit!"

A winning smirk came across my face and it would be one of many through our love and hate relationship. There were many who used to think Paul and I were like a cat and dog, and we were, but we were also the best of mates for sure and despite the cat and dog tag we worked very well, we each had our strengths and weaknesses but we were an awesome team. Paul made a quick phone call to Jassim and the meeting was arranged for the afternoon.

Jassim Al Misnad, a Qatari national, CEO of Qatar International Trading. I had only met Jassim in passing one day, quite a simple and straightforward man, did not talk too much, was to the point which suited me.

We sat down and went through the formalities of what he wanted me to do. He had been happy with all my previous work for him and it was quite simple to conclude. He did however state a very important and interesting point, for sure I had to consider the unknown and he allowed me twenty minutes to think it over. The simple part had been done but I was curious why he had offered me such a lucrative deal; I did not question it but the statement he made at the end made it easy for me to understand why the deal was going top drawer.

Jassim said, "Gary, if you are able to tender for this business and win the deal, you have to go to Iraq with Paul. I think you will have to go to Dubai for a few weeks to mobilise all this, you will have to meet Red Sea for a prefabricated building and use all the contacts you have for the equipment you need and purchase everything you need in Dubai because it has to be shipped on trailers to Iraq. You and Paul will fly to Iraq, arrive in Iraq before the goods arrive, put the building together, set it all up, teach and train the staff and manage the business for me."

I had never been to Iraq before and I had never served time in the military. I had been to other countries such as Oman, Syria and Lebanon but those visits were not at a time just after a war and they were not occupied by foreign forces, it was unknown. I made my choices, decided I would go, the project was interesting and many challenges ahead, the financial part was attractive and an adventure with experiences was on the agenda for sure.

Tender documents in hand, Paul and I worked our way through the pages and put pen to paper, considering all the risks and costs, we came up with the plan of attack. A week later the proposal was submitted and now it was a waiting game to see what materialised if anything. I did not have time to think about the eventual outcome of the process as I was busy looking at options to where my next move would take me.

Qatar was on the verge of entering the good times, the country in general was buoyant across all sectors and everybody wanted a slice of the cake of the American military business, whether that was in Qatar, Iraq or Afghanistan.

The second week of September 2003 I was in a cybercafé, the phone rang and it was Paul. "Hey where you at Gary?" I replied, "I'm at the café, having a brew and doing some stuff, what you up to, what's new?" Paul responded "Man, you better get packing we are on our way to Dubai in a few days because next month your sorry ass has to go to Iraq, damn Gary we won that contract and Jassim is well happy, it's on."

Paul and I booked flights to Dubai and we expected to be on the ground for a week or so. The laundry facility shell was being manufactured by Red Sea out of Jebel Ali, Dubai. The dimensions could be no bigger than 8 x 12 meters (96 square meters). Red Sea would be making the building in two halves (4 x 12meters), each half transported on a flatbed truck from Dubai to Iraq. It would be delivered to Baghdad first and then from their it would move South to Nasiriyah and delivered to Tallil Air Base.

The design was a tight fit to say the least, right down to the last millimetre and no stone could be left unturned. The packing list was unreal to be honest, right down to crazy items such as safety pins. Finding an equipment supplier in Dubai who had the correct technical specifications in stock would prove difficult but through my contacts we made it work. The lead time to get the facility up and running was tight, time was not on our side, the days and hours were going to be long but we had to get it right. The hard work we put into the organisation was critical and proved to be the case when we arrived in Iraq, buying things in Iraq is not easy, whether that be the availability or the high prices, the mobilisation in general went like clockwork.

On our return to Qatar, I sat down and went over the shopping list again and again. As well as the building being shipped out of Dubai to Iraq by road, we had to arrange a shipping container full of goods. These goods included laundry powders, fabric softener, all sorts of stationary, engineering tools, uniforms and working boots for the workers and a few other luxuries such as Walkers Crisps amongst others.

Red Sea in Jebel Ali, Dubai had been the company to manufacture the building and support the whole logistics plan, great company to work with and I would be meeting one of their main guys again in Iraq an American national who I would end up driving crazy at times, more of him later.

The estimated time of arrival of all the goods was given, which meant Paul and I could plan the flights to Iraq and we were looking at mid-October. The goods would be moved out of Dubai to Saudi Arabia, on to Jordan and then across the border to Iraq.

I never had a worry about the goods arriving at the border of Jordan – Iraq in good order but from the moment they crossed the border, in Iraq, I was sceptical how they would survive the journey from the north of Iraq down to the south of Iraq. The shipping container was placed on a ship in Dubai, best choice for the sea to look after it rather than the road, bandit country would have a field day getting their hands on my goods.

Our own departure plans had been made. We planned to fly from Qatar to Jordan and spend a few days in Jordan as we had some locals to meet and needed to book our flights in to Iraq through Royal Jordanian Airlines.

Royal Jordanian Airlines at that time were the only company flying to Iraq and commercial flights were crazy dollars, they must have made a killing during this period. Flying us into Baghdad International Airport in an aircraft with an elastic band propelling us there, not my first choice to be honest. We knew we had a little relaxation time so maybe we could fit in some tourist time before entering the land of the unknown. QIT staff in Iraq were supporting us on the ground in Iraq, making various support services ready and I knew they had arranged our accommodation, I would be living in a villa in Nasiriyah whilst I was in Iraq, now I was considering my venture.

The Coalition Forces had seized control of Iraq three months before I was assigned the project and to the best of my knowledge and due diligence, I believed the country was relatively safe. There had been some isolated incidents and attacks on military positions, convoys and civilians targeted from time to time but it would not stop me from working in Iraq. I knew that I would be spending most of my time at work on Tallil Air Base and not too much time to myself and of course we would be staying in the general population in a nice villa in quite a good area of Nasiriyah.

My decision had been made already but as the weeks progressed, I paid more attention to the news, trying to keep myself updated to the changes. I was not going to change my mind; I was going to finish the project but I had to make plans.

I sat down to write out a will of testament and handed it over to Essam who also worked for QIT in Qatar and was not travelling with us. Essam became a good friend of mine, a Jordanian national with a great sense of humour and for a big built man, had the personality of a gentle giant, truly nice man but did love a glass or ten of Jack Daniels or Jim Beam.

It is quite an experience sitting down and writing a will on the back of travelling to a country but Iraq is not just another country. From the first day of Paul mentioning this project to me, the unknown was always there and it grew day by day, from the reality of what I had signed up for.

The facility was so much different to the others I had designed before, the preparations to mobilise like no other because it is not easy to access supplies in Iraq and then on top of that you have the security issues. I had been to many countries in the Middle East since 2001 and Iraq was going to be added to that list. The unknown was the surprise package though, I wasn't scared of going, I knew I would be switched on, after all I was going to a country that had been deprived for years by a dictator and money speaks volumes when you are in need, children have to be fed and a roof over heads has to be given. I read up on the history of Iraq to try and understand it more, tribal for sure over the years, with many religious sites all over the country and one in particular in Nasiriyah that I would learn about in my future.

4 JORDAN HERE WE COME

October the 13th 2003, Paul and I step onto an aeroplane and the destination was Amman, Jordan. Arriving in Amman, we grabbed a taxi to take us to the Intercontinental Hotel where we would be staying for four nights.

The following day we had to book our flights to Baghdad and the only airline we could use was Royal Jordanian Wings out of Amman Civil Airport. The flights could only be paid for in American Dollars, so Paul and I went along to their local office. We took a ticket and waited until we were called and did not have to wait too long.

We sat down at this desk with a nice smiling lady. After exchanging information, the lady sparked up with her verdict, "Gentlemen the flight leaves at 7am on October 16th from Amman Civil Airport and the total fare for one-way travel to Baghdad is $6,000 US Dollars, which is three thousand dollars each." Paul and I simultaneously brought our heads back, opened our eyes and swiftly turned to look at each other in a world of shock. After restoring his composure Paul placed his hand in his newly found man bag/pouch and produced $6,000 US Dollars, brand new off the press in $100 US Dollar bills. Tickets printed, top money paid, so now that's me on the plane and can't see me pulling out now and waving goodbye to that sort of money for a one-and-a-half-hour flight on a twenty-three-seater aircraft… geez that is some serious profit taking place.

That night, I sat with Paul and slipped quite a few glasses of Jim Beam down my throat with some nice flavoured South American cigarillos, a nice combination which relaxed me enough to take Paul to task on a few issues I had.

In conversations with Paul, he made it clear that we would always have security wherever we were, travelling in the cars and at the accommodation. Paul had a past with the American military, he was a soldier himself and served as a Doctor in the American Army, not that you would have known because as far as I was concerned, he knew fuck all about medical shit, me on the other hand had no Military background, just a few years in the British Police Force.

I took him to task again and asked him the security plans and his reply was swift, "Gary, you ask me that one more time I will shoot you myself, stop bitching me about this and trust me, damn." I replied as normal, "Fuck you, make sure you don't forget and fuck up. If I am not happy with what I see I will let you know prompt." All I got back was a chuntering under his breath and a deep forehead frown with a side stare, followed by a smirk as he knew I was 'no/yes' man to him.

The plan on arrival to Iraq, we had planned to stay in Baghdad for a few days in an area called Al Mansoor and wait there until a man from Red Sea would arrive, we would then travel down to Nasiriyah and set up camp there in preparation for the goods to arrive.

I did not want to be in Baghdad any longer than I needed to be, Nasiriyah in the southeast would be far safer and I wanted to get on with the project so I could finalize it all and get back to the UK to enjoy Christmas.

The next day we had a lovely breakfast in the hotel and then decided to try and find a taxi who could take us on a guided tour and we got lucky with a young Jordanian lad called Maher. We offered him $50 US Dollars for the duration, sat down with him and made sure he knew the plan for the day. He was happy with the schedule, so off we went.

We asked Maher to take us in and around Petra, allow to visit the place where it is said that Moses looked out on the promised land and then onto the Dead Sea to have a float about on the water.

The views at Mount Nebo were breathtaking to be honest but I could not quite buy into the other parts of the story that were scrolled all over the rest of the museum we went into but the views were something else, very pretty.

Then we had the visit to the Dead Sea to look forward to and have an education and experience in doing so. After stripping off down to our shorts we made our way to the shoreline of the Dead Sea. It was a boiling hot day and we were ready for the plunge. I had read about the Dead Sea and how dense it was with salt, so I was prepared for the moment, well for most of it.

Rumour has it that the mud of the Dead Sea is very good for your skin and so I decided to go for the all over body mask, top to bottom in this mud, sat on the side of this bank plastering it all over me. As quick as the wet mud was going on it was drying out on my body, I must have looked a right tit!

I was not aware that Paul was going to try and reinvent the wheel today. The clue of the Dead Sea is in the title, it is dead and not a lot of things can survive in it due to the density created by the extreme high levels of the salt. The water feels like cooking oil to the touch. Paul thought it would be a good idea to make entry into the water by diving! What is he like?!

As his body hit the water's surface, he kind of bobbed and bounced back quite quickly, like a yoyo effect, because your body just wants to float on the greasy surface and then he went into a frenzy because his eyes were stinging from the salt and he had to get to the freshwater showers to rinse his eyes from the burning salts!... this is a doctor; I will have you know! I helped him to the shore and then he ran for his life to the shower to rinse the salt from his eyes, all the time he was whining like a bitch. Quite funny to see if I'm honest and I was pissing myself with laughter.

Paul returned to the water and stood beside me as I started to rinse the mud off from me. He tried to defend his action but I just stood laughing and smiling. The banter was to the full for a few minutes.

Paul was standing quite close to me and I started to have a not so pleasant feeling. My backside was on fire, my ring piece was stinging like crazy and as I bitched to Paul, he started to laugh and agreed he was suffering the same fate. Both of us made a rush to the fresh cold-water showers on the shore and the relief of the washdown was amazing. We returned to the changing rooms, had a nice clean shower, got dressed and jumped into our awaiting taxi where Maher dropped us back to the hotel.

A nice evening meal was washed down with Jim Beam and my newfound friends, American cigarillos to relax me before going to bed not too late. We had to rise at 0300 hrs to catch a flight at 0700 hrs.

We checked out of the hotel and jumped into Maher's taxi again to take us to the airport and on arrival a weird feeling happened, we were wondering why the airport was like a ghost town? Hang on a minute, this does not make sense, an airport that has its front doors locked? Out came the flight tickets.

As we looked at the tickets telling us clear in black and white, "Amman Civil Airport, yella Maher my friend quickly to the other airport! How long it will take us?" Maher did not look back, just made the choice of slapping his toe on the gas, "It will take me forty-five minutes I'm sure no more, it is ok Habibi (Habibi means my good friend) we have plenty of time."

Well, what a start! Is somebody trying to give me a subtle warning here? Typical we get the wrong airport but luckily, we started out earlier than needed.

We arrived at 0530 hrs and made our way quickly into the small grounds of the airport but I made sure Paul got it in the neck for not checking the tickets and I got a Paul reply, "Don't start your whining like a bitch!"

The approach and front entrance of the airport reminded me so much of Wellingborough train station, looking like nothing had been replaced or renovated since 1935. That smoked brick look, ornate woodwork, complete with bulky wood swing doors. The inside of the airport was extremely small, six hundred square meters at the most, rows of seats against the walls and central to the room. In one corner I could see the luggage scanning conveyor and above the doorway a sign stating, 'Departures'.

As I looked around the room there were mainly Arabic families, except for a huddle of men and I knew they all had been booked on the same flight as Paul and me. They all stuck out from the crowd, short haircuts, black holdalls and desert boots. They were all Aussie lads, private security company, ex Aussie military and seemed to be in good spirits. Like me and many others, these lads were on the great gravy train that was leaving for Iraq.

We were only allowed 20kgs in a suitcase plus one piece of hand luggage. I had my briefcase and Paul had his man bag!... love him. The other luggage we took with us had to be loaded into a 4 x 4 Landcruiser and taken from Jordan to Iraq by road. I was not keen on this option but I did not have a lot of choice, the 23-seater aircraft had a restriction on weight and judging by the size of my mates on the aircraft that was a good call!

A message came over the airport tannoy system for all those travelling to Baghdad to make their way to the gate as the aircraft was ready for boarding. A bus drove us to the aeroplane, we boarded, the elastic bands of the propellers started and we taxied to the runway…. there is no going back now Teeley!

5 ARRIVING IN IRAQ

The flight to Baghdad went quickly to be honest and I managed to grab about a thirty-minute nap during which I was stirred by the steward as we were ready for landing. Mission unknown had started.

I had read quite a few incidents where aeroplanes were being shot out of the sky on the approach to Baghdad International Airport. Wonderful! RPG's and mortars had been successful taking down some big birds and as we came down closer to the runway, I just wanted the pilot to get the damn thing down and out of sight.

Moments later we were walking down a smartly placed ladder, led across some tarmac to a receiving area and my eyes quickly pounced on the number of armed guards. A private security company judging by the choice of dress and carrying unique types of guns that are generally seen by these types of companies, unique in their own way. We were directed towards passport control where I had my photo taken and then off, we went to collect our luggage with no scanning. I thought this was weird but many things over the months would be proved to not make much sense either.

We walked out the front entrance of the airport and I was looking for some protection whilst we stood waiting for our taxi. Directly outside of the airport was known as, 'Snipers Alley' and I did not fancy being on the list of those fucked up and shot dead or injured at the entrance.

Immediately to my right was a thick concrete pillar, an excellent place for me to be or maybe back inside, but Paul the numpty just stood in the wide open. I felt fine behind the pillar and could not resist a light-hearted joke, "Hey, let me know when the taxi arrives and I will come out!" Paul replied,

"Don't be a stupid fuck and get here now!"

It's funny, me and Paul are the best of mates but like cat and dog, arguing the fuck about many things and many of those in our company would always ask, "How the fuck are you two best of mates?" Trouble is, Paul was so easy to wind up and who else better than me to take advantage of that situation? I was so used to have him at breaking point with banter and Paul never learned his lesson with me.

Eventually a red GMC pulled up and stepping out from the driving seat was Mike, all six feet four inches, dark grey hair to the base of his neck, early forties but no smile. Fuck my luck, another Paul!

Mike was decked out in a pair of desert boots, bullet proof vest on the outer part of his shirt and combats. Mike was carrying what looked like an MP5 Heckler and Koch with a short stock and strapped to his leg he wore a handgun and looked like a Browning 9mm. Mike walked to the back of the GMC, opened the boot and our luggage was quickly chucked into the back. Mike said "Ok lads let's get going. This place is not the best place to stay for too long. Gary, get yourself in the back seat, no need to buckle up, all the weapons are loaded and safeties are all on, take what you want."

I did not bother entering into too much chat about weapons training at this stage, I just thought let him drive as fast as he can and safely. I stooped low in my seat, making sure the doors were unlocked and keeping the top of my frame below the window level.

At this stage I really knew I was in a completely different world, jokes aside, there had to be about seven or eight loaded weapons under my feet, mainly AK47's and the feeling is quite uncomfortable. On top of that, my mind was thinking that we are being watched and maybe there are gangs plotting an ambush at any stage.

Whether I liked it or not I was already in fear of the surroundings and the thoughts that someone could be now watching us and have a high-powered weapon, or maybe there are many of them who are going to ambush us down this road or shortly just after. It is difficult to hide the fact that your heart beats faster, your body heat changes, hot flushes run over your body and your eyes are constantly scanning everything.

Within five minutes we were on Camp Victory, a huge American military base and I felt safer. I had passed my second test.

Mike started to explain to us that the base had been attacked quite regularly with rocket and mortar attacks; the thought of my safety left me again. We drove around some areas of the base that Mike thought we should know for safety measures and where we should go in the event of an emergency. We then drove onto the offices of QIT.

I soon saw some familiar faces, Bilal, Ahmed and Salam who I knew from Qatar. Bilal and Ahmed were Jordanian, both in their late twenties and had left Qatar for Iraq, looking for the big payoff. Salam, a Qatari had also joined them in search, I'm sure, for a nice pay day. Yet here is a man, since I had known him, who was very loyal to QIT. Salam was a diamond geezer and knew how to have a good laugh also.

We were all stood outside the office block having a cup of tea and grabbing a cigarette or two and then suddenly… BANG, WHOOSH!

I found myself bending at the knees and arms coming up and over my head, crouching down and ready to hit the dirt. "Salam what the fuck was that?" Salam moved slow and cool, placed his hand on my shoulder and said, "Gary look over there, they are blowing up weapons and ammunition they have found, this happens quite a few times a week, relax." I kept my eyes in the direction he was pointing in and this huge plume of grey smoke started to push its way towards the sky, reminding me of the time I watched on television a bomb being dropped on Japan in the 1940's. It could only have been about three kilometres away maximum, but the reality is that the ground shook around my feet and the noise was intense to say the least. I was the only one to jump out my boots, it seemed all the others were so used to it now.

Over the next two hours it happened twice more at the same kind of distance and I was ready for the last one. I saw the red and orange colour on the initial detonation, then the grey plume of smoke, followed by the sound of the explosion and the ground shaking under my feet. I thought to myself, I wonder what this would feel like if I was only fifty meters away. Little did I know in the future I would experience this.

A few hours later we moved out of the base in a Landcruiser, Paul and I were joined by Salam and Ahmed. The car again had quite a few weapons inside, an old AK47 was under my feet and Paul seized the chance to drag it in to his clutches. The conversation then moved on to understanding what type of automatic weapons they all had chosen. Salam and Ahmed both had the 'John Wayne' leg holster, a kind of sling, same as Mike the Brit who picked us up at the Airport. It is quite a funny thing trying to get used to the guns in and around you all the time, a completely different way of living, not really comforting and relaxing to be around.

After a few hundred meters after leaving the base, we came into a built-up area with the streets full of children playing in their rag like clothes and their parents going about their everyday life, shop fronts looking like they had taken a battering over the years. Streets full of rubbish, dirt and dust filling the walkways and the roadside lined with derelict looking houses.

Many of the houses seemed to have the same pebble dash design but not to be confused with the pebble dashed council houses that were built in the UK in the 1950's, this pebble dash had come from ammunition being blasted at them. Everywhere I looked there were piles of building remains, heaps of rubble and I was not too sure if this was caused by military hardware or building projects. I would go for the first option. There was wasteland full of rubbish, scattered about with stray cats and dogs scavenging for food scraps, locals searching and collecting scrap metal and/or cardboard to either recycling or use to patch up the house.

Five minutes later we pulled on to a carriageway, three lanes of traffic at a steady flow. Most were old clapped-out taxis and by the state of the bodywork and the design I would say most of them were at least thirty years old. I noticed there were many small vans, like your typical minivan fit to carry twelve to fourteen passengers, decorated in a multitude of colours like something from the 'flower power' era. One of the fashion trends in Iraq has to be the windscreen of the vehicle. Whether that is a small crack, to a hole or holes and even completely shattered with a two-inch clear view of what is outside. Unbelievable! In years to come, the sales of replacement windscreens, car horns (as they use them all the time) brake shoes will be huge business. Indicator bulbs, like most of the Arabic world, will stay on the shelf as it seems they don't understand what indicators are used for.

The standard of driving was not a shock to me. The entire Gulf region is the same. White lines that divide lanes and stop lines at a roundabout? Forget it!... they make up their own rules as they go along. Pick up and drop off points are on the roundabouts, its madness for sure.

Ahmed in general was not hanging about, which was just fine by me, let us get to our new home, I needed to eat and clean up. We came off a series of carriageways and began to enter a built-up area and it was busy and chaotic, this area known as Al Mansoor.

Al Mansoor was the area where Mr. Ken Bigley was going to be staying,

Ken was also a civilian worker out of the Gulf States. Ken was taken hostage in September of 2004 with two Americans, Ken unfortunately would not survive his ordeal. I didn't know Ken in person but for me not to know about his ordeal was going to be impossible because of my own future experiences. The BBC contacted me in the September 2004 and wanted to interview me when Ken was being held, I declined the offer to do so out of respect to him and his family. Ironically, I would suffer many sleepless nights when Ken was being held, it brought back memories for me for the first time, I became part of his family and it really fucked my head up. I had a good idea what he was going through and to make matters worse for Ken he was being held by Abu Musab Al-Zarqawi who found the group Jama'at Al-Tawhid Wal-Jihad. These lot were associated with ISIS and Al-Qaeda, not the ideal situation and Zarqawi would see the end of his own life in 2006 in Iraq… Rest in peace Ken.

As we passed through the streets in this area, I began to notice that our car was attracting more interest and the stares had a purpose about them, if the stare could talk it was saying, "What the fuck are you doing in this area, who and what are you?." One thing that did become apparent to me, I could not see any coalition forces around the busy streets. Sure, I could see tanks and personnel carriers set up at the busy intersections off the carriageways and they were all American but it would have been nice to see some bulked-up security near my fixed abode.

We came away from the busy streets and entered a very quiet road, immediately the type of buildings changed dramatically. Either side of the car my eyes were invited to view the plush villas and I was shocked to see the extreme contrast. Moments later Ahmed steered the car to the right and to a stop, before sounding the horn.

A set of solid gates opened and on entering an armed guard greeted us, complete with webbing around his waist which was finely decorated with grenades, he wouldn't have looked out of place as an extra on any Sylvester Stallone film set. He could hardly walk due to his bulged pockets, filled with ammunition and his AK47 slapping against his frame. As I stepped out of the car this guard shouted out to his left, raised his AK47 to his shoulder, pointing it directly in front of him and then panning to his left and right as he was joined by two other guards, all going through the same drills.

Salam ushered me in to the villa and suggested that he would show Paul and I around immediately in case something happened. We needed to know where to go and how to react.

QIT had decided to rent out two villas, side by side, one for management and the other for workers and guards. Each villa was designed in the same way, seven rooms on the ground floor and ten rooms on the first floor. From the first floor there were a small set of stairs that led up to a flat roof. I knew I was going to be in Baghdad for a few days so I wanted to have a good look around, just in case the shit hit the fan, I wanted to know where I could run or hide.

On the ground floor at the rear of the building a solid steel door opened outwards and outside was a pathway, to the left it led to a dead end and to the right an open back garden. The garden was protected by a concrete wall, damn the thing was high, I would estimate it to be 5 meters and on top of the wall was a barbed wire and glass had been set into the concrete for good measure. The state of the garden suggested we did not have a gardener to feed, it was a space for the guard dogs to have a run about.

The dogs stayed on the roof, left to roam free and bark freely. The guards on the roof were the babysitters for the dogs, good to know we had these ugly, snarling K9's up top. To my surprise, the roof housed three serious looking weapons, long rifles supported by a tripod, fearsome looking things that looked like they would spray bad news with big bullets, so we had quite a varied cocktail waiting for those who wanted to try and have a wild party on our rooftop.

From the front door of the villa to the large solid steel gates was a five-meter-wide driveway and stretched a good twenty meters in length. The gates stood about three meters and either side of the gates was a solid concrete wall, not sure three meters being high enough for me, only time would tell.

We ended up being in Baghdad for five days. For 24 hours a day the three-armed guards were at the front of the house, two always walking about and the other was viewing the security screens. There were security cameras all over the place which was a good thing to see.

With not too much to do in the daytime other than keep looking over the plans for assembling the laundry facility, I made it part of my day to go out to the guards on the roof and at the front of the house to make sure they were not sleeping on the job.

All of us who stayed in the villa went to bed with a loaded weapon beside the bed which was quite a funny feeling to someone who had never been involved with guns in his life. There were loaded guns all over the house, if you did not have yours on you, another was not too far away.

My weapons induction course lasted for two hours in the garden. The noise was deafening as the rounds hit the banked soil at the back of the garden, the smell would not leave me for a long time, a smell that I would experience again and for a lot longer in a completely different environment in the not-too-distant future.

I remember two nights where there was some small arms fire, just outside of the villa and other explosive sounds from a distance, quite normal in Iraq. We blow out candles on our birthday cake, they empty a full magazine from an AK47! Thankfully we never had any full-scale attacks on the villas, the days went slow and was pretty boring most of the time, I just wanted to crack on with completing the job.

To hear noises from weapons made my mind go into overdrive, my imagination would kick in, I used to think of the worst at times but they were a good thing and I did not take it for granted that nothing could happen to me. I said to Paul one day, "These Iraqi guards could set us all up, do a deal with a group for a nice pay off!" Paul just lifted his eyebrows and carried on reading his book. Typical! It was different for Paul as he has served in the American Army for twelve years and although he had not experienced firsthand combat, not only did he have the training to see him through it, but I also felt he wanted to experience it, just not at my expense.

Finally, the luggage had arrived from Jordan and along with it an American whose name was Rick. Rick had been assigned by Red Sea out of Dubai, the company who had manufactured the prefabricated building. Rick had been sent to make sure the jigsaw puzzle was going to be assembled correctly plus he had some other business to attend to with other units they had on Tallil Air Base in Nasiriyah.

Rick and the luggage arrived early morning, so I knew it would not be too long before a long wheel-based GMC was loaded up and we would be on our way to Nasiriyah, thank goodness. Rick told me that he planned to be in Iraq for only 7 days but that would change for him, little did I know that he would continuously bitch and moan! Being from America and from the south Rick had this drool. Standing at five feet ten inches and approximately sixteen stone with a grey and brown beard, he reminded me of Stinky Pete from Toy Story 2!

6 LOCATION NUMBER 1 - NASIRIYAH BOUND

We rolled out of the land of leisure in Al Mansoor to make our way south to Nasiriyah, travel time estimated to be four hours. Lovely.

Rick sat with me in the back, Paul in the front passenger seat and the driver was an Iraqi national. I said to Paul, "Where are the guards? Why am I sat in a car with two Americans and an Iraqi but no other cars in front or behind us, we should have a security crew?" I got nothing back in reply from anyone. Paul sat in the front with the sun visor up, so his face was in full view. Stinky Pete had decided it would be a good idea to have his window down probably because he was smoking like a chimney. The car had curtains on the windows and I thought it would be best to have them drawn closed but what is the point when Paul and Stinky Pete are advertising us to the world? Even so I decided to have my drawn shut.

We had to travel right through the very heart of Baghdad or so it seemed. Everywhere looked the same, the telltale signs of bullet holes all over the buildings and children playing on the sides of the street with no shoes and dressed in rags. What a complete shithole, excuse the pun but it did look like a bomb had hit it all. As far as the eye could see, adults and children standing on the side of the road with jugs, bottles, jerry cans and anything else that would hold petrol. Petrol stations had long queues, Iraqi's arguing about who was first in line and how little they believed they should be paying.

The country is bursting at the seam with oil and everyone is struggling to get petrol, what the fuck is going on here?!

We had been in the car for an hour making slow progress. It seemed that every man and his dog wanted to move south today. It was hard going and then suddenly, we came to a standstill. We were on a two-lane road but as usual the locals made four lanes and we could not move two inches to the left, right, backwards or forwards. Either side of the road you could not move for the busy restaurants, market stalls selling fruit and vegetables, small industrial units filled with hustle and bustle, the whole area was filled with activity. Although we had the air conditioning on in the car, I started to feel very agitated about the situation. For the first time on this car journey I felt at risk, my heart started to pound and my breathing became heavier, I did not like it. I tried to leverage my body about to see if I could see what was going on ahead of us but with no success however my movements for some reason started to get more attention from outside, stares increased. I sat nervously thinking that anyone could easily just walk past the car and easily pick us off, we are sitting targets for sure.

It was getting out of control, I started talking to myself, running through drills in my head, thinking of which way I would run, where would I go? Would I try and hide somewhere until darkness fell? Fuck all this, why is my imagination taking over me? I'm sweating like a twat, full on hot flushes, this is not fucking normal and I sense we can be taken out any second!

Then relief! The traffic started to move and moments later I could see a bridge ahead and at the entrance to the bridge I could see it was manned by American soldiers. As we approached Paul wound down his window and one soldier said to Paul, "You will have to go back that way where you have just come from.." Paul quickly responded, "Sir, we have an appointment at Tallil Air Base with Colonel Ladston, there are two Americans in the car and one British.." The soldier looked into the car, smiled and just said, "Ok you are good to go Sir, no issues, have a good one." He stood to one side and allowed us to pass.

Extra relief for sure but also quite bizarre that this soldier actually believed Paul's words, we could be anybody! We were allowed through without any ID checks. Nice one but that didn't make much sense to me. Either way.... we were back on our journey.

For the next three hours we continued to make our way down to Nasiriyah and part of the journey took us through Najaf, not knowing at that time a local and prominent figure named Muqtada Al Sadr would want to try and know me better. Muqtada Al Sadr being a Shia Cleric, close friends with Hezbollah and Iran.

For the best part of the journey, the road was a two-way scenario with the odd part of a dual carriageway, desert around us with the odd house here and there. The roadside was littered with burnt out tanks, personnel carriers, jeeps, aeroplanes, a massive metal graveyard the length and breadth of the country.

The driver let us know that we were now entering the outskirts of Nasiriyah. The lay of the land was similar to the rest of what I had seen in the country, the only difference is that it looked a quieter place than Baghdad. Before we knew it, he was pulling over to the side of the road in front of a set of large gates, the gates being part of a wall surrounding a large villa. To the left of the villa was some waste land that had piles of rubbish, a pack of dogs and to the left of that, oh my God, I could not believe what I saw, an open fronted laundry shop… well let's say 'shack'.

All I could see was a small washing machine/dryer, with an ironing table to press clothes and something that had an appearance of an open bread oven but why would you have an open bread oven in a laundry? I would find out later.

The 'bread oven' was actually a man-made boiler which produced steam for working the steam press.

The only problem is that the fuel was paraffin. Without going into the design of this death trap boiler, Paul came to me after just a couple of days and said to me "Fuck me! Smell these clothes man, they smell like petrol or diesel, what can it be?" I looked up at him and said, "Stupid fucker I told you not to take your clothes to that laundry because of his pressing machine, the paraffin he uses comes through his pipework with the live steam! It's paraffin! So don't smoke or sit near others who are smoking!" Paul retorted "Well fuck you Gary, you didn't fully explain that to me and why did the housekeeper take them there? "I responded as usual with gusto "Ah ok so now it's my fault because I didn't write it all down! Fuck off numpty and go pick a fight elsewhere, dumb septic! "Paul sighed, "Yeah, yeah and stop saying septic because you are going to get me and Rick in deep water with others on the base if you carry on with your bullshit Brit talk!" I could not help but laugh because his shirts stunk to high heaven of paraffin! It was going to take a bloody good soaking in vinegar and baking soda to get rid of that smell!... serves him right for not listening.

We were greeted at the house by Hussein and his wife. Hussein had been given the General Managers role in Nasiriyah for QIT, his five-month stint was coming to an end and Paul was taking his place. Hussein was a Kuwaiti with a plastic American passport, a lovely geezer who made me laugh and made it feel like home as best he could. What was a shock to me is that he had his wife with him, a white American lady, blonde hair, blue eyes with a petite figure. Who in their right mind would have the wife with them in Iraq? I could not come to terms with this decision, crazy and unbelievable.

After unpacking we had some lunch with a cup of coffee, quick cigarette, forty winks and then to Tallil Air Base for a meeting with the contracting office. Hussein was going to be sticking around for another two weeks as a handover to Paul, plus all the other bits of shit that came out of the woodwork.

I made the decision that I was going to sleep downstairs in the living room for the duration I was there, with a mattress on the floor with a blanket and pillow. The room I was offered was on the second floor, it was one of two rooms. On the first floor another two bedrooms and a living room. On the ground floor was a kitchen, dining room and living room, so I was going to bed down in the living room.

From the second floor up there was a small set of steps that led to a flat roof with a five-foot wall surrounding the roof top and to get back to the ground floor from the roof you would have to jump. Paul also decided to join me in the living room until such time that Hussein had vacated the bedroom which had an ensuite on the ground floor. Bastard!!

It was a simple choice for me, if someone wanted to come into the house, I wanted to hear them and that would be a lot harder to do when you are two floors up. I needed to be prepared, I have five exits on the ground floor, the floors above were not as attractive. The villa was plush compared to others in Nasiriyah, the bathroom was cleaned every day by the cleaner, there was a shower and a washing machine, which was a luxury in Nasiriyah.

Once Hussein had left, we had to make drastic changes to the food and cooking. Fucking hell! Every day for dinner we had eaten chicken, salad, potatoes, rice and Arabic bread! I was fed up with the sight of the same food, it drove me mad!!

Rasak was our cook, a nice man who had a good sense of humour but had no idea of the word hygiene.

No more reheating food or leaving food out so flies could shit and vomit on it! He had to be taught to clean fruit and vegetables before anything else, luckily, I took some sanitizing tablets in my luggage. I showed him how to make a homemade cleaning solution to be used all over the kitchen. We emptied everything and cleaned everything in that kitchen, I had six on the job. Rasak now had a clean kitchen and a great menu plan to follow, how to store food, how to cook it, how to use an oven and not just fry everything.

I called for a meeting with everyone that was staying in the house, we all needed to know the house rules in general, so I put myself forward to making those rules. I used Osama as my translator so everyone knew what was expected, especially when it came to the kitchen and bathroom.

Osama was an Egyptian who was working in Qatar, I knew him personally and employed him for this project. Rasak in fairness was a great young man, big build but soft at heart, he always looked after me, making sure I never ran out of cigarettes and spoilt me with treats such as chocolate. Paul would bitch that he was the boss but Gary got preferential treatment, I baited Paul and suggested that it is obvious the Iraqi's prefer the Brits to the Yanks, which went down like a lead balloon.

Flies in Iraq, oh my goodness! From day one they would be a pain in my arse, wherever you go in Iraq there are flies in abundance and they all have attitude, they simply do not know when to fuck off! The big problem in Iraq is the lack of a good sewage and drainage system across the whole country and the dumping of rubbish on wasteland, unbelievable!

The shops in Nasiriyah are for general bulk foodstuffs and canned goods and possibly a chilled drink (and I do mean possibly). For fresh fruit and vegetables, you can only buy from roadside food stalls or 'grocery shops' (well shacks!). These fresh fruits and veggies were infested with flies and not a pretty site to say the least. Thank fully we could get supplies on the air base. Chunky soup, corned beef, sausages, steaks, chocolate biscuits, cheese and lots of other goodies, plus the military field packs. I had been given boxes of military field packs for free, just add boiling water, wait for the chemical reaction in the pack and it heated the food so fast. Very tasty.

For the first two weeks in Nasiriyah I was sat around quite a lot, just waiting for the trucks to arrive with the laundry facility and shipping container. I had arranged my laundry workers through local Iraqi businessmen, something I decided to do before I even arrived in Iraq. Ahmed and Bilal helped us in networking, which worked well for us. QIT and Jassim had suggested that I took Asian workers to run the facility, but I wanted to do this properly. It was agreed that the project was mine, so I overruled the suggestion and did it my way. I thought it was the right thing to give the work to the people whose country we are in, after all they had suffered for years in the south under the control of Saddam, he really made them suffer.

I recruited fourteen Iraqi nationals, ages ranging from twenty to thirty-five. Some of them married with children, others single and living at home with their extended family to feed. I interviewed each one properly in the villa and always had Osama with me as my translator and also involved Ram who was a Nepali national.

Osama and Ram were taken out of a commercial laundry in Qatar which was owned by QIT and they would work together side by side as supervisors whilst I was there and when I left. Both of them had never held a responsibility like this before so it was new to them both and they had to learn quickly. I took them both because of the mixed skills. I needed two men who knew me, liked and trusted me. They had to be good hands-on workers, I needed them to help me teach the Iraqi nationals to understand how military work has to be processed, with fast hands and minds who knew that time was key. Osama was important for speaking Arabic, although saying that some of my workers could speak English and as time went by, they learned English quickly.

I interviewed every man. I was very open with them and wanted them to feel relaxed with me. They were instructed they had to follow my instructions at all times, no fucking about! I held group meetings with them and I went over the same things to be honest but I thought that repetition was key with these guys, you had to keep repeating the same thing for it to stick in their minds, Iraqis are hardheaded, unreal at times! I would find out that they understood better when you shouted at them and borderline threatened them but that is not what I wanted for many reasons, it is not a nice environment to work in, not for them or for me, very stressful. I kept on telling them I was their manager yes but also your friend but you must respect the border between friend and manager.

They were told from day one their monthly salary would be $100 US Dollars, plus a bonus of $70 US Dollars but they would only get the bonus if they came to work every day, they were not late, they completed the daily work and they were on best behaviour when they were ever near the coalition forces. It does not sound a lot of money but when you consider the average monthly salary is only $90 US Dollars, another $80 US Dollars per month is a game changer.

I decided to make this policy to reward them for their physical hard work and also for good behaviour and actions, facing up to the real responsibilities for a better life, they deserve it. They were issued a company uniform, white polo shirts, black dress trousers and black shoes. The group talks included how they should arrive each morning for the bus, clean body, shaved or a groomed beard or moustache, short hair off the collar and no bad body odour. They should know how to speak to soldiers, when to sit, stand, walk, talk, the full drill of discipline. I wanted my lads to be the talk of the base and I wanted others to see them as normal men and respected them for what they are. I knew the dress code and appearance would stand out from anyone else on the base, which were not only Iraqi, most from India, Nepal and the Philippines. The choice of dress code was important to me, I wanted my boys to stand out. To this day I'm very proud to say that many military personnel and other contractors passed comments on my boys, highly praising them, especially the escorts we had with us ten hours a day, 7 days per week.

The escorts were American Air Force soldiers and every day we had a minimum of four escorts to control my team when they were on the base. We tended to have the same soldiers, male and female, most of which were great but also some morons unfortunately, I had some incidents with a few of them but that is for later. From the moment of getting on the base at 7am to 5pm, it is hard work. Not only are you doing the job of getting through the workload but you are constantly watching your staff and the soldiers. At times I found myself in the middle of arguments, not taking any one side, being neutral and seeing both sides, then making my own decisions. It has to be said, during the eight weeks with my Iraqi crew, I was so pleased of what they became, they maintained the dress code, there general time keeping, there standard of work whether that be quality or speed, they were a credit too themselves and to me, very proud of them!!

Albeit hard work for me, to train sixteen workers in eight weeks, it was one of the most enjoyable and satisfying projects I have ever done. In my past I had worked with some very good production crews and I would put this crew right up there with them. I remember quite vividly, the times I would stand in the laundry just watching them and not quite believing the quantity and quality they were getting out the door, they were immense. If you lead, others will follow. Some would say that they had no choice, everyone has a choice and they well and truly made theirs.

27

7 UP AND RUNNING

It was 0700 hrs on November the 7th and Paul's phone rang, he looked at me and Rick, sat up and gave us a thumbs up. Cancelling the call, he said, "We're on, it's here, let's go to the base." I replied, "Why have we got to go now, it is seven o'clock and you want to go fucking around now in the dark?" Paul came back, "Gary for fuck's sake just get dressed and drive the car!"

We got into the Landcruiser and drove at the usual 160 kilometres per hour! If anyone is going to shoot at me you better be quick! Whether it was light or dark I drove at high speeds.

When you arrive at the entrance of the military base there is a massive car park and this is the area where you start to be booked in. The car park only has a few lights and it was not easy to see the units, so we would have to use the car headlights. We asked the drivers to drive over to the brightest area so we could take a closer look at the equipment. Fuck knows what Paul wanted to see at seven o'clock at night in the dark but as the trucks shined in the lights, "Oh Fuck me!" They had been damaged, how on earth could they have managed that? There was nothing we could do now so we had to wait till morning to see the full extent of the damage.

All the way back to the villa Stinky Pete was on one, fuck me it was relentless. He had spent the last two weeks doing my head in, moaning and whining at everything. But... saying that he was putty in the hands when it came to baiting and winding him up.

An example of this would be when Rick had started to make his own iced tea, all homemade, however I was not aware that he was making it and storing it in two big jugs in the fridge. I thought Rasak was turning his hand to tea making so I helped myself. Rick went mental one evening and a right old onslaught took place where Paul had to intervene! It was quite funny to see some silly old fucker upset over a few glasses of missing iced tea.

The trouble was he showed his true colours once too often with me and of course I would not turn down the chance to bait him. Sometimes I could hear Paul at times talking to him and my name would crop up. It was quite funny to hear Paul talking about me as we were so close but he said nothing bad, just true words. "Hey Rick man, you need to chill out with Gary, fuck dude he will play and jump all over you to wind you up, trust me he is one of the best I have seen at it, he does it with me and if you go fishing with him, he will send you nuts, don't give him the line."

Rick had been sitting around for two weeks now, the work he had to do on other units was simple stuff, lasted for about a day, then he was done, he was just waiting for more units to come in and sort. It was a daily thing for him to bitch and whine about the same stuff, asking "why it is taking so long?" and "why can't we try and phone the drivers more?", he went on and on. Morning had arrived so off we all went up to the base to crack on and assess the damage what had been done to the units that we had found the night before.

The two halves of the building units had been sheeted over with extremely thick plastic and it was almost like a proper tarpaulin. We had learned that the drivers who had been driving out of Dubai had arrived at the border of Jordan – Iraq and refused to go any further. Red Sea did not inform anyone about this, they just keeping it hush hush until they could find other trucks and drivers. The choices they made and people they involved, nobody thought or knew how to lift a building that is 4 meters by 12 meters, correctly, so hence the damage that was caused.

After stripping the plastic sheeting away, Rick went to work to have a full check. He found that the undercarriage had been damaged, mainly the steel beams. They had hairline cracks due to the intense pressure the building was put under when they were offloaded from one flatbed to another in Jordan and they did not use a special steel beam that was supplied with the units. This steel beam used to make sure the building would not come under any additional stress whilst being lifted.

The drivers wanted us to take them off the trucks quickly so they could leave but that was not going to happen. We already had in place a well-designed concrete base to put the units onto but the steel beams underneath needed some welding work before Rick was willing to try and lift. It took a full day to lift the units into place and have the correct welding measures put in place. The drivers had also managed to wreck the gable ends of the building and they just happened to choose the area where the electrical panel had been fitted, coincidence I would say. The damage had not completely fucked us but we had to complete some rewiring and replace all the conduit.

Before we officially opened the laundry, we had arranged to put some actual hands-on training in place with the staff, live training so they could understand the significance of it all. Osama and Ram had been doing training with them in the villa as best as they could, inventing role plays for the processes we had, it was going to be run like a high street dry cleaner. Seven days after the trucks arrived, we were up and running, full steam ahead, I could have done without the holdups after they arrived but hey-ho this is Iraq, and it could have been worse.

I would never suggest that I'm an expert on Iraq but of course from being there, I'm in a better position than some. During the many years of Saddam Hussein's rule, the south of the country did not get a fair rub of the green, when you compare to how the north was treated. During one of the days at work one of my workers came to me and asked if it would be ok for his eldest brother to come and meet me at the villa, he said, "My brother would like to meet you, he would like to know you and ask you something. "He explained that his brother had left Iraq many years ago and had only returned now for the first time to visit his family. It was stated that his brother had moved to America some years before. For me I had no issues with him coming to the house and agreed he could visit that evening but not too late.

Evening time had arrived and the guard came into the living room and explained that four men had arrived and wanted to see me. I followed the guard outside to double check who it was, I recognised three of them as they worked for me, so obviously the other man was the new visitor. They came into the house and I invited them into the dining room, made them all a cup of sulaimani tea and we sat down.

Now forgive me as I forget the name of this visitor but he spoke very well for an Iraqi. He explained that he has been in America for the last seventeen years and now was the first chance he could visit safely. After they left, I spoke to Paul and explained that I had sat with three of the workers and their brother, who is visiting from America, he came because his father had sent him to meet me. I said, "Paul his father would like me to be a guest in his house, he said that his father would be very honoured to meet me." To which Paul replied "If I'm honest I don't like it, you don't know where they are taking you, what happens if he is lying or it's a setup? Call them back to the house."

Paul and I sat down with the visitor and Paul just came out with it, "My friend, Gary wants to go but you have to understand we are taking a risk with this one, he is going to be travelling alone in your car at night, you are taking him to an area I don't know, so I'm telling you that you will have to travel with a guard following you and the guard will also have to be in the same house all the time with Gary. I want to know the address and I want telephone numbers."

Everything was agreed with smiles and handshakes, so the next night I would be going to this house to meet his family.

They came to pick me up just before 2100 hrs and one of the guards sat in the car with me, feeling quite proud that he was my bodyguard for the night. Another car with another guard followed us. The name of the guard with me in the car was Mohammed, he was thirty-two years old and a former soldier in the Iraqi Army. Mohammed always tried to find ways to get my attention and I was told by Rasak that I make Mohammed laugh and made him feel like he was one of my best friends. He also told Rasak that he felt it was his own mission in life for now to make sure I was safe because he saw me as the man who gives work to Iraq and for this, he respected Gary, so I guess there was another who felt the choice was a good one. The biggest joke I shared with Rasak, was the brand of cigarette I was smoking, "Ishtar" but we will come on to that later.

The journey took about fifteen minutes, when we arrived, the car pulled into a long driveway and under a canopy. I was walked into the house from what appeared to be towards the rear, from what I could see in the faded light the building was concrete block built and there were no signs of damage through any type of war or weapons, good sign. I was led into a room, approximately 4 meters by 8 meters, the walls decorated in pictures, small rugs and at the base of the wall all around the room were cushions, so you could sit and lean comfortably.

When I walked into the room, I could see all twenty sets of eyes on me as they huddled around me smiling and wanting to shake my hand, the younger children hanging off my arms and legs, I could not believe how many people were in the room. I was introduced to the father of the house, an old man whose warmth I felt from the moment I locked onto his eyes and shaking his hand. I remained standing until the father sat down, a sign of respect but what was to happen next was quite unbelievable.

My guard Mohammed poked his head in the room and asked me how I was, I covered my heart with my right hand and nodded at him, followed by an ok hand signal. The door remained open and what took place was unreal. A huge plastic sheet was brought into the room and laid down, then tray after tray of food was brought out and presented right before me, it was a spread fit for a King and I truly felt like one. It was astonishing the quality of the food when you consider the difficulty to find such quality in Iraq.

It seemed like everybody wanted to be near me, the kids were that close they were nearly in my pockets, quite funny to be honest but made me feel special. I waited until his father took his food but the father suggested he would fill my plate for me, he would serve me in his house. I did not know what to say to the American translator, I felt it was wrong for him to do but he said, "I cannot explain to you how happy you have made my father, please don't deny him this honour." I nodded and smiled in agreement and his father filled my plate, the same volume you would expect on a healthy serving of a British roast dinner. The centre of attraction for the spread was a whole sheep on a bed of spicy Arabic rice, as I said it was for a King.

We sat and ate for just over an hour and then we sat and spoke for another hour about many subjects.

The father sat in front of me and my new friend to my right but everybody else was trying to get as close as they could, the kids were the funniest, I guess it was the excitement of having the first Englishman in the house. We spoke about many things, our families, our lives, how he felt about the soldiers coming in the first Gulf War and the most recent where Saddam had been removed. He explained to me about the time Saddam Hussein came to power and how happy he was when he was toppled and killed.

Saddam was in power from July 1979, removed from power in April 2003, he was captured on the 13th of December 2003 and executed on 30th December 2006.

He told me of the time when he was a young man and forced to join the army, he did not want to and proved to be the case after a few years when his wife became sick, he wanted to look after her and comfort her as she was the future for him. Just after he was given permission to leave, he had a visit from Saddam's hench men and they put four bullets in his stomach. As this was being explained to me through his son, he pulled up his upper garments to expose what he had suffered. I could not believe what I saw, four holes where the bullets had entered. I began to feel sick in the pit of my own stomach, so angry of the fact that these injuries prevented him from ever working again.

I had to explain that I had to go home as the clock was ticking and I had to wake early for work. Through his son the father suggested that I sleep in his house for the night. I froze fractionally and had to be careful how to react, I did not want to offend anyone, especially after such a memorable evening. I explained that it would not be fair to Paul and he would worry. We all have to respect that, we had a special evening and let us be thankful we enjoyed it.

I had found my safety in the villa and no way was I going to start a new chapter for a temporary bed, plus I knew I would not be able to sleep, no way would I be able to fully relax, plus Mohammed my guard would not like it. Luckily, the father nodded in agreement and spoke a little further but he found he was distracted by some activity behind a door in the corner of the room. I could hear giggling or should I say gigglers, all different types of tones and speeds of the giggles. The door was ajar and all you could see from the top to the bottom were eyes, quite funny to see. The father spoke and the door was opened, in came the ladies of the household, they made up the forty-two of the total household, four generations in one house. My American friend explained to me that his father had given special permission for the ladies to come into the room and also no need for them to cover their faces. He allowed them to come in and say hello, he had been kindly pressurised to do so by the family. It was explained to me that my visit was historic, an Englishman visiting the house was an honour and his father would speak about it for years to come. He would tell the village what had happened, he would have bragging rights.

Translated the father said, "I don't think you fully understand what you have done, you have given work to three of my sons and I know you are paying them good money. I also know from you are looking over them and protecting them with the soldiers, I know you are educating my sons to be better men, to be smart and clever, so I cannot thank you enough. The money we have coming into the house is a dream for us and I can never forget you for doing this." He walked closer to embrace me, which is not normal for Arabic men, normally it is a handshake or a simple kiss to the side of each cheek or they touch noses but a bear hug, I have never had before in the Middle East. Being humble, it was not so easy to accept but the reality of this, is that it is true, it is the real world he is experiencing and when you realise that your choices and decisions change others' lives so much, it is a funny feeling but a nice one.

I got back to the villa around 0100 hrs and Paul was up watching television, he went ballistic and blasted me, I said I was sorry and then a swift "Fuck off and mind your own business!."

We would go into the city of Nasiriyah quite often in the evenings, visiting a simple internet café. A small office type of set up which had about six or seven booths. We would park the car up and walk the three hundred odd meters through the busy streets.

The stares from the locals were a mixed bag, from, "Are you stupid?" to "Who the fuck are you?" to "What are you doing here?" Responded with a "Nice to meet you" and a full-on smile.

8 LEARNING CURVES

Did we feel scared? I'm not sure to be honest but for sure my radar was working overtime to make sure that any threat was neutralised. As far as incidents... they were scarce. We never went anywhere alone; we were always accompanied by others and I guess as far as I was concerned, I felt a lot better with Paul beside me.

I remember one day I left the base, travelling back to the villa in the Landcruiser and there were roadblocks all over the place that had been set up by the Italian military and Carabinieri (the Italian Police).

I finally arrived back at the villa but on the approach, I could see two helicopters flying nearby. I parked up and asked Rasak what is happening? Five hundred meters away from the villa was an Italian military base and someone had decided that they wanted to bomb and kill eighteen Italian soldiers. I knew many of the Italian soldiers through business on the base and general small get togethers. No death is good but I was hoping that none of them were close to me.

I sat in the villa and took stock of the incident, it was the first major problem since being in Nasiriyah and it unsettled me, plus it was right on our doorstep, maybe these fuckers were staying close to us, maybe they are our neighbours? What made it worse for me, Paul had travelled to Baghdad and was due back the following day. I would not sleep well that night.

The morning arrived and I made my way to the base. I knew I would be visiting the Italian contract offices but how was I going to react? Were the deaths going to be personal friends of mine or were some of the soldiers close to my friends? Either way I was not looking forward to this. On arrival

I went to the contracting office, after paying my respects, I found out that none of my personal friends died but the base was a very sad place to be in.

One night we were sat in the living room and suddenly there was the tell-tale noise of screeching tires and heavy gun fire, I knew it was just outside the front entrance. I have never seen Paul move so fast. He jumped up in one swift motion, pointed at me and said, "Stay right here and don't go near them windows, stay down. Don't fuck around now Gary."

The look on his face said it all, he ran to the kitchen door that led out to the front gates, from the kitchen door to the gates was only ten or so meters. The living room was situated at the front of the villa and it had two exits from it. I walked over to one of the doors and opened it slowly to try and get eyes on what was happening but was useless as I could not see over the solid perimeter wall. I tried to listen in to any talking or shouting, I wanted a better idea of what was going on. I could see Paul stood by the gates but inside the boundary, he was stood by the guards.

I walked towards the gates and now I could clearly see Paul with an AK47 in his hands and his pistol shoved down the back of his jeans. I stood in the same spot for about a minute just watching and then walked to where Paul was standing. Mohammed (my guard friend) tapped Paul on the shoulder and pointed in my direction, Paul turned and snapped, "Are you deaf and fucking stupid, get the fuck in the house now!" Calmly I said, "It's ok for you, you can see what's happening, I have no idea what's going on!" In typical Paul style he retorted "Gary! Not now and get in that house before I shoot you myself!"

The whole incident lasted for about fifteen minutes; it was all over an Iraqi who owed someone some money, the grand total of $10 US Dollars!

Another night we had a similar incident. Sat in the living room watching a movie when we heard gun shots. We knew it was not close but the sound of the gun fire was heavy, this was no birthday celebration. The following morning in the laundry, all my lads were talking about it.

A local politician, come cleric, went to a man's house with approximately fifteen men and the cleric was telling the man inside this house that it was wrong to be drinking alcohol, becoming drunk and making a nuisance of himself in the streets. The drunken man basically told the cleric to fuck off, it's a free country and he could choose what he wanted to do, which is a fair comment. The cleric left but returned later with an array of weapons and started to obliterate the man's house. As drunk as this man was, he was still able to hit this cleric straight between the eyes with a direct kill. The story goes that the Italians arrived and said, "Hello hello, what's going on here then", nobody spoke, no arrests were made and life went on… amazing.

In Iraq you quickly learn that Iraqis do not do things the way westerners would. I was told a story one day by one of my lads.

A taxi driver went to his friend's house and asked him why he had not paid him $2 US Dollars, the man turned and walked into his house. The taxi driver was thinking he should stand and wait as his friend was going to get his money but unfortunately his friend was only going to get a full magazine of bullets to fill him in with. All over $2 US Dollars!… you can make your own mind up, which will probably not be too far away from my reaction.

Unfortunately, the tribal violence will go on for many years after the coalition forces have left, trust me it will never change.

The day Saddam Hussein was captured, every man and his dog were on the streets of Nasiriyah, firing off rounds into the sky, celebrating. I was in the villa watching BBC news and they were explaining that he had been captured and how Nasiriyah was delirious about it. The celebrations continued into the early hours of the morning. The following day my laundry lads were telling me how happy they were that Saddam had been caught and were hoping that the Americans would allow the people to choose his fate. As said before, Nasiriyah had suffered for too long and in their eyes, Saddam was only good to those in the north. Now it was payback time.

The laundry had been up and running for two months now and it was a great success but hard work for sure. The soldiers made some great comments of the service, in short most said that it was the same as the service back home and in some ways better. Although the contract stated that the turnaround time of each order was forty-eight hours, I told Osama and Ram to take that luxury out of their heads and only to think that it was twenty-four hours and that is why it was so special. I did not have the storage space for more than twenty-four hours, so that is why the service was unique. The space for goods on hangers or flat packed was tight and there was no way could we store it.

Before it had all started, I remember telling the Colonel of the base from day one that I needed more space next door to store items, especially for hanging items as I knew his soldiers would not collect when they should do and I was right. After two weeks of opening, we had a tent erected to deal with the overspill. We were that efficient at turning it around, a nice situation to be in.

With the huge success of the way it operated, QIT were able to offer the services to other soldiers from other countries. QIT made more money and the US Airforce also picked up commission on those additional sales. A win win for everyone.

The main difficulty I faced over those two months was the weather for sure. I could not believe how cold and wet Iraq would get. The nice desert surfaces became boggy conditions, it was unreal. The mud at times was piss wet and a good 30cms deep in some places, it was nearly impossible to keep my lads dry from the time we entered the base to the laundry facility. They would step off the bus in the main car park and immediately walk through a mud bath and that continued through all the check points to the laundry. It got to the stage where I decided to buy my lads proper work boots, like 'Doc Martens' and carry their black shoes in a bag. Along with the mud we had freezing cold conditions, it could drop well below zero, something we never planned for, none at all.

As time went by, the base became busier with the number of workers they had to bring on. Most of the contractors were the big shots from the USA, KBR (Kellogg Brown & Root) being the biggest for sure. The management of KBR all being ex-military, many of them in my opinion thought they were a law unto their themselves. I happened to be the only British National and never far away from some good old banter or light-hearted fun.

Now I don't make the rules but for one reason or another, the Colonel (who I got to know for the wrong reasons, which I will come to) decided that the laundry workers should be a priority to come on to the base and start work ASAP. For a few weeks I had become the target for abuse by these ex-marines and because of their overpowering loud voices, they thought the Brit would be an easy target and the Yanks would have a field day. They thought that trying to bait and mock the me with the history of how the Brits had their butts kicked out of America in 1783 was going to get the better of me and I was going to bite. A quick reminder was given that they had to make a phone call for the French to help them over the line!!

That first morning the new rule came in to play, I walked in as usual to the desk where you register that you have arrived and then you join the queue. I turned away to go over to my lads and suggested they go back to the bus, wait there as I thought we would be delayed. I decided to grab a cup of tea at the small café and lit up a cigarette. A call came over the system, "QIT laundry all good to enter, Gary move the guys, let's go."

I turned to Ram, asked him to go to the bus, I was finishing my tea and fag when the Texas mountain approached me. 'Cowboy', yes Cowboy was his nickname (I never thought to ask him his real name), walked over, tilting his Stetson and wearing a big frown, spray on denim jeans and his designer KBR boots. Cowboy opened up, "What time did you arrive? I don't believe your guys arrived before my crews?" I replied, "The word is good morning geezer and I have been here for ten minutes I think, does that help you in anyway?" I think Cowboy was slightly confused with what I said, which led him to walk over to the desk and start his inquest of how I'm allowed to move up the queue. After a conversation with some American soldiers at the desk and not low key, Cowboy walked away from the desk and I heard him say to his colleagues, "Damn fucking Brit, who does he think he is just strolling in like that?" I thought it was funny to hear, it made me laugh. Cowboy for sure thought that an American should take precedence on an American base, why does the Brit get to go before him? I should have let it go but I was not going to miss out on this opportunity after the shit I had taken over the weeks from many of them.

Ram came back with the lads and on his return a soldier at the desk made an announcement to those that were in the room. The Staff Sergeant stood on a desk and said, "From today you need to be aware that we now have in place a priority list of services, in short this means that certain services come first and those companies involved with those priorities come on to the base first, it is not about who arrives first. Gentlemen you will find these new rules and the priority list on the information board. We will also be emailing your head offices of these changes, thank you for your cooperation."

I walked up to Cowboy but had to stand back by a meter so I could look at his face without pulling the muscles in my neck as he stood about six feet five inches tall. I sparked up, "Well, it looks like the damn Brit has the priority! Lads come on I don't make the rules but have to follow them, I'm sure you won't be waiting too long, have a good un now." As I smirked at Cowboy, he cut back at me, "You need to be reminded of manners and the way you should go about your business on base and stop disrespecting American soldiers, remember who your friends are, you are too quick to take their mother fucking side." I knew what he was talking about and it was a cheap childish shot at a time when he was pissed off that a Brit put one over on him and his mates. I retorted, "Think as you like, they work for me and are paid through the services we provide and while that is happening, I have every fucking right to stand my ground and protect them, they have done nobody any harm from day one, I'm their voice and I will not have any of them spoken to like a piece of shit. I'm busy and if you are that concerned that I argue with the American escorts, maybe they can help me to stop some of the bullying."

From day one I had been tight lipped, ignored the shit I was taking, but this day it changed. They can all go and fuck themselves.

As previously said, most of the time the escorts were great and they engaged with my lads, they were nice to them but there were times when they would speak to them in a bad way and I was not going to have it. Cowboy had obviously heard about these arguments and thought he had the right to comment on them. Fuck him.

The damn flies!! When the weather was hot, they were just a nuisance, they would be everywhere and all had bad attitudes. It got to the stage in early November that we needed to deal with these flies in the laundry and through talking to a soldier he informed me of a place on the base where they could help us. Paul and I drove around the base to find this workshop and it took a little while to get there. The base was massive, I would have liked to have seen it from the air to fully understand how big it was. To get to from one place to another, you had to consider all the check points and then had the huge convoys going backwards and forwards. The place was a small city.

The Americans had most of the base but there were also other soldiers from other countries, South Korea, Holland, Poland, Italy and even a few British soldiers. We arrived at this office for pest control and it was a special unit set up by the Americans. I was blown away by the size of the set up and the work they did. I knew flies were a problem but after seeing their set up and listening to the stories. These guys had projects going on where they were tracking, following various swarms, understanding where the nests are and how to destroy as many as possible.

They had a truck outside, it looked to be approximately five tonnes and attached to the cab of the truck was a tank, like one of the many typical water/petrol tankers. This tank was full of industrial fly killer and is discharged by a special hose/fogging device. One man told me that the spray was activated by remote control and that they would park the truck up and only activate the pump when they were at a safe distance. He showed me some quick videos they had and the volumes of flies they would kill. It was a good visit anyway and I went shopping in their secret cave and bought all sorts of killing strips to hang in the laundry and general sprays.

Coincidentally, on the same day in the evening, I was sat in the kitchen smoking a cigarette, drinking a cup of tea, the back of my chair rested against the wall, so I just put my head back and then my eyes zoomed in on the ceiling. These rooms all had high ceilings, so not always easy to see what was on the ceiling and why would you? it's not normal to keep angling your neck at 180 degrees.

The light bulb was covered by a dome shaped lightshade and it was plastered with flies, you could hardly see light for the flies. How long they had been there I have no idea, we had ourselves a mini nest. I knocked on the door of Paul's room and dragged him out, him whining that I had disturbed his beauty sleep, "Damn Gary, do I have to do everything around here what is it now?" I pointed to the ceiling and said, "Now wind your neck in and think how we can get up there, we can go to the shop tomorrow and ask them if they have any fogging equipment?" The cogs were turning as he scratched his eyes, he was still waking up, "Fucking hell mate!! How the fuck did we not notice before? Maybe we could use a ladder or scaffold?" I replied, "Are you on drugs or something? What are you on about? Fucking waste of time asking you! It's ok I will deal with it tomorrow. With the ladder you are three meters away and where the fuck are we going to get scaffolding?" I shook my head in disbelief but he had only just woken up to be fair. I would hopefully be able to set up a fogging machine tomorrow evening when nobody was around, close all doors and blast the fucking things! My friends at the pest shop had a hand-held fogging device that could spray a mist twenty meters high… job done. It took me 30 minutes… mission complete. The floor was covered in the fuckers, they had made a nest around the light fixture. I tidied up and filled half a black refuse bag.

Ram and Osama had done very well, they had gone through the learning curve of moving into management, hopefully they would not leave their hands-on approach and sit back. Paul's methods of management very different to mine and he was even honest about that. When Osama and Ram were working for QIT in Qatar, their monthly salary was $250 US Dollars and through their promotion it was increased to $3,000 US Dollars.

On top of that they were going to get better free food, free travel, free accommodation. It was funny trying to explain this, especially to Ram, he could not grasp what I was saying. It took me three presentations to make him understand and when he finally got it, he started to cry and ask why I wanted to do this for him? What had he done to deserve this? Sounds silly I know but it is the reality of these situations, you change people's lives for them.

Paul and I worked very well together, we knew each other's strengths and let things play out. Paul would never argue or meddle with me when it came to kicking arse, it was not one of his skill sets, so he would always leave me alone when it came to moving mountains. We argued like cat and dog at times but when we did it was always good natured, we never used to take it to the extreme where we fell out, never.

Thanksgiving Day, I had been set up… hook line and sinker! Well nearly all three but as usual I was not going to be outdone!

Every day on the base I went to the food hall, a huge tent where the soldiers went to have their food and I had permission to use the canteen, along with Osama and Ram. Ram used to make me laugh. Like most Nepali nationals, Ram could eat a whole plate of rice, had a separate plate for meat and veg and let us not forget his dessert. The system in the canteen was that you could serve yourself, so Ram would pile the rice high on the plate and think nothing of it. Twice the Executive Chef came to me and asked me to speak to Ram about the portions he was taking. I have never had an issue confronting anyone but for some reason I was not looking forward to this. I knew how much he not only loved rice but I knew he needed it to keep his energy levels up. I had to pick the right moment to sit him down and explain.

Ram was not happy. He asked if I could speak to the Chef on his behalf, Ram wanted to suggest he was paying for the extra rice but the Chef said no, so back again I had to say no Ram, enough is enough.
Rasak would be the man to save the day and top up Ram's daily intake!

On November the 4th Paul came into the laundry and suggested that we should sit and eat lunch together in the canteen, so we walked over and was joined by a few of Paul's military friends. We walked in, washed our hands and then went into the canteen area. It was a big space which seated 350 at any given time. Paul was acting a little strange, he walked to the trays and passed me one, he even picked up my cutlery, there you go mate, on you go I we will follow." I joined the queue who were making their way down the line to help themselves and then I noticed that we had servers and not just any ordinary servers. What the fuck?! Colonel Ladston was standing there, the first of the service crew, standing nearby Captains and Lieutenants. I turned to my left and said to Paul, "What's this about?" Paul replied, "They do it sometimes, you know, leadership, inspiring others." Paul's mates were in front of me and were having their plates filled, I could see it was roast turkey with all the trimmings, nice one.

My turn… I was stood directly in front of the Colonel. I had met him a few times and shared some good banter with him as he knew us Brits were in the minority on the base but he knew the laundry was a success. I put on the best fake smile I could and said, "Colonel Ladston afternoon to you Sir, I do like a bit of breast you know." Trying to keep a straight face with my opening line but struggling to hold the laughing back, more than Paul and his mates did as they heard what I said. "Good afternoon, Gary, we shall come back to that comment in a minute, anyway I need to ask you something." He took off his serving gloves, put down his carving knife, large fork and folded his arms, the whole place fell silent, I'm stood their trying not to laugh, so hard to hide my smirk. "Sure, Colonel what would you like to ask me?" He asked "Gary, do you know what today is? what do you think we are celebrating?" I looked at Paul, motioning my head about, revolving my hands in front of me, gesturing for someone to help me out but help was not coming and to be honest I did not have a clue but I could not resist to say, "I think I know Sir, today is the day that Americans celebrate the day you kicked us Brits out of America but you couldn't do it alone, you had to phone French, otherwise we would have won." My words certainly got a mix of laughs, oohs and ahhs. The Colonel carried on trying not to laugh but swiftly corrected my accounts, "No Gary not that occasion. Sorry to say it is something else, today is Thanksgiving Day." I replied, "I knew really Colonel but I thought I would just test your history but as you know it is not really a test when your country only has just over two hundred years of history to talk about, unlike us English but saying that Sir, Happy Thanksgiving Day to all my friends here with me, now can I have some turkey Sir, breast please?" He put his gloves back on, picked up his serving tools, placed two nice sized slices on my plate, gave way and laughed, "As always Gary, you never let us down, enjoy your dinner." I smiled and said "Thank you, Colonel, it looks great. Happy Thanksgiving Day Sir."

9 TIME TO SAY GOODBYE

My last day at work became quite an emotional affair. All day my lads wanted my time, attention and I got fed up with everyone asking me when I was coming back. I had told Osama and Ram that I would never be returning but we had to tell the lads that I would return in about six months, I'm lying for sure but it would do no harm, it would keep them happy knowing they would see me again.

We shut the shop at 1700 hrs and locked up for the journey back to the city. When we were on the bus the lads were like a bunch of school kids, the many raised voices were not normal, so I intervened to try and get the volume down but Osama explained.

As he started to talk, the laundry lads were coming closer to my seat, I was not sure what was going on. Osama shouted them down and then said, "Boss please, they are all sad and excited too, these gifts are for you." Osama handed me two parcels. I was shocked to be honest and did not expect it. On opening them I was bowled over. One of the gifts was an Iraqi soldier's decorative knife, not cheap at all, quite expensive and original. The other gift was a set of brand-new Iraqi bank notes, one of each denomination, again not easy to get with the face of Saddam Hussein on each one.

I was choked up. I have never found it easy to be the receiver of gifts and I was humbled in many ways for these men to spend their money on me. Tears cannot be hidden, it does not matter where you are from, they speak louder than any words. I wanted the bus to get back to the city so I could get back to the villa and away from the emotion. Along the way, the bus stops and drops the lads off, at each stop each one wanted their bear hug and their tears came also, powerful moments.

It was not an easy situation to deal with. I'm just a normal man on the street and I have sixteen men feeling that they can never repay me, sounds silly but is true.

Finally, I got home and could finish off my packing. The journey to Baghdad would start early, I needed to get an early night as I did not want to sleep in the car on the journey.

It was just past 2000 hrs and Osama came to me, "Boss please don't be angry but Sameer is outside he needs to see you, just two minutes please." Exasperated I said, "Osama you know this is tiring, I'm not sure I can do this anymore today; I don't mean this to sound bad but it is very emotional. Since day one, I have tried to stay away from the reality of the way these people live and try not to get to involved. He replied in his broken English, "Boss forgive me but I need you to just stop, look at me for one minute, then you can choose what you do." I said, "Ok Osama you have one minute, be quick."

"Boss, I knew you before I came to Iraq in, I knew you as the man who designed Magic Laundry in Qatar for QIT and I witnessed with my own two eyes what you did for that laundry and I see every man in that building respect you more than our owners. You say you have not got involved here but you have and you don't know because this is so normal for you to help people, you leader man and you protect us all, you are a crazy man sometimes with this soldier if they speak bad to the men. Many times, the men say to me, Osama, Gary is crazy man, why he keeps fighting the American for us and I tell them because he has good heart, yes sure he makes you work but he is a good man. I sorry boss but I have to tell you are wrong, you make me strong enough to be confident to tell you, you are now wrong and walking away from your responsibility. You made this situation and you have to accept it, these men love you boss. They see you as the man that came and gave them a chance, you made them feel like men again, you educate them from A – Z and you feed their children and their families. I'm sorry if it makes you cry but you create this. Boss you waste your life sometimes, you are true a leader and these men are upset, respect that please."

Paul overheard and he came in the room. I looked at him, he nodded, reshaped his mouth and said, "How does this work? You are one son of a bitch and they curse you from making them sweat but they are going to miss your sorry arse, man come on! I will sit here with you, Osama show Sameer in." In walked Sameer but he was not alone, the kitchen was filling, what the hell was going on?! "Guys no! What is going on? Osama outside please, why did you not tell me the truth of what is happening?" Osama replied, "Boss how can I explain? Not possible."

We walked out the villa, Paul followed. The lads had all come to the villa to say a last goodbye and also brought their families with them. We estimated that we had about 200 people in the yard. It's not possible to remember every word but it is a night that will always stay with me. It was not fake, it was all true, honest and relevant. Whether Paul and I liked it we had brought this moment on ourselves.

We stayed outside for about fifteen minutes and then made Osama agree that if Gary said a small speech, they promised they would go home. So, I said a few simple words, covered my heart with my right hand, momentarily kissed the tips of my fingers on my right hand, ushering my hand in their direction, I think that said it all.

Stating the obvious, any war is bad. Even if the war is required to fend off the attacker, it is one of the regrettable things of our existence. These moments are rarely shared or seen, this group of people were the winners for that moment from the war because for once they had the chance to show what they can do, the chance to learn and develop, the chance to give good food and keep their families healthy and safe. To be part of something like this is life changing, my conscience is clear that I have given something back in my life, I can sleep at night.

The 18th of December had arrived. All the bags were packed and I was putting the luggage in the car, ready to start the journey back home.

The schedule was, Nasiriyah to Baghdad, Baghdad to Jordan by road, Jordan to Qatar by aeroplane and then Qatar to UK for Christmas. Paul came out to see me off. Not a lot was said, I sensed he did not want me to leave and if he had the chance would have offered me some kind of new contract there and then but he knew that I had some other offers to take care of.

I travelled in the car with four Iraqi's and the trip went very well and seemed quicker than the inbound journey. I arrived at the villa in Al Mansoor, Baghdad early evening. So, one night in Baghdad and then next morning travel to Jordan. The night came and went, morning was here and I was taken to Camp Saliya, where QIT had offices.

I sat around for about an hour but was given some coffee with a nice twist of brandy, courtesy of Salam. It was time to go and as I went outside, I saw Mike who I originally met when first arriving. Mike had collected me and Paul from the airport. Mike was going to be making the trip with me to

Jordan as he was also going home for a Christmas vacation. So, we threw the luggage in the rear of the GMC and rolled out of the base, ready to make the journey and what punishment it would turn out to be on my backside.

10 ON MY WAY HOME

I asked the driver how long it would take and he suggested nine hours should do it, so not to bad but he underestimated by four hours... it turned into thirteen damn hours!

To be honest the journey was not too bad because we had a brand-new GMC to travel in but the delays at the petrol stations and the border was punishing. Again, I witnessed the Iraqis arguing the price they were paying for the petrol, a bunch of head cases, they would argue over a fly crawling down a television.

Most of the journey was just open desert roads, very lonely and long, nothing to see but sand; and the conversations inside the vehicle you could not exactly call them riveting. I'd had many conversations with soldiers and civilians about taking things out of Iraq and everyone had a different story to tell.

I had two sets of brand-new bank notes, one of each denomination. One set with Saddam's face and the new notes where his face had been removed, both sets were going into a frame. I also had my Iraqi military decorative knife and two Iraqi bayonets, so I thought I would be ok, no issues. At the border we had to get out of the car, pass over our documents and wait until they had finished their checks. It was absolutely freezing cold, we were at the Iraq – Jordan border, with the Syrian desert very close and this is where the ice-cold wind was coming from. The guards wanted to check our belongings and they seemed to take great pleasure in turning out all my stuff but I had the last laugh, they did not find my knives. I managed to get my knives to Jordan, then from Jordan to Qatar and then the final destination of the UK... result!

We arrived in the early hours of the morning in Amman, Jordan and checked in at the Intercontinental Hotel. I took a quick shower and then thought I would just casually mooch about the hotel, grab a beer at 0700 hrs, have a cigarillo and a few Jim Beams. Why not? I'm on holiday now.

It felt good for once to be able to fully chill out, 0700 hrs or not I'm having a good drink. It had been an eventful 2 months, busy every day, not a lot of time off, just a few hours here and there. It was tiring if I'm honest because most of the time you have to be switched on for varying reasons. I had my moments of fear but nothing to serious. It had been an experience, would I do it again? I wasn't too sure but at the same time it was not on my agenda and my contract had finished.

After grabbing some breakfast and saying goodbye to Mike I made my way to the airport to fly back to Qatar. On arrival I went straight to the QIT offices, signed off my contract, got paid off, happy days.

Then I was on my way in taxi to the airport and catch my flight back to the UK for Christmas. I checked in and then decided to go to the lounge where I would be able to enjoy a few drinks where I could fully relax with nothing too serious to think about and no need to be watching my arse all the time.

It did feel very different, which made me think there must have been a fear within me but I did not really recognise it until now. I had thought about it too much before, it could have affected me. I closed my eyes for a while and thought of the times where I thought it could have got ugly but worked out fine and thought of the lads that I had spent my time with. The project had been a success in so many ways. I had delivered on so many fronts and made the laundry a very profitable business for QIT. We achieved high standards of service and quality with a team of Iraqi nationals that knew nothing about working in a laundry. Ok, so one used to press a few paraffin flavoured shirts! Which reminds me I did manage to salvage Paul's shirts! Ha!

I had breathed life into sixteen families and that was probably the most rewarding thing to be honest.

I had experienced working in a war-torn country and turned negatives into positives. I think I took my management skills to another level. Tribal personalities are not easy characters to deal with. Good job Gazza! Onwards and upwards!

11 BACK TO QATAR

I was in the UK until January 25th. Christmas was Christmas. I had not seen my son Christian and wife Lisa since September, so it was a nice reunion and it was Christians first Christmas.

Many wanted to know about Iraq. I spoke about parts of it but did not touch on the sensitive and emotional side, I did not see the point of talking about it and upsetting myself once more, no need, want is done is done, it is history.

I travelled back to Qatar on the 25th of January 2004 with Lisa and Christian. Paul wanted me to stay at his place to look after it, which worked out well as it gave me time to get back on track with Bassam who I had met in September 2003. I needed time to work out what I wanted to do, working with Bassam was on the agenda and that was a given but what else would go with it?

Paul and I were in regular touch for one thing or another. He had recently moved from one villa to another and he needed a bigger place as his contracts had expanded. He was doing some great work in Iraq, building a nice empire for himself and I was happy for him. He was the General Manager for QIT in Nasiriyah and he really wanted to be in Baghdad where the bigger contracts were, which meant supplies and services on a bigger level but he had to be satisfied with Nasiriyah and from what he told me he was making it pay.

By the second week of February the next few months had been planned. I had agreed to start officially with Bassam in April. He had some things to sort out and I also had a chemical supplies deal on the table to work on. Paul phoned me a few days later and explained that he was a Daddy again, he wanted to go and see his wife and newborn son in Kyrgyzstan.

I said, "Hey mate congratulations to you both, great news!" then words came I did not really want to hear. "Hey, mate I have been here in Iraq since October and I'm ready for a break, what with Donald coming along it makes sense for me to go and see them both, mate I want you to relieve me for just a month." I came back to Paul, "Mate it's not that I won't do it, you have a big group in QIT, I'm sure there are a few who can cover you?." He replied "Gary, I have worked so hard to build these contracts, I trust you and you only to look after them mate, I don't trust any other fucker. If I'm honest I wanted to talk to you about another deal and contract, work with me all the time. I need you to do some extra training for the laundry as I have some new staff, there is also some arse kicking I need you to do with Ram and Osama." I cut in, "What do you mean arse kicking with them two, for what reason?" Paul advised "Both have got a little lazy and taken the foot of the pedal." So, I retorted, "I fucking hope not I will go fucking mental with them." The final line from Paul was "Gary, there are quite things I want you to do, the list is quite long mate you are born to sort this shit out. There is some preventative maintenance lists and schedules I need you to work on for the laundry and other contracts I have now."

I was fucked. He had sold it to me. Plus, he came up trumps with what was on offer financially. I came off the phone and I could see Lisa wanted to know what was going to happen. Whether this is right or wrong I told Lisa that I had made my mind up and I was going back for a month. Yeah, for sure who am I not to discuss the decision with her but that is what I chose. The main problem was that I would be gone for a month but work is work and other factors had to be considered. At the end of the day, I went back because Paul wanted to see his newborn son and needed a break from Iraq. I for one experienced that and I knew he would benefit.

Paul went out of his way to help us. I did not ask him to allow me to stay in his house, I did not ask him to go out of his way to give me employment and he did not ask anything in return, so I had to return a portion of that. We spoke a few days just after his initial request and he mentioned again the fact that he wanted to talk to me further about joining him full time so we could be looking at a much bigger picture. I said, "Let's see."

It would take me a month to arrange various things in my life before I could step on the plane and head back to Iraq. I went to see Bassam a few times where we sat and discussed how we would move the Jeeves of Belgravia deal ahead; he was ok for me to go for a month. I sat down once more to make a new Will of Testament, easier this time, more or less a copy and paste scenario.

I had one dreaded thing to do on my list and waited until the very last moment to do it. When I originally went to Iraq my Mum was not happy at all and when she saw me at Christmas, she asked me to make a promise that I would never go back. I did not use the 'promise' word but I said that it is highly unlikely that would happen because I had other things to do and I couldn't do them if I was working away in Iraq. On the 15th of March I made the call to Mum and did not beat about the bush. I was slightly heartless about it but I just came out a said I was going; I had decided a month ago and could not back out. I homed in on the fact that I was going to help Paul as a mate because he stood by me and that I had to repay him, that is what mates do for each other. I asked her not to talk too much and told her that Iraq was still the same more less.

I did not want a long talk on the phone and I certainly did not want her crying. Easier said than done; I knew she would cry. Before we closed the line, I said I would call her when I could, told her not to worry and said the month will go quickly and I would see her in the summer.

12 BACK TO IRAQ

On the 16th of March 2004, the driver from QIT was coming to collect me and take me to the airport just after 0800 hrs. I said my goodbyes to Lisa and Christian. I did not dwell. I have never been one for goodbyes and was not going to start extending it now.

I caught the 1100 hrs flight to Kuwait and on arrival a friend of Paul's picked me at the airport and drove me to the Sheraton Hotel, where I was going to stay for one night only. I spent the afternoon chilling in a nearby shopping mall (which is not like me to do at all). I hate shopping malls to be honest but I'm glad I broke the mould for the afternoon. I had never spent much time in Kuwait and I was taken aback that the ladies in Kuwait have open and western-like dress codes, faces exposed also. Although the air conditioning was fine inside, these ladies definitely increased the warmth in the building. I have to say that many of the Kuwaiti ladies are seriously hot and classy; an afternoon well spent wouldn't you say gents?

Morning arrived and at 0700 hrs I knew the same driver who picked me up at the airport would be coming to take me to the border with Iraq. The drive would take us about two hours. Paul told me that I would be met by Ali and Abu-Haider. I knew both of them from my previous visit and had met them on various occasions.

At the border you had two routes to choose from, military and civilian. We chose the military. The rules say if you take the military route you need to show and prove you have a guard(s) to escort you on your journey. I had to go through the paperwork system at the border office and once they were happy that I had the correct procedures in place I was sent on my way.

We came to the meeting point, a large car park where there was a lot of activity, so not easy to find anyone. Eventually we were able to see each other. Ali and Abu – Haider (Abu H) were stood by the rear of a Landcruiser. I got out of the car, handshakes all around, I thanked the driver and now it was the journey to Nasiriyah again. Before we left, I wanted to buy some water and snacks, which was all easy to do with the local roadside stalls. There were some kids hanging around trying to either get some small change from you, or any treats or souvenirs they could entice from you.

There were many pockets of media dotted all over the car park, easy to identify due to the dress code. Pockets all over their trousers, shirts and jackets, like someone going on safari. They were hanging around, waiting for the teams of escorts they had arranged, taking them all over the country to report back to the world what their eyes were telling them, what was going on in this apocalyptic country. We got back into the Landcruiser and headed northwest to Nasiriyah. I was back in Iraq. Sure, I had to pinch myself but hey there is no drama, I have done this before. I'm technically a veteran now, lol.

After about ten minutes, Ali who was driving pulled over into a petrol station, he stepped out of the car and walked to a man who would fill the car with some fuel. Abu H was sat beside me in the back of the car, he could speak a little English, it was broken but we could always get by. Abu H was approximately 6 feet 4 inches, I would guess 18 stone and had hands like shovels, but he was another of Iraq's gentle giants. He had been in the Iraqi army but when the army was disbanded by the Americans (big mistake) he started to do private security work, so QIT had hired him.

He turned to me and said to, "Mr. Gerry many men speak good about you, I'm happy I meet you now, I promise you, wallah lazeem (means like I swear by Allah/God) nobody will come to you or hurt you when I'm here." I knew what it meant and I could see his sincerity. Abu H would come into my life again, more than I would know at this time.

For most of the journey it was open desert like most of the roads in Iraq once you get out from the cities. Every now and then I could see food stalls, people standing about selling petrol, once more in different types of vessels. Still, for some reason there were issues with petrol, I should have asked why but I was not sure if I would be able to deal with the bullshit answers.

The Iraqi military vehicle graveyard was seen all too often. In the UK, when we were kids, we would play a game called 'eye spy with my little eye' in the car on the way to the coast for the summer holidays. I'm not sure it would last too long here as once you said 'tank', 'sand' or 'personnel carrier' the game would be over as that's all you saw on the journey and they were all over the place! Probably more so than between Baghdad and Nasiriyah. Surely it would make sense to have a good clean up in order to forget the memories of the past. You say you want to clean the country up? Well start with the military junk, sewage and refuse collection.

The stares of disbelief when Iraqi's see a 'western face' in a moving vehicle, that had still not changed. Some of the stares were born of hatred but many had a smile, there were two sides. The journey was a good one and we entered Nasiriyah; no big changes from what I could see. We drove down the road where I had stayed last year and as we reached that villa we turned right, fifty meters on took a left turn, straight on for one hundred meters and then at the T-junction a right turn. Immediately on the right there was a small driveway and a set of solid iron gates. The gates opened and we pulled on to a longer concrete driveway. I stepped out and walked into the villa. Cool and familiar territory for me.

Just after arrival I was treated to some lunch… and yes! you guessed it, chicken, salad, chips and rice! I remember thinking "Are you having a laugh? This is a wind up for sure!" I genuinely thought that this was a piss take on the instructions of Paul! Paul arrived midway through the lunch and joined me, along with five others. Not too much serious talk was going on, it was more chit chat… why he decided to move from the previous villa, who was staying in the villa, the surroundings, what Nasiriyah was like now, how the base was… just general small talk.

After lunch Paul walked me around the villa which was slightly bigger than the previous property. A ground floor, level one and level two. From level two there was the familiar set of stairs that led to a flat roof but what greeted me was something else. No guns or guards, just a dog, a German Shepherd and it was as big as a lion, it was fucking massive! Initially I shit myself as the thing hurtled towards us, snarling and foaming, baying for blood. Surely this is not happening, why is this fucking dog not on a leash? As the dog got closer, Paul confronted the dog by shouting at it and gave it an almighty slap on the head. Fuck me! The slap was a full-on slap that jolted the dog to calm down a little. I say calm but this dog was on drugs!

I did not really know how to react and I was very unsure even though Paul was there. I asked "Paul, why don't you have that fucking thing on a leash?" Paul replied "Gary it's ok. The dog is mine and he won't bite you whilst I'm here, so just relax." Incredulously I said "Relax?! Are you fucking serious?! It's a fucking liability! It's a killing machine! Where the fuck did you get it?" Paul responded "If I told you, you would not believe me. I will show you the dog's papers when we go downstairs. All I ask is that you don't attempt to come up to this roof without me." I replied "Why on earth would I want to come up here? I can't exactly play tag with the fucking thing! It's on fucking drugs for fucks sake! It needs an injection to put it to sleep!" We went back downstairs and Paul walked to his bedroom that was just off the main living room. Ground floor, the same as he chose in the other villa.

He returned to the living room with some papers. The papers showed that the seller of the dog was the American military. They had seized the dog and kept it in custody until they could find a suitable owner. Paul found out about this, got talking one day to someone who shared the information about the dog to him and Paul was mad enough to take on the challenge of handling this nutcase on the roof. The paperwork also showed who the previous owner was. Paul pointed at the box where the previous owners full name was and read, "Uday Hussein." I took a long look at Paul, twisted my mouth, and frowned hard, "Fuck off! Not THE Uday Hussein? Bullshit! So, you are trying to tell me that dog was stroked by Uday and his Dad Saddam?" Paul smiled and said "Gary, I know it sounds off scale and yes, I also questioned it, but it's true and that dog, believe it or not, obeys me and only me. Yeah, sure it's wild; it's a nutcase but not many people will want to get onto that roof!"

Paul had employed five Iraqi lads from Baghdad. I had met them before on the base where they were doing various mechanical jobs for some companies. All of them were good mechanics and knew a lot of shit about American cars. Paul had won a contract to supply cars to the American Air Force, leasing out just over 100 vehicles; Ford Expeditions, Ford Explorers, Landcruiser's, Pick-Up trucks, minibuses and a few other vehicles and he needed a maintenance team to look after that type of fleet.

Paul hired Ali and his team full time. They would look after all types of maintenance and engineering, whether that would be on the vehicles, laundry or even portable toilets. Ali was the boss who managed 'Small' Ali, Bessam, Muthana and Mohammed, good lads in general. Their standard of workmanship was very good but several times they had to be brought back inline. They were like kids and they tried to reciprocate what they saw between Paul and I but of course that cannot be allowed. Some reminders were needed and most of the time a good use of NVC's were enough to straighten them out. I treated them no different to my laundry lads and why should I? They were doing a job and being paid for it but I needed to make sure that I kept the distance from them and the trust can only go so far here.

I can't remember a time where they let me down to the degree of disaster but this is Iraq and it is not easy to find these types of lads at this level, so it could be worse. They would go out their way to help me, quite a caring set of lads. In the evening time they would like to make sure see if I wanted beer or something. I could get more out of them than Paul could. Paul was easier on them, probably because Paul's role was not as hands on as mine.

Paul would spend a lot of his time sat in front of a computer looking at all the contracts that were on offer, service contracts and general trading. Every day he would be sent enquiries from various military offices, inviting to tender for supplies of various goods. The list was endless for the different sorts of requests, you name it Paul would try and find it and supply it. He would network on the base with all the departments and offices and why not? He is American and so are most of the end users.

When I came back, Paul always had me watching the boys, making sure what had to be done was being done. They had it easy for some time and they tried every trick in the book to soften me up and try to get on the right side of me thinking that I would relax my opinion on the work to be done but it did not work.

One day, Ali went to Paul in an attempt to get Paul to speak to me. Paul said to me with a smile and a chuckle "Hey it seems you are pissing people off and pushing them to hard and maybe you should chill a little?" I replied, "That can only be Ali coming to you, complaining for the famous five. I tell you what we will do, we will have a meeting tonight here in the house and I will chair, if you don't support it then I will release my own burden of managing them, it's that simple really." Paul came back "When did I say you are wrong? Or how did I deserve to get your backlash? I will support you always but I want to make sure that you are not going over the top and need to understand this is Iraq, not London." I replied, "Well I'm just putting it out there now, I will chair the meeting and will do so in a civilised manner but we do it my way because you will just beat about the bush." Paul said, "We all know your thoughts on how much ground you will give, so I can safely say we will be looking for a new crew soon if you piss them off too much." I said, "Just trust me, let me deal with them and stop bitching about a new crew."

At the dinner table I told them we will have a meeting in the living room. An hour later the scene was set. I knew Paul met Ali just before so I knew what was coming, so, I let it play out. Paul didn't give me the chance to start the meeting, he was clever enough to make some fun and laughter about a few common things. That was his intro, to create a mood where the famous five could use their kid like humour to take away the seriousness of what they should be doing, so I just went along with it.

Ten minutes had passed, I had not even opened my mouth and was hoping that my introduction would happen through one of the five, not Paul. Paul I'm sure was trying his hardest to keep my input away from the talks and he knew to ask me too many questions would not be helpful. There was one particular topic that they all seemed to want to talk about and it was the main one for me. That was how they spent their time and as luck would have it, Muthana who was sat beside me, patted me on the back and said in broken English, "Habibi Mr. Gerry, what's wrong, you so quiet, my goodness you know you keep work so hard since you come back. I not surprised you tired, you need to slow down, you know my good friend is good to have you with us."

Muthana was a good actor, that speech with his white toothed smile and head nodding around the group, he could have got an Oscar on another night but not this one. He carried on, "Mr. Gerry, so come on, speak up my good friend and put your hand in to say this is good way for us to do these schedules, you agree with the schedule?" The look on Paul's face was a classic and he had a good idea of what was coming.

I spoke up, "Muthana, yes, my good friend and friends you are indeed but also remember we have many contracts to take care of. Whether you like it or not there are weaknesses. I have seen more than enough over the last few days to know what is required and I will tell you how it is going to be. Ali, you have to sign off a daily review sheet at the contracting office. The answer to that is yes, which means my neck is on the line which means my rules apply. There is a daily plan and schedule for each one of you and you can find it on the wall in the kitchen. It is subject to change if I have any type of breakdown at any time of the day. If you don't want to be on the schedule you can simply cross out your name on the wall chart. Simple." Ali replied, "Yella, then is ok, we agreed, so as you say, if we not agree we can just put a line through our name for the daily timings, hours we have to do but as long as we go to work and solve the best we can." I replied, "Ali, if you cross off your name no problems but after going in the kitchen to cross off your name, make sure you take your suitcase in the kitchen with you and carry on walking out the back door and away from the villa. If you cannot work to an agreed system that is no good to me, my laundry lads do the same, they have a system and so will those who work in maintenance, take it or leave it." Paul's face was a picture, not a happy look but there was no way he was going to take their side and no way he was going to disagree with me, he was going on leave.

Deep down he knew it was the right thing to do, he knew that laziness had crawled in and discipline was needed. Paul turned to Ali, "Ali, at the end of the day it is Gary's call. I asked him to look at operations for me, if he feels this is needed, I have to respect that and I think it would be better if we all know what everyone is doing, so I'm sure Gary will tell us when it all starts!" I said, "It starts in forty-eight hours. So, good we got that out the way, let us crack on and get these service issues up to date and back on track."

The main problem for Ali is that he wanted everything his own way. The four other lads worked for him in Baghdad where he was the boss but he forgot that QIT had a structure and he had to respect that. What he could not accept was the discipline. He wanted a more relaxed environment where they could come and go as they pleased... no fucking way. Gradually as Ali spent more time with me, he learned many things which would help his cause further with QIT, not just in Nasiriyah. He adapted and started to show more respect for me.

The very first night I came back, Paul and I sat up quite late. We agreed that he would leave on the 23rd of March and he would concentrate on getting his paperwork up to date for a smooth handover. He wanted to introduce me to all the contacts and clients and we did that for a full day. It took us twelve hours to meet and greet everyone on the base. Some changes were also going to be made for the better and Paul was excited and happy about them, so were the clients.

At the same time of relieving Paul, I was also covering Osama who had decided to go for a vacation at the same time as Paul. I was not happy about this; I only found out about it when I arrived. For the first four days I was leaving the villa at 0600 hrs and returning at 2200 hrs; there was a backlog of work in the laundry, just my fucking luck!

Osama had managed to convince Ram that everything was hunky dory and it would all work out ok. He had taken his foot off the gas a week before as he learned that I was coming over. Whatever was he thinking for fucks sake? He must have thought that Gary had a magic wand and he can easily get back on top of the work within thirty minutes of using his wonderful brain power! How fucking wrong! I went ballistic at both of them. Osama had offered to delay his vacation and help me clear the backlog. I simply said, "Osama it's simple, I don't need your help, I will do it myself and I will deduct from your salary, live with it." Osama said, "Oh please no no Mr. Gary it's ok I will help you, I'm sorry this happened is confusion." I came back, "Osama, no confusion here, learn the fucking hard way. Never take your foot off the gas. You are lucky I do not replace you, now fuck off out of my face!" Ram then got the wrath of my tongue for not speaking out and being a soft touch. Ram did the right thing though and said fuck all. He just made sure he grinded his body into the ground to pull it back.

During one early evening Ram said to me in his broken English "Boss please, when Mr. Paul leave 23rd April, I don't want you help me, I'm ok I can do all, I can do work for two men boss, I don't want you doing too much, you have too much to do." And that is exactly what happened. Ram did manage to take care of all matters relating to the laundry, he did not let me down with that, he only needed me a few times to kick some arses. Ram just worked. You feed Ram three times a day, make sure he gets his rice and he is like a 'Duracell' battery, he goes on and on and on.

Whilst I had been away, Osama had recruited four other workers from Iraq. Paul told me these four lads had unsettled the other workers in the laundry, so over those first four days I came down on these four like a ton of bricks, they needed to understand I do not allow bullies or attention seekers, I have a business to run. They were brought back inline, very quickly.

With these extra additions, it had created an unbalance to the workflow, so the knock-on effect is that at times they were standing around with nothing to do, taking extra breaks. It was not their fault; it was Osama and Paul's. I decided to pull them out of the laundry and use them on another contract Paul had won and that was for the portable toilet units. These units are best described as a toilet in a toughened plastic 'telephone box'. I never knew how challenging it was to clean these things on a daily basis and Paul had two hundred of the damn contraptions on rental!

The 'toilet' team consisted of two tankers, one to suck the shit out of the storage tanks and the other a freshwater tanker so the toilets could be cleaned and then refilled with fresh water, all with the support of a specialist disinfectant. The tanker drivers needed the cleaners to help them do the cleaning. One of these new workers was a right cocky little shit, eighteen years old and he thought he was a young up and coming 'Rocky Bilbao'. I swear he reminded me of Stallone in the first ever 'Rocky' movie, mainly because he wore these black leather gloves with the fingertip part cut off, a black bandana, black monkey boots and wore his QIT Polo Shirt with his collar turned up.

First things first, I asked ram to call him over to me. I had to stop myself from laughing because he strutted over to me with a right attitude and it really pissed me off but I had to keep it together. The main thing was to bring this little fucker down to where he belonged before he infected all my lads with his cocky nature. "My name is Gary and I believe your name is Amer?" He replied, "Yeah I know your name what can I do for you?" Biting my tongue I said, "If you don't take off your hair band and gloves these soldiers will take you off the base and you will never work for QIT ever again. "He took a long hard look at me, moved his head around a little and had this irritating smile on his face. He was looking for attention from the room and trying to remain the ringleader. Clearly enjoying the moment, he thought it was funny to keep me waiting but unknown to him I had a soldier watching him and without saying a word, the soldier walked into the laundry and said, "Gary, is this the man you would like removed from the base?" I did not have to answer as dickhead removed the items, at the same time I lowered his collar.

Later that day I had a phone call, asking me to return to the laundry. Most of the lads were taking the piss, going to the toilet more times than they needed and found it funny to try and take a snooze whilst having a shit. This is a complete no no. I was fucking livid, more so because I had never had these issues before and now have all this shit starting, I was going to read the riot act now. Fuckers!

I calmly explained to the guards that I needed to urgently close the doors to the laundry for five minutes and to be pardoned for my outburst but it needed to happen. I got them all in, closed the doors and went ballistic. I asked them what the fuck they were doing and who they thought they were? My dream came true and 'Mr. Macho' was going to make my moment. He thought it was funny, as soon as I saw him with his cocky smile on his face, he was mine. I walked over to him, "So you think it's funny Mr. fucking hard man? I tell you what, let you and me go around the back of the laundry now, just you and me and let us see who laughs there?" I had been told that he did kick boxing and he fancied himself, hence the fingerless gloves. He stopped and took the smile away and said, "No it is ok I don't want to." I responded, "Let's go around the back now or we meet tonight, bring all your friends so they can see how fucking hard you are." He did not like it and Mr. hard man was now seen for what he truly was, a typical bully but for some reason my lads thought he was funny. I said, "Listen all of you! If you don't like working for me, fuck off and I will bring in others, if you want to leave you can leave now, so what do you want to do?" The guys could see that I meant it; they had never seen me this way and I knew they would not walk as they knew they had the best jobs in Nasiriyah. It didn't make sense, the more you spoke to them like shit, the more they understood, damn mentality on them, they drove me mad with moments like this.

So, March the 23rd had arrived, Paul had packed his stuff and he left early, now I was on my own.

I had the famous five from Baghdad but it is not the same. It is a completely different level of trust and of course I have Ram to rely on. Most of the time I would be on the base, which was a good thing, the work keeps you busy. I was left with looking after the villa, the vehicles, the contracts… no drama. I just had to stay switched on, the rest is easy. Paul got away on time, his ride took him to Kuwait by road and then he was able to fly out to Qatar and then on to seeing family.

13 LIFE WITHOUT PAUL

The villa was situated on a corner plot and there were roads directly to all sides. On the ground floor there were three exits and nine rooms. On the first floor there were another five rooms and then you went up to the flat roof to visit 'Danger', Paul's dog. I was tasked to feed the fucking thing, so we left the dogs bowls near the doorway where you would go out to the roof, this was so I would just have to walk a quick 2 or 3 steps, grab the food and water bowls, go back inside, fill the bowls, then quickly put them back out and not think that I was Danger's idea of dinner!

Outside the walls of the villa was a large garden and surrounding the grounds was the perimeter wall which was approximately four meters high with no gate. The only gate was the one located in between the two driveways, that were a double set of solid iron. In the grounds there were some outhouses that Paul had converted to make rooms for Ram and Osama. The villa was guarded 24 hours a day and we always had two guards on duty, mainly situated at the main gates but also making regular walkabouts around the perimeter. I used to tell Paul there should be more but he felt it was ok.

Abu H was one of the guards and many times he would tell me never to worry, no man can come through him and I believed him. I used to look after Abu H because I knew how he felt about me. He came to me one day and asked for some of my time, he wanted to bring his son so he could meet me. I agreed and he sent for his son immediately. Abu H came in with his sixteen-year-old son and a translator, he looked nervous but carried on smiling all the time as usual.

Abu H spoke through the translator in broken English, "Mr. Gerry he is only sixteen, he has never had a real job, he has a good heart like his father but I want him to be smart like my brother. Please Mr. Gerry take him for my family, he will listen and learn from you. I tell him true, if he honest and work hard for Mr. Gerry he will start to grow to a clever man." I could not say no to him, there was something about Abu H where you could see the truth in him, or otherwise he was a fucking good actor and had put one over on me, but I don't think so, his eyes told me differently. I said, "Abu Haider, he can start tomorrow but you know my rules about hygiene, to be on time, work's six days a week, he listens to me. He does not speak to the soldiers unless they speak to him and if he has any problems, he comes to me. I will put him with the tanker drivers, I will give him responsibility." Abu H said, "Mr. Gerry you know how I feel about how good your heart, many men truly love your heart for how you look after us, like your sons. My son is your son Mr. Gerry, if you want kick his arse you have my permission, you can. Thank you so much, I promise he will not make any bad things, I will explain your rules to him, thank you Mr. Gerry. I love you my brother."

Arabs always say Gerry and not Gary. I kind of got used to it, no problems with that but the words of loving me, that I'm still not sure how to take. A few days after this meeting I came home one day and as I walked into the kitchen Bessam was sat at the kitchen table with the new chef. I could see the chef was wearing a brand-new blackened eye and a nose that had been re-arranged by a baseball bat. I sat down, listened to what Bessam had to tell me about the incident and my heart sank as I knew what I had to do. There was no other way out of the situation.

Later that evening Bessam came to see me, he told me that Abu H was here to see me. We sat down and Abu H explained that he knew what I had to do and told me not to worry or feel bad that I had to sack him. He said that he was so happy how his son had a job and said he would always be thankful for my kindness to his family. He said, "Mr. Gerry is not your fault what you have to do. I know you have to teach the right and wrong thing to do. I do bad, I know I do bad, I'm sorry what I do to this man." To this day I would trust Abu Haider with my life and little did I know after that evening how he would once again come into my life and touch it in such a way.

The following day brought another big test for me and a personal loss to me of my own items. I had moved my stuff into Paul's room, there was an ensuite bathroom and I had left my 22-carat gold bracelet on the sink, now it had gone missing. I waited until everyone had returned to the villa and held a meeting in the yard. I said to them all, "If one of you has taken it, make sure you put it back in my bathroom in the next hour. If it is not returned then for the next week, all of you will not receive an evening meal from the company. You will not have the use of free drinks in the house, no television networks to use and no bonus this month, all that will go. The bonus payment will be cancelled and do not try and use the kitchen to cook anything, no cooking, you get your food outside."

Ali came to me and said, "You have to do this, this is the only way they will understand and my guys agree with me." I replied, "Ali, the same applies to you and your lads, all five of you, if I don't get my gold back then you are treated the same no different." Ali's face contorted "Gerry this is not fair on me and my guys, I know our bonus payment is more than the laundry, Paul would not agree to this." I replied, 'Ali, Paul is not here and I decide until he comes back, help me find my gold and your bonus is paid, no gold no bonus. Ali, I think you are missing the point here, these changes are for everyone, my gold has gone missing, it could be something of yours or someone else's that could go missing next week! Maybe in your culture, your values or non–values it is ok for you to accept someone to act like Ali Baba, for me no and I believe as senior management I feel the need to try and create awareness of what is right and wrong. You always talk the talk Ali, come across as a man who really cares. If you want to do the right thing for me then listen to me. QIT has invited all of you as guests into their villa, free of charge. You clean, feed, warm yourselves free of charge and are welcomed as guests and that is paid back by someone stealing my gold bracelet. You think I'm not fair, what planet do you come from Ali? If you really want to prove yourselves and do the right thing, have a meeting with all of them and between you, find my gold."

Unreal! I go out of my way to look after these guys, someone steals my shit and all Ali can see is his rights. Fuck right off! Funny part of all of this, the chef was happy, he would only be cooking for me and not the other fifteen. Rams face was a picture, he could not believe it. No dinner?! WTF?! Ram said to me, "Boss I need talk to you." I replied, "Ram if it is about your food don't talk to me, I don't care, you want food, find the person who took my gold, now go away."

My sleep or lack of it changed. For years I was a heavy sleeper but I moved over to a light one. I went to bed in a clean pair of jeans, T-shirt, pair of socks with an AK47 under my bed and a pistol under the mattress which belonged to Paul. I would change the patterns of my sleep and change the times I would leave the villa and return. If someone was watching the villa, I would not have a set pattern. I was always being cautious, it was important to me that the others followed my thoughts, including the Iraqis.

Gun culture for the Iraqis is a normal way of life but for me I was not happy from day one. Who could be happy with guns in their face wherever you go? It wasn't for me but whilst I'm here they were needed. Sometimes, I used to wake the house up at night, when I heard gunfire, especially if it was too close, these lads had to try and change their mindset. Every day I would travel to the base with one of the famous five. We would use different routes, leave at varied times, I love routine but I felt it could compromise things. I would always drive the car. Why? Because I know my own ability. I know I'm able to drive fast and safe, having previously served time being taught how to drive in the Police using roadcraft techniques. The locals were not used to brand new 4 x 4's driving around at speed, and especially not the speed I was holding, at around 160 kilometres per hour in built up areas. This was not normal but it was for me, you want to try and hit me you will have to be an amazing shot. I stopped for nobody, even at junctions I would take control of the road with the size of the car, dominate the space, and just pull out with sheer arrogance.

A problem we always faced was that we could not take guns onto the base, so we could not keep them in the car. I used the car all the time when on the base, hence why I used to drive at high speeds.

On Monday the 5th of April 2004, I had two important meetings booked with the main American Air Force contracting office and then I had promised Ram he could have an early day, so I would cover him. I therefore decided that I would leave the house around midday because I was going to be working in the laundry until 10pm. I woke up just after 9am, took a shower, got dressed in a QIT white polo shirt, pair of blue jeans and trainers. This was one good thing about doing this work, no need to put on a shirt and tie. A look at the clock told me it was 1150 hrs and it was time to be off so I gathered my papers, picked up my sunglasses and cigarettes, walked into the kitchen, placed the stuff on the table, called out the name of Little Ali.

The only known people to be in the villa, Little Ali, the cook, the cleaning lady and myself, everyone else should be at work. Ali walked into the kitchen and I said, "Ali come on I'm ready and need to go, yella let's go." Ali came back, "Gerry please give me five minutes, I need to check the oil in the car, just five minutes, go smoke cigarette and then we go." Impatiently I said "Ali, be quick please I have meetings, yella come on."

I moved back into the living room to do as Ali said. The living room was a big old room and like many Arabic houses, windows were not in short supply, it was like a green house in there. No sofa in here, just large cushions placed on the floor against the wall, the floor covered in various large rugs on a wooden floor.

From walking in through the back door, you walked into the kitchen, then walking straight on, out into a hallway, two strides and you would come to a door and walk into the living room. From walking into the living room opening up to the right was the living room and an instant right a door led into Paul's bedroom, to the left of the living room door was another door that led into our small office we had and that room also housed a massive safe 600cms x 1000cms, this was one serious lump of metal, goodness knows how much it weighed.

One thing I did know, is how much money was in that safe, just under $500,000 US Dollars! I know what you are thinking but it is true and I was not happy that I would have to look after it, I had the key. I had to sign for it to say that I recognise that this money was is in the safe but it pissed me off. For me it was madness beyond all belief to have that kind of cash readily available in that safe. I don't care how heavy and solid the damn thing is, that money should not be in this villa.

I lit up a cigarette, paced around the living room, thinking about my meetings and how I should approach them.

14 UTTER MAYHEM

For what you are about to read, to this day I have not been able to explain to anyone how I really felt because it happened so fast and my mind went to a place, I never thought it could go to.

From the corner of my right eye, I could see bodies directly outside the windows, dressed mainly in black clothing, faces covered running at speed with large calibre weapons. I guess the best way to explain this is that I just froze. I was in shock. My mind said run! Yeah, sure but where the fuck do I run? There is no secret underground room, run upstairs to what? This is not a movie, forget under the bed or behind a curtain and the roof is out of bounds, unless I want to get eaten alive by the fucking dog! For some reason I ran into the office, opened the drawer to the desk, a handgun was in there. Gazza take it and get out of there!

I picked up the gun, then dropped it! But why drop it for fucks sake? Am I scared? Am I a true man and need to have a full-on battle with these fuckers, go out in a blaze or do I do different? Am I a bigger threat to them, armed or unarmed? If I was them and see others with guns, would I react differently? Your damn fucking right I will but I have nowhere to run! Yeah, sure I'm 37 years old now but I know I'm still very quick off the blocks, not be many of them would be able to keep up with my speed, no fucking chance but I'm fucked and have no place to run! Gaz wake up and shape up you twat, switch on or else you are fucked son. The heavy sound of gunfire opened up all around my space outside of the villa, it was so close and the noise was deafening. I had never experienced it this loud before, what the fuck are they tooled up with?

'WHOOSH!!'... What the fuck?!

A volley of noise exploded around me, smoke and dust filled the air, my ears were ringing with a sharp piercing noise as the living room door flew through the air, just missing me. Concrete was flying all around me, I couldn't see anything, I just covered up to protect my face as much as I could, my body was low to the ground, my throat was struggling to keep up with the small amount of oxygen I could gather in. Fuck am I hyperventilating here? Fuck, am I going into severe shock?

"Yella! Yella! Fucker! Fuck you! Down! Down!" I was trying to get out the office as quick as the words were being said. Easier said than done. The sound of weapons had been taken over by many voices, all hollering in Arabic, a crossfire of words. There must have been ten officers and no soldiers in this set up, the traffic of voices had hit peak time. As I came out from the office, I tried to get a fix on who was in the room but I could see fuck all for all the smoke and dust, it was so heavy. Gaz for fucks sake stand up, look up mate, get a fucking grip! The smells around me were horrendous. What is that smell? It was like a gas smell or like eggs, but from what? The shouting got closer and more hostile, there must be at least twenty voices hollering bollocks but with a clear message towards me, "We fucking hate you!" I had to look up. Perhaps I could make a run for the front door without being seen, surely no one can see one meter in front of their own nose?

'SMACK'!!!... Hands! Pushing, pulling, slapping, punching around my head, just continuous hysterical abuse in a mix of English and Arabic, fucking hostility on steroids! There was no pain at this stage, I was too afraid to think of any pain. The shouting was mental. These fuckwits were totally out of control and looked like there was not one strong leader between them who could take control. What is going on? Are they just some rogue group or are they a switched-on mob who just have no leadership?

They were now behind me. It was like a ruck and maul. My body was kicked and punched into the corridor. Crossing into the kitchen, I tried lifting my head, maybe Little Ali would be there? Again... 'SMACK!'... Fuck me! What just hit me? Whatever it was took me to the ground. I waited for boots to follow in or worse, then my ear popped and began to sting like fuck. I was dragged to my feet but these fuckers were obsessed with my body stance, they wanted me walking but no eye-to-eye contact.

I was trying to understand how many of them were around me. I'm thinking there is about six of them but where is Little Ali or the cook? Where had they gone? Where the fuck are the guards? Dead? They were throwing me all over the place in their quest to get me moving, they were pushing, punching, slapping me to the double gates and as I got through the gate, again I tried to look up to see my surroundings. I could see Little Ali to my right, ten meters away from me. I tried to move towards him. They were kicking the fuck out of him; he was on the floor trying to shield his head. Mother fuckers let me be close to him! I needed Ali near me. Ali locked his eyes onto me and for a moment I thought he was trying to speak but both of us were under heavy physical abuse, Ali more so than me.

I was dragged to the left of the gates and away from Ali. I was being frog marched across to the other side of the road where several white pickups were sat. My eyes were panning left, right, all over the place trying to understand the situation. Within eye shot, my mind was counting thirty people. In each direction there were black dressed bodies, on one knee, hugging an RPG into the neck. Fuck me, these lot were covering every angle. To take this lot on it had to be a military force, where are the Italians for fucks sake? They are supposed to be in control of the city, the bridge is just 100 meters away and they have check points on the bridge, why have they not heard all the gunfire? You would have to be deaf not to have heard what has been going on for the past five minutes! Fucking unreal.

I tried to scan around further. I clocked the two guards we had on duty; the fuckers were stood about 20 meters to my right, leaning against a shop fronted building, they had company themselves with armed bodies standing around them. I hope they get what is coming to them! Paid to guard in my book means paid to open fire on such occasions, not fucking throw the towel in, the fuckers! Some fucking guards they turned out to be! Fuck! Where is Abu Haider?! My friend I need you now, fuck the difference of being right or wrong, I need you here, how the fuck are you getting out this shit Teeley? I don't think I will.

The way these lot had gone about their business; this was not there first time at the rodeo. They have done this before; they did not learn this in their bedrooms. These fuckwits continued kicking me all over the place towards a pickup, twin cab for sure. As the rear door opened, I was bundled inside, followed by a person to the left and another to the right of me, two others jumped into the driver and front passenger seats. The passenger seat had been filled by a feral Jundi, whose barrel of an AK47 came up and pointed straight at my head and for good measure a bitch slap planted to the back of my head, signalling for me to look down.

As they struggled for supremacy in the pickup, again the volley of shouting escalated, not that there was any calm since they had attacked the villa. I could hear and sense activity directly behind me in the back of the

70

pickup, the damn truck was rolling all over the place, so the dickhead with the AK47 on my head was not able to stop it prodding all over me, the fucking thing could go off any time! My head pointed downwards, my back arched, I could feel a heavy weight on my back, was it some kind of chain? I could hear the rattling sound of metal, the roof of the cab was being pounded by a heavy weight, what the fuck are they doing? Hang on a minute, these fucking nutters I am sure, have bad news assembled on the roof, the rattling sound is a chain of bullets hanging down into the cab! Fuck these lot are serious and not just some street kids. This feral prick better have his safety on! All I need is for him to have a fucked-up weapon or maybe he is some crazed trigger-happy twat! He would wipe out everyone in the truck!

We were on the move. The driver sped off. Switch on Teeley! Follow the vehicles direction. If I focus, I can get an idea of where we are going, the feel of the ride, there are good road surfaces and wasteland. The ride was rough for the first one hundred meters, the driver then made a one-hundred-and-eighty-degree turn, turned right and then left, he is headed for the bridge, over the Euphrates! The Italians will have the checkpoint at the bridge! They have to be there! Fuck this pickup is going to take incoming. Fuck me! My heart is all over the place, I can hear it booming in my ears, I can't fucking breathe. Am I walking into a shower of bullets?!

Gaz! Switch on, fucking wake up, deep breaths and get ready to make a run for it! If they are there, maybe the pickup will be forced to stop, maybe the stop will be non-aggressive and they just have to hand me over. Fuck, I hope so. We could only be one minute from the bridge now, the checkpoint I know is halfway over the bridge, I had been through it many times. The sound of the tires had changed, we were on the bridge. We slowed down and came to a stop. I moved my head to the left by one degree, pushed my eyes as far as I could to my left, who was at the checkpoint? The window came down, the talk was Arab on Arab, what the fuck?!

Where are the Italians? Have they lost the bridge? Are you fucking serious?! This is not happening, how the fuck can you lose control of a fucking bridge? What the fuck am I going to do? I can't do this shit! The car began moving again and we reached the end of the bridge, turned right, straight on for hundred meters, left turn and then another left, we stopped, then moved forwards again by ten meters, coming to a grinding halt.

The door to my left opened and I was dragged out of the cab. I was being forced forwards, I looked up and took advantage of this. I raised my head fully to see the party of blacked dressers had increased. Fucking hell there are loads of them! For sure one hundred plus, this is an army of some kind

71

but which army? I was marched through a concrete yard and in front of me was a huge building, the yard being surrounded by a wall which had to be five meters high and one particular area decorated with bullet holes... not a good sign!

The looks I was receiving were scary. Men standing around, smoking, drinking. I had never been looked at this way before in Iraq, I had some looks of curiosity but these kind of looks are not good. Funnily enough, I remembered past times working in Abu Dhabi, in the UAE. The industrial estates were heaving with all sorts of heavy trucks, plant equipment for rental and the hirers being from Afghanistan/Pakistan. Those boys for sure did not like having us Brits in Abu Dhabi, why I don't know as I had done nothing wrong to them, the looks were similar.

These fuckers all seemed to be carrying the same piece on them, AK47's. What is wrong with these lot? Can they not move forwards with the times and buy something different? I guess not. They wanted something free, cheap, or stolen but I know they like them for reliability, what more do I know?

Every single one of them had webbing on of some description. Some had a normal amount; others were definitely looking to get themselves in the frame for the next Stallone movie. They were smothered with hand grenades. What have I got myself in to? Who are they? If this is Zarqawi's outfit I'm not surviving! What the fuck have I got myself into? What do they want from me? Will I be beheaded on video or maybe used as a human shield? My mind was going crazy, my body temperature was at boiling point, my heart rate off the charts, I could hardly catch my breath. In the last ten minutes my life has gone from thinking about looking to start another service on the base into a gang fuck!

I was waiting to be shot in the head at any time. Mentally I was already drained, physically I was fine and had reserves for sure but mentally I was struggling, or was I? I started to think of family, my kids, my Mum and Dad... I have let them all down, I will never see them again, I don't want to think about the facts of how I was taken and what happened, not now.

I was taken into the building, walking through a corridor on the ground floor. There were rooms to my left and right, people everywhere, a busy place. I was pulled back, stopped dead in my tracks, swung round to face the wall and then a stabbing to the back of my neck. Fuck it! A gun to the back of my head! My muscles were so tight, afraid they would go into spasm and bring on exaggerated cramp. We are surrounded by a hundred or more of his mates and he needs to have a gun pointed at me? Fucking prick.

Two minutes later I was pulled away from the wall, my left arm was grabbed, swung around the back of me, I was pushed up a stairway and within a minute I was being led outside onto a rooftop. I was pushed with some force towards the edge, a two-meter-high wall stopped me falling over the side. As my eyes adjusted, I could see Little Ali and the cook. A blanket lay on the floor and I could see some garments. I was sure I was looking at some dish dashes (a dish dash is a male dress, ankle length). Why do they have clothes on the blanket? I'm sure I would find out.

Switch on Gaz, you need information from Ali, maybe he will know what is happening? I needed clarification for the immediate future. I was close to Ali, he was just two meters away from me, he had no smile, I was trying to read his thoughts by his facial expressions. I said, "Ali who are they? What will happen to us? Will I be killed?" Ali replied, "Gerry, they take you to protect you, they will not kill you, don't worry." With that he turned his head away from me, threw his guts up and the cook quickly followed to show me his breakfast.

Fuck I can't believe this, they are Iraqi, me the Brit, I'm in more shit than they are and they are throwing up! Then again, why are they being sick? Is Ali keeping quiet from telling me the truth? What does he really know?

The blanket and the dirty dish dash made my mind go into overdrive, what was the blanket for? To soak up my blood and roll me up in? The clothes to be used to disguise me? Maybe all three of us would be executed away from the eyes of the world's eyes, here on this roof. I was in a shit state. I had a full packet of cigarettes in my pocket, Ishtar brand, thank fuck I had Ishtar, stronger than a Marlboro Red or Gitane with no filter. Even the Iraqis could not smoke these fags and many wondered how on earth I managed to smoke them without batting an eyelid. I was lighting one up after another, being watched all the time by my captors, dotted and huddled over the large area of the rooftop. The stares telling me, "I hate you! I want to kill you and I hope I can!"

I had never been in this type of situation in my life where the odds are stacked against me. I hated the feeling of having no control of the situation but worse of all, waiting to be shot or losing my head by some massive fuck off blade!

Ali and the cook were ordered to sit down on the blanket, they came closer to each other. I was pushed towards the door which led back down

73

the stairs. Another man came forward, started to shout at me as he pointed to the ground. I sat down, his gun came to my face so I turned my face away from the nozzle of the barrel and my body tightened once more. I took a deep breath, closed my eyes, waiting for the impact. I sat there with five or six standing around me, them finding it funny that their guns should be pointed in my direction. The feeling of the guns on me all the time was horrendous; my heart was pounding out of my chest and I was so hot, my mouth felt like the bottom of a bird cage, to spit would have been a miracle and to swallow was painful. I never knew until now how long I could take a long breath for, it felt like I was going into a deep meditation.

Ali and the cook were moved to where I was and as he got into earshot I said, "Ali what is going on? what are they talking about?" One of these nutters walked closer to Ali, "Americi? Israeli?" This ugly looking fucker stood in front of me, "You are Americi?!" Fuck me he thinks I'm American! I replied, "La la, I'm English man." (La means no in Arabic). He carried on speaking to Ali and the word Israeli was hot on this fuckers' lips. I said to Ali, "Ali, you tell him I can prove I'm not Israeli, you tell him I will show my dick too prove I'm not circumcised." What a gang fuck this is, I need to get myself down the pecking order. Logically a Brit will live longer than an American or a Jew. If these nutters had a 'Top of the Pops' top ten list, a Brit would not be number one, not in my book.

The conversation was then interrupted by an evil looking fucker in white. On any other day he would look like he was selling ice cream but today the ninety-nine cornet was replaced by his snarling looks, black 'Dr. Martens' and a Freddie Mercury haircut, fearsome looking. Fuck me he looks like bad news; I wish I didn't stereotype in life but was hard not to with this fucker. He stood shouting out to others, like he was giving orders. The groups around him who were talking, abruptly stopped their idle chit chat and listened in to this ugly prick. He even looked at his own the same way as he did me, by the looks of things he would not have an issue putting a bullet in his own mates. With his rhetoric he suddenly dropped his weapon downwards, pointing it in my direction, choosing to shake his arm alarmingly, thrusting the AK closer to me and I could not even succeed with a proper gulp, my mouth and throat was too dry.

Ali turned to me, "Gerry they are taking you now, taking you away to safety he is saying, he said they are leaving me here and that Allah is with us all." I replied, "Ali you don't know this for sure, you need to get word to Paul. Tell my family I'm sorry and I love them, tell them I'm being as strong as I can." With that I was picked up, forced down the stairs.

It would be the last time I would see Ali and the cook; they were released two days later, safely to their families.

I was pushed and shoved all the way out of the building. I thought, what the fuck is Ali talking about? How the fuck do they want to keep me safe when every man and his dog is taking the opportunity to keep punching and kicking me to fuck as I'm walking? Ali was not being straight with me. To keep me safe would be to take me to Tallil Air Base and let me be with my own kind of people. I'm fucked and all the time Mr. Ice Cream man is around me. What a fucking nightmare!

As we got outside, we turned right and walked towards a blue metallic saloon car; a four-door vehicle, with the back door open. My head was pushed down and I was forced into the back. I had a babysitter sat either side of me and in the front a passenger and driver, all tooled up for the journey that was ahead. The gates opened and we pulled out slowly, we turned left but carried on very slow. I managed to get an eye on what was around us but had to be careful so I would not get a beating in the car. In front of us was a white pickup, which had about ten men in the back of it, with a big weapon setup on top of the cab. At every junction we came to, they all bailed out of the back and quickly became the cannon fodder for the pickup and my chariot. I was quite happy to see this as in my mind I was hoping that the European military boys could be out on patrol, see these nutters and hopefully challenge them when I could then seize the chance of getting out the vehicle. They would hit the pickup first surely. Keep going through these head drills Teeley! You need to keep with it and think that something will happen, something will go in my favour, I must be ready to seize that window of opportunity.

The next thing I knew, my head was covered with a ghutra (an Arabic head scarf). It was put on in such a way that my entire face was covered and I could see nothing. A voice said, "Keep head down and have no problems." My body temperature was ever increasing with this head scarf over me, the temperatures at that time of the year was about 35-40 degrees celsius and the shit heap I was in had no air conditioning.

The route we were taking was mainly on the back streets, they were keeping off the main road. We picked up more speed, I heard quite a lot of activity outside, the sound of car horns of the vehicles with my captors inside joining in. I took the chance to raise my head a little to understand what the party atmosphere was for. What the fuck? White pickups everywhere! There were people lining the streets, dancing in the roads and all these pickups were all equipped with heavy weapons! Where the fuck are the Italians or

Americans? How on earth can the streets be dominated in this way by the locals? This is my worst nightmare happening right before my eyes! Word has surely got back to the base on what is developing here in the city. Every day I normally see truckloads of Italians in the city and they choose to have a bank holiday today?

We came to a standstill. Yet after about two minutes, why no movement? I arched my back, brought my neck back, shrugged my shoulders. Oh, that feels good to stretch. A quick peep to my left showed that we were at a roundabout and close by a disused hangar, what it was used for years ago I'm not sure but I recognised the location. Moments later we pulled away, went straight on then within a few meters the vehicle jolted as the wheels drove over an obstacle, maybe a curb? We moved over an uneven surface, this went on for about ten minutes, stopping every so often. What the fuck is going on? Maybe they are trying to find a perfect hideaway?

I was doing my utmost to keep my senses together, trying to keep my focus in an attempt to visualise my whereabouts. I had to remain upbeat. Come on Gazza, if the chance allows itself and its safe to run in the cover of darkness, not a lot is going to keep up with you. I still have my trainers on and to keep up with me in Jesus boots or desert boots will not be easy.

My mind was drifting to back home. It had been at least two hours since I had been taken, I'm guessing it's about 1400 hrs or just after. Had word filtered through the base to my lads? Is Paul aware yet? If Paul knew, for sure my family would know, unless Paul chose to keep that quiet for the first 24 hours to see if anything changed. If the news of my abduction was out, why the fuck are the streets not full of military? My mind was on steroids, I was shattered mentally, the physical side of me started to take its toll now, I had not had any water for two hours plus, if I'm not careful I will dehydrate I'm sure I will, I was dry as fuck.

Two men were in the back of the car with me so I tried to keep them both talking. One of them did understand some words, so I said to him, "I will be shot, yes? You will make me dead? I am finished, yes, or no?" Whilst saying this, I was pointing at his gun, then pointing at him and then me, running my hand across my neck in a cutthroat expression. He started to smile at me and said, "La la, ma fi mushkila, is ok, you ok, we are not bad man." (ma fi mushkila means no problem in Arabic).

I maintained our talks, "You have babies? You have wife? "Smiling at them, cradling my arms as if I'm holding a baby, pointing at my finger to identify a ring for having a wife. Let me see if they have a sensitive side.

Maybe, just maybe I will find a weakness with one of them. I was talking about the lads who worked for me, explaining they are Iraqi men and how important it is to give the work to these men. I was selling myself; I have to find the weaknesses.

The car finally came to a stop, the ghutra was placed back over my head and I was led out rather than being kicked and punched. The ground was uneven so I knew we were out in the open a little, I could hear the voices of kids quite close to me, perhaps they were out playing. Head down, I was walked over an open ditch, not to deep but about 50cm wide, so a big stride and then up two concrete steps, turned right, then up another two steps. The sunlight vanished.

'Smack!'... they walked me into a wall, my nose taking the brunt of the force! They corrected my movements, walked straight on through a doorway, taking a second right into a room. My ghutra was taken away and one of them gestured for me to remove my trainers. I shook my hands to suggest I was ok to have them on but a furious handshake followed, he wanted my trainers off the fucker. A thin mattress was placed on the floor and I was ushered to sit on it, so I pushed it further in to the corner and sat down and instantly lit up a fag; the floor would be my ashtray for now.

I sat up against the wall, raised my knees to my chest, keeping my feet flat. I really wanted to put my legs out straight in front of me but if I did the soles of my feet would be facing them and the last thing I wanted to do is offend them (to some in the Middle East, if you have the soles of your shoes showing to your audience it is offensive). It's crazy to think that I should be thinking about something like that but I'm glad I did, I had to do as much as possible to keep them on my side, to like me as much as they could. I was shattered and wished I could have a soak in the bath or a sauna, oh my goodness what I wouldn't give for that right now.

The room remained busy for about two hours, many different faces, most of them had removed their face masks but to be honest this did not make me feel any better. I was analysing everything. By taking off their face covers and showing their faces, it's not an issue for them to be recognised? Maybe they were thinking, it's ok, a dead man cannot talk and give evidence against us, so no worries, let us walk about as we like.

I was watching their body language towards me, the expressions on their faces, the direct staring, the looks away from me and of course every time a gun came close to me. Fuck I did not like that at any time and my heart would race. I was trying my best to smile at them, hoping that I can find one or two of them with a weak link, just a crack of the mouth or the cheeks moving to single a smile, I have to get close to one of them, make a friend. I need to mix it up a bit, keep the smile up but also show them I'm a normal man, a family man and that I'm afraid and just want to go home to my kids.

The activity slowed down in the house and I was joined by four of them on my mattress, then another came into the room, a very well-dressed man compared to the others, cleanly shaved and when he walked in the others stood up, he was obviously senior to these lot. I decided to follow suit and stand for this man.

He said, "My name is Mohammed, these four men will be with you most of the time, you will be given food and water. If you don't have cigarettes, I will tell them to make sure they bring you. If you have money to buy Pepsi, chocolate or chips they will bring for you, we are not bad people. We will all leave now and be back shortly if you need anything say now?" I replied, "Yes Mohammed thank you, my name is Gary, I'm from UK. Thank you for asking if I need some things, I need water now, nobody has given me water. I have money, I want some cigarettes, Pepsi and chocolate, maybe some fruit." I continued, "Mohammed, I don't understand what is happening today, why have you taken me away from my work? My family will be worried about me, so you have to let me go home, I have done no wrong in Iraq, actually I give work to the Iraqi people, this you can ask to my workers, they will tell you this is true." He replied, "Gerry you talk too much, we know your name, we know you are a strong man but not as good as you say, we know how you have hard ways with Iraqi also. You are safe with us, we are good men, give this man some money and I will tell him what you need, he will bring later." I said, "Very kind Mohammed thank you, sorry one more thing, you work for who please? You have a company or group here?" He replied, "Gerry, I tell you, you talk too much now, no need for this talk, you understand we are good and you are safe now, we will let you know if you can go home."

With that, I gave Mohammed $10 US Dollars and he gave my list to one of the men, not sure what he would be bringing me back from Tesco later. Tesco... I wish they had a Tesco. The solid iron door to the room closed, I heard them lock the two mortis locks and I was alone for the first time. I scrambled for my back pocket and then paused. I walked over to the door.

To the right of the door was a two-meter square window, bars had been placed either side of the glass, this was a typical cell. On the other side of the glass, I could see a staircase, going up to the right of me. Beyond the staircase, directly in front of me was a door into another room. To the right of that room, I could see that you could make a right turn down the corridor, so there must be a rear entrance. I looked up the stairs as best as possible, I could see a window above me going up to the next level and to the left of that I could see that the staircase was of a curved design.

I waited another five minutes to make sure I was safe to take out my wallet. They had given me a metal tray to use as an ashtray. Out came my wallet, I had to act fast. I took hold of my lighter and began burning items on the metal tray. I had business cards from American and Italian soldiers, plus other cards from divisional heads, my Department of Defence card that had my name, date of birth and a picture of me standing in front of an American flag on it. Everything burnt to a cinder, I crumbled it into ash, pulled away at the seam of the mattress, poured some water onto the ash and then shoved it into the padding. Job done, all I had to do now was smoke like a chimney to remove the smell of plastic and paper. I also put some money into the mattress.

15 LOCATION NUMBER 2 – SETTLING IN

I began to drift into a sleep which I felt comfortable to do as I didn't have to keep watching those around me, wondering what would happen if I took my eyes off them. If I was going to die, I wanted to see it coming.

But I could not fully drop off! So, I stood up and began to pace the room, trying to take stock of the situation. I lit up my fortieth cigarette of the day. I liked a smoke but had never smoked like this before. I had now been held for at least six hours. What is their plan with me? Who are they? Who is the ringleader? Did they want to keep me safe? For what? To sell me off? Surely by now word has got back to Paul and my kids, how much do they know?

I needed to keep positive. I kept telling myself… Keep your fucking chin up mate, it's a fifty-fifty challenge on the football field Gazza, you always won them mate, keep that adrenalin and thought process but control it. You have to be smart, have to keep selling the sympathy vote, a married man with kids, have a Mum and Dad. Keep looking for the weak one in the pack, maybe one of them can lead me to freedom for a small reward but be careful, don't piss anyone off.

I needed to get my body temperature down, get as much water as I could, eat when given food but try and calculate the bad that will give me the shits, maybe worse. When I piss, look at the colour and listen to my body. I cannot afford to dehydrate, get exercise in if I'm allowed to. Whether I liked it or not, I was now facing the toughest mental challenge of my life… Don't dwell on this too much Gazza. Easier said than done as not much to keep me occupied.

If only I had left the villa ten minutes earlier, these lot would have arrived to execute my kidnapping but find out nobody is at home. Maybe then this warning would have prompted me to seek protection and move onto the base.

I spoke to the big man (God)... Ok Big G, many say you exist, apparently you see everything, you made everything and you can help anyone. I'm asking you to come forward now, get me out of this shit, turn my fortunes, if you don't....

I started to hear children's voices very close to me, I placed my plastic cup to the wall and could clearly hear. When I first arrived here, I could hear children's voices in the street and now I can hear them in the room next door. If there are children in this house then I'm sure there is a mother, if a woman saw this happening, surely, she would not agree and go tell someone.

If I was in their shoes, I would be smart, I would think to go and tell the military forces. I was hoping that they would be thinking if I do this, I can get a reward. This is positive thinking. Maybe this has already happened and military forces could be using this intelligence to make a sweep of the area. They must be looking for me. I know in the past the Italians had their arses kicked, lost control for a short while and now it seems it has happened again. I could not get this out of my head. How the fuck can all that military clout on Tallil Air Base have their arses kicked out of Nasiriyah? How the fuck did you lose control? It's not rocket science! Would the British military get involved and send in special forces?

From what I had seen today, the streets had been involved in a massive fancy-dress party, everyone decided to wear black, cover their faces and pickup all sorts of heavy weapons.

I know this is not some two-bit mob who are bored and thought they would have a one-day attempt at stardom, these boys had numbers and tools to take control but who are they and who has the muscle and the money?

Mohammed who spoke to me, what the fuck was he on about? Stating that he knows me and my hardline ways, what the fuck is that all about? Is that just a coincidence or does he know about my recent tough management decisions or does he know something from those who work for QIT? Do these lot have someone on the inside who was pissed off from my no-nonsense decisions?

I could hear a car door closing, feet on concrete, someone is coming, please let it be good news. The door was unlocked and in walked Mohammed with my four babysitters, they all had a quick look at me and walked back out of the room, except Mohammed. He took off his sandals and sat with me. He said, "How have you been?" I nodded downwards and smiled back at him. Mohammed spoke again, "You will now eat some food and we will give you some more water but first I need you to empty your pockets." I took out my wallet and started to go through my items. I explained the photos of my family, I had $200 US Dollars, my UK driving licence and my business cards, thank goodness I had burnt my other items. He put all the items back in my wallet but pocketed $100 US Dollars and said, "Ok you will not say that I have one hundred dollars."

Son of a bitch! I hated this prick now. I have no power at all. I have to suck this one up for now as I hold no aces. I then said, "When is my release? How long will I be in this room? Why have you taken me as a hostage? What have I done wrong? I think you should answer; you have just taken one hundred dollars from me?" He replied, "You have been taken for your safety, inshallah you will be released in two days." I replied, "If that is true, why not just come to my villa and tell me I'm in danger, then I can go and stay on the military base. Maybe you think that the military are going to attack me? If you are as good as you are making out, that you are doing this all for my safety, why come to the villa with guns beat me and why steal one hundred dollars from me?" He replied, "I did not steal from you, that money is Allah's money because you take this money when you are in Iraq and also there is some political things which does not make it easy." I looked him straight in the eyes and said, "Mohammed I need to know if I will be killed, so tell me." He snorted, "We are not animals or terrorist, you will not be killed, our mighty leader by the power of Allah, said Muqtada Al Sadr will not hurt you and will show you the bad of your ways. I have brought you a radio and television, just be quiet, be good and everything will be ok for you." I nodded and smiled, to make him feel that I understood. So that was me set for the evening... a television sat on top of a metal bucket and the world service broadcast put on hold for now as there were no batteries in the radio.

I could see and hear activity across the corridor in the other room and I started to smell food. Minutes later in walked the makeshift 'chef' with a metal tray that looked like it had been stored under the tracks of a tank. He placed it on the floor by my mattress and I began to frown and my stomach shit itself for what was coming to greet it. Fried eggs and onions sat in three inches of cooking oil; my stomach was fucked up as it was but I had to eat something. Three bags full of Arabic bread were thrown in front of me and my babysitters, one of my friends passed me a rounded slab. Cucumber and tomatoes were also on the menu and these were on show on another plate. The salad was covered in shit, the skins were soft and slimy, so no salad for me.

I dipped my slab of bread into the tray, scooped up what solids I could and then used the bread to wring the oil. I promise I will never complain or never hear another joke in my lifetime about a motorway fry up on the A1, North of Peterborough!

My newfound friends were offering me the salad so I gestured they should eat my portion, fuck that. The water jug arrived so it was now time for my first game of charades with them and the response was, "No! No bottle water!" Fucking great, no bottled water, which means this is tap shit! But I had to drink. Fuck I'm going to be bad in the coming days.

Mohammed came into the room, "Ok I go now, see you tomorrow." I replied, "You said I can have Pepsi and chocolate so where are they? I gave you ten dollars to bring." He replied, "Yes here is your cigarettes, the other items if you are good, I bring tomorrow." Cheeky fucker, I have been good all day and I want my sugar treats! This was torture knowing that I had to wind my neck in.

I had to start drinking this water, small amounts at a time, I didn't have a lot of choice. I had to drink to keep hydrated. I was not only dealing with the heat of the country, but I was also trying to deal with the heat caused by my new holiday adventure, anxiety and stress.

After we had eaten, I settled in for the evening, my captors were also ready to settle with me and enjoy the evening viewings on television. There were three Iraqis and one man from Sudan. He had come over to Iraq recently, like many other insurgents, he said he had come here to pick up arms for the cause of Islam and Mohammed. The three Iraqis were very young, aged between twenty and twenty-five, I could not believe how young they were. With no guns and no one outside I would have fancied my chances if I had a plan at this stage. But the guns were always with them and I was not aware of how many guards would be at the front entrance or in the area, so what would be the point of an attempt? None.

I was back to playing charades. I needed the bathroom, so once they guessed the actions I was using, I was guided to the 'little boy's' room. The door to the room had an old-fashioned latch design. I lifted the latch and opened the door... the stench hit me. Fuck my old boots! I never knew urine could be so stale, it was borderline ammonia. The ceramic 'toilet' surround was set flush into the concrete floor with a hole in the centre with no chain to flush the damn thing, just a disgusting plastic jug full of water to clean myself and flush the waste away. I straddled the hole, aimed and unloaded. I began to clean myself with water only as there was no soap or tissue paper. I decided to use all the water so I would have to refill the jug. I wanted to try and get the freedom to wander. I went back to my cell, walked in and tipped the jug upside down to inform them the jug was empty. As I turned around Mr. Sudanese walked in front of me and pointed down the corridor. Good man. Yes! I have the go ahead to wander.

I walked on and turned left into the makeshift kitchen. As I thought, they were using it to cook with a two-ring gas burner, I also noticed that a disgusting sink was in use. The room had one window and on the other side of that window I could see a wall. The wall was a meter away from the window itself, so there had to be an alleyway there. I filled the jug with water and quickly came out, shuffled down the corridor and on my right was a door which opened into a storage room. I thought I would take the chance see this last room, I kept the door open, the door hid me, I quickly went into the room, empty more or less, nothing of importance, a few mattresses and another window no back door. Back into the corridor, I approached the toilet, I could see in front of me a doorway into a small porchway, to the right of the porchway another door. I could see the light coming through, so there would either be another window or a door with glass panels, I would guess a window based upon what I have seen of designs in Iraq. Back into the toilet, the stench hit me again!!

The television was flicked from station to station, I was looking for the news channel, all Arabic, no BBC news. I was trying to understand what was going on through the pictures and the reactions of my room mates.

I sat there hoping that coalition forces had not been killing anyone or anything else that would piss them off, I didn't want to be the guinea pig for any revenge. I didn't know how long I was going to be with my cell mates, so I assumed it could be for some time to come. I had to make a friendly situation with them, it is amazing how you can understand each other through broken language and the magic of charades; I could have had Lionel Blair in my back pocket.

The discussions were about many subjects, such as where we were from, what work we did in our past, what they thought of Saddam Hussein, if the country is better now than before, what I thought of Bush and Blair, the reasons for the invasion. We talked about many things, except their families. I spoke about my family as much as I could, especially my kids, I didn't care if they were sick and tired of hearing it, I need to keep beating that sympathy drum. I was glad the subject of their families didn't come up, maybe some of them had died from bombs or coalition bullets.

I started to drift off to sleep but just the odd ten minutes here and there. Something in my deepest reserves told me to stay awake for as long as I could because I simply did not trust these lot, plus there was a part of me that sensed that the hours of darkness could prove to be a secret weapon for me, who knows. Through the late evening and early hours of the morning, I was drifting in and out of naps, I was shattered but I just could not fall into that deep sleep. They took it in turns to sleep which pissed me off. My body temperature had changed slightly, it was coming down but this was now worse, now I was cold. I sat watching the television as the daylight started coming through the window at the top of the stairs, I would estimate the time would be 0500 hrs and coincidentally the television told me it was 0515 hrs. Well, there you go, good guess. The Imam from the nearby Mosque had started the early morning call to prayer, the mats came out and before I knew it, we were having breakfast. Yes, you guessed it! Fried eggs in a tray of oil and the other lovely side dishes. It would have been nice to have some salt or even some fresh labneh or fresh breakfast cream, so I could eat with my Arabic bread, oh and some honey.

The day came to nothing of importance, my captors were very lazy, not wanting to stretch their legs, no showering, no nothing, lazy fuckers. The television told me that it was just after 1230 hrs, so twenty-four hours had gone since I had been taken. I counted my empty packets of cigarettes of which there were five. Five empty packets! Yes, I had done one hundred cigarettes in twenty-four hours! I had never surpassed forty in one day in my life. If these lot don't kill me the fags will for sure at this rate.

The radio was turned on, oh hurray they had batteries! So maybe I could get the worldwide listening service, who knows? There was another call to prayer so the mats came out again and I had to wait for some time before I was allowed to try and tune in to something. After they had prayed, I came across some lively Arabic on the radio and it had a happy feel to it. It had been on for about three seconds and these fuckers all of a sudden went berserk at me, hollering and shouting. Allah this and British that, what the fuck are they going on about? Mr. Sudanese grabbed the radio, turned it off and continued to vent his anger at me. Fuck me he was foaming at the mouth, out of control or what? So, it was time for charades again to explain their mental breakdowns! In short, I was told no music after prayers or during prayers unless music of Allah. I had been in the Middle East since 2001, this was the first time I had heard of this. For fucks sake, just as I get a release to try and make myself feel better, we have some new rule enforced.

For some reason they decided to pray again. It was on mass, loud and seemed to have rhetoric with it; it felt like there was a defiance behind the delivery and when they had finished, they left me alone, closed the door behind them and locked it. Wow, this was an extreme level I was seeing, these lot are hypnotised I'm sure, obsessed with it, what the fuck have I got myself into? This is something I had never witnessed over the years with the many Muslim friends I have, totally different to my friends.

After about thirty minutes they came back into the room and wanted to play charades to explain the reasons for the prayers. They placed a few smiles in the talks which told me that they were ok about the situation but Gerry needs to understand that it is Allah who decides and nobody else. I nodded in acceptance of the explanation and all was back to normal. I could smoke to my heart's content but still I had not seen any sign of my Pepsi or chocolate. My shopping list was going to grow, the need for soap. I'm pretty sure I would be wasting my time hosting a training seminar on how to use 'Domestos' and how it cleans all germs dead in the shithouse.

Whilst watching the news in the afternoon, the pictures showed the faces of three Japanese men. My captors looked to be enjoying some banter and something had made them laugh, they were enjoying the show for sure but I was left out, so cue the charades. They were laughing and mocking the likes of contractors coming to Iraq and that their leaders were taking hostages. The orders and plans are working, it is only a matter of time that they will win. One of the captors said "Muqtada Al Sadr, he knows, he knows, you see Mehdi Mehdi!" I had never heard this Mehdi, so I asked "Yahi, what is Mehdi? Tell me what is." (Yahi means my very good friend with a touch of brotherly love). He came back to me, "Now Mehdi army, we are the good one now Iraq, you see now what happens to make Iraq good, Muqtada Al Sadr will also make you happy."

Only time will tell if Muqtada Al Sadr spring breaks would be a success and I was not too sure on his marketing team but at this stage the housekeeping and food and beverage teams were severely lacking and the entertainment was not a lot better.

I then remembered where I had seen Mr. Muqtada before, I had seen his mug shot on various billboards all over the roadside near Najaf when we had to go via Najaf to get from Baghdad to Nasiriyah.

The clock was ticking toward dinner time. Oh, the pleasures of life looking forward to the culinary delights! Maybe today it would be edible. My body temperature was back to high once more. Sure, it was hot outside and there was no air conditioning inside but I should not be this hot. My heart rate had not changed that much but I have to say it had reduced from when I was first taken, hopefully in the future my heart would not have to deal with that kind of experience again.

My only real enjoyment was the smoking. If I did not have the fags, I would be in the shit but luckily for me, my friends also smoked but could not take the power of the Ishtar cigarette. They had to go to the shop to buy their own cigarettes as they could not smoke mine, so they got me my own cigarettes. The Ishtar brand is made in Jordan, what a great cigarette, but only real men can smoke them, at the time I loved them, the best I have had for sure and now they were my vice. Saying that though, I was missing my cigarillos I was buying from the base, from the US, flavoured cigars, a lovely tasting smoke.

I was quite hungry now, which can only be a good thing and I was hyping myself up to enjoy the gourmet feast. Dinner came in… fuck me, same shit, no difference at all! Are they fucking serious? And I'm sure that's the same salad that we did not eat at lunchtime! Before starting I went to the toilet, my piss was like orange juice! Not good Gazza! Fuck it I'm going to have to bite the bullet, take on board more of this shitty water or else I could have other issues and I don't think they would be considering taking me to the A&E that soon. Right! Fuck these lot, I'm going to eat this salad, throw it in, wash it down. So, shit and slime in and more shit to flush it down. I fucking know my body is going to react to this before long.

16 THE BATTLE

Midway through this delicious meal I could hear gunfire and it seemed a little close to us. It was the first time I had heard such activity since being here. The noise levels picked up somewhat, perhaps they had a street party for a birthday?

Moments later a huge noise came from the front of the house, 'BOOM!' like a mini explosion and I could feel the floor vibrate. My babysitters looked at each other, shuffled to their feet and as they did, they were joined by a frantic Jundi. What the fuck was going on? It was something serious for sure as the gun fire continued. Bastards, they locked the door, fuck!! Why didn't they leave it? Aarrgghhhh, that was a chance to move out this room!

Within minutes bodies were racing past the window and running up the stairs. I could see them carrying wooden boxes and all sorts of heavy weapons. Fucking hell that is serious kit they have there. Box after box followed and I could see what looked like mortars and RPG launchers. What the fuck is happening here?

I had the luxury of being able to be at the window to watch more closely. My captors for now had far greater things to worry about than me standing near the window. The noise was getting louder and louder, the gun fire was relentless, I would not have a clue to estimate the numbers of people firing but I had never heard anything like this, never.

We went to the next level and above me I could hear the pounding of a downward force, directly above my head, a huge "BOOM!" every twenty or thirty seconds and along with this a distinct noise of a heavy calibre weapon. As the minutes passed it was beginning to get intense. Fuck me, the building is shaking, how the fuck can it shake? Suddenly, in the far-right corner of the room, I could see dust and concrete fly off the wall after a huge thud had hit the exterior. Was it a full on hit or a ricochet, I was not sure if we had an adjoining building. The noise was deafening, it felt like I had high quality earphones on and was listening to the scene in Saving Private Ryan when the small boats landed on the beaches, it was that real.

Fuck Gazza you got to get both of these mattresses and cover yourself up in the corner. Fuck me what happens if these walls or part of the ceiling comes in, I'm fucked for sure. The door opened to the room, a body rushed in, smashed the light to the room and then he quickly left locking the door behind him. Fucking hell, these thick fuckers have no logic at all but they are always locking that door, fuck me their arses must be on the line if they lose me for any reason, that is perfectly clear now. The light bulb had shattered into pieces across the floor so I took one of the pillows/cushions in the room to use it as a makeshift brush.

The battle was on. Yes, it was a battle and this house is in the middle of it for sure, what a gang fuck, this is bad fucking news, I need all the luck I can get and hope this ceiling does not bury me. Who is the battle between? It has to be the Italians or maybe the British have mobilised, this is not just some street party gone wrong. The building continued to shake from the activity on the roof where they were sending mortars and fuck knows what else to the others. I could hear the incoming ammunition on impact, hitting the walls and nearby ground, the ceiling was taking a pounding, I cannot compare any noise like it, this is out of my league. The room was filled with dust, small pieces of concrete falling from the ceiling and walls, I can only hope that my mattresses will hold firm for what is about to be thrown at me!

More boots could be heard pounding the steps on the stairs, boxes followed suit, the thuds on the roof increased. There would be some soldiers that could never experience this. Training they would have to try and replicate these conditions, the only thing I had experience of was paintball with my mates ten years before in the woods near Bedfordshire. I hope this is not a battle between tribal groups. Fuck me all I needed was another group of nut cases to try and take control of me, it must be, just had to be western forces, come on lads, you know I'm here, that fucking door has to fly off the hinges soon and I can be dragged out of here by a crack group of our lads, fucking come on.

I had seen some special forces around the base before or lads that looked in that ilk, of course I can't say for certain but their dress code and weapons being extremely different to regular soldiers, it isn't rocket science. It had been the longest time I had been alone, so technically the best time to sleep but how the fuck can I sleep in a building that is integral to this battle, it was like being inside a firework as it explodes. The only thing I had were my two mattresses that I pulled around my frame, which meant I was sat on this cold floor but what can I do? It was more important to protect my frame, the farmer Giles I could deal with at a later date (farmer Giles means piles). I needed the bathroom badly, so I wandered over to the far side of the room, the shit food and water was kicking in, I would have to sacrifice my boxer shorts as I don't have enough water in the room to clean by arse, I need the water to drink. I covered up my waste as best as I could to prevent the smell echoing in the room, my hands had to wait to be cleaned, what can I do? I don't have this luxury. The smell of my waste was not an issue, none at all at this time, my priority was to stay alive during this battle.

Back to the corner and hiding behind my protection, I lit up another fag, how can I be in this mess, it's not real, I'm just a normal man in the street and yet here I am in the middle of this battlefield. I looked up at the corner of the room and remembered a phrase from a book I once read, I'm not sure of the book to be honest but the words I remember, it was a true story. The man was saying he looked to the corner of the room and said out aloud, "God if you are real and you are this most powerful man, then get to work now because so far you have not picked up the gauntlet mate, you have not delivered the goods." For me there was no such thing as a God, as an Atheist my only type of God was my Mum, closely followed by Bobby Moore, Sir, Geoff Hurst, Sir Trevor Brooking and 6 foot two and eyes of Blue, Billy Bonds coming for you, legendary West Ham football players.

If family knew I was going through this what on earth would they be thinking? I cannot imagine what they are going through. I was not only dealing with my own crisis with the situation I was in, but I was also dealing with thinking about my family and what they were going through and of course I did not know, I knew nothing and had control of nothing. I knew my Mum would be going through hell at the moment, I'm sure nothing could console her. As I type this, tears roll down my cheeks to this day and I can never forgive myself for putting her through this, Mum I'm so sorry. I don't mean disrespect to any of my other family, not at all, I just hope that someone was with my Mum all the time to watch over her, keep her strong and convince her to take some tablets to sleep. Keep strong Mum because I'm coming home, yes you are going home Gazza, you must believe this. Fuck this, come on, stop these thoughts now, focus on the shit you are in now, you can get out of this. Being alone made my mind wander a lot more as there was no television, no charades and nobody for me to keep looking at and keep me active. I was analysing my childhood, my career and thinking of some great times watching West Ham United, the births of my children.

The battle started to fade, it was not as ferocious as before but it was still going on, maybe they had run out of ammunition, maybe there has been to many deaths but to which side and who were the other side my captors were fighting against? I decided to turn the television back on, maybe the television could give me updates, who knows. The television informed me it was 0300 hrs, the gunfire was still rapid and had now gone on for eight hours, where the fuck has that time gone and how much longer will it go on for?

More importantly, who is going to be the first person walking in the room, friend or foe? If the opposition were the Italians or British, how the fuck could coalition lose such a battle, they have tanks and other armoured vehicles, plus more troops, how the fuck can they not win? I continued to doze off for the odd two or three minutes, I was that shattered but of course the louder bangs would keep disturbing the deep sleep and cigarettes were more or less one after the other. So far, I have done four packets again, by the time lunchtime comes around its going to be five packs, so I'm going to be averaging 100 a day from now on. Fuck that is frightening to think in the future, how can I carry on smoking that volume? How will I get that one hundred down to 20 again?

The corner of the room was calling me again, as I downloaded it was liquid, fuck it! Bad timing, my body was now changing, it was only a matter of time, I knew it and no medicine is available. My boxers would not be able to deal with all the mopping up, so I had to use my hand, no way I was going to use my mattress, I didn't want to be sitting on it. I had to use 100mls of my water, so I was now down to about 200mls for drinking. How much more of this do I have to take? Fucking hell, I remain in control of nothing, come on son keep with it, keep with it. I clenched my fists and let out a loud roar, "Come on, lets fucking avit! Come on!" Fuck, I'm losing the plot here. Sounds daft to say but it is amazing what that adrenalin rush did for me, I simply cannot give up, cannot and will not, fuck them Gazza.

During this battle, why could this house not take a direct hit? But in some bizarre way break up to suit me, so that my corner stays intact but the impact makes an escape hatch for me. If I did get the chance, one thing is for sure, I will be running right when I leave the front entrance, I more or less knew where I was geographically. The volume of the battle was coming down, as I looked up the stairway, I could see the window was allowing daylight in, the television told me it was 0530 hrs. The mortars and the other heavy explosions seemed to stop around 0300 hrs but the sound of small arms fire never stopped, they must have run out of ammunition. I'm not fucking surprised after eight hours. I sat down on the mattress and did not feel the need of my barricade. I need to check my body, so back in the corner for a piss, fuck me its dark orange and my forehead could fry a potato into a crisp.

I sat back down and drifted off, my body had to sleep, it had to switch off.

17 BACK TO REALITY

The next thing I knew, I woke up and I was looking at Mohammed. I was thinking is this real or am I dreaming? This must be a dream, I'm sat here waiting for the military to walk in, western soldiers, what the fuck is going on? I sat up and said, "What is the time?" He replied, "It is 8am, you will clean up your mess, you will eat and drink, I think today you are moving from here." I shot up to an attention, "You mean I'm going home?" Mohammed said, "No not home, maybe tomorrow, I'm not sure but their again maybe you will stay here another day." I wanted to know about the battle "Mohammed I know for sure there has been a big battle, where are the four men who have been with me, they are ok I hope." He came back, "Gerry your military men we fight them, they are weak and stupid, they think that Muqtada Al Sadr and Mehdi Army will not fight strong, we defeated them, the four men are ok and be here soon, many others survive but many Italian soldiers are dead, I'm sure."

Mohammed walked out of the room. I walked over to the corner of the room so I could not be seen through the window. I cradled my head in my hands, how the fuck has the coalition forces not beaten these fucking morons? Is Mohammed telling the truth? The soldiers have not come to free me, I only hope that not many of the Mehdi Army were killed last night, I don't need these fuckers trigger happy and maybe take their emotions out on me. I assessed my general physical condition, I had to get my urine colour back on track, I was simply not taking in enough water and the time has come where I need to insist on bottled water or my Pepsi and some chocolate treats. My neck and shoulder muscles were coming around to the abuse they had taken in the early hours of when I was taken, the punches, rucking and rifle butt shit, not too much I can do about this, no medicine or deep heat to rub into it. Other than that, I only have to control my body temperature but my fear is making it so high, the unknown of how many twists is in front of me.

The television started to show pictures of the Italian military and Muqtada Al Sadr. I knew the voice on the television was talking about the battle, I recognised the Italian uniforms and the word Nasiriyah city was said constantly. I was still struggling to come to terms with how a twelve-hour battle could not be won by the coalition forces. I'm no military expert but I knew that in the area there was at least fifteen thousand troops with all the gear necessary to flatten this city, if I was asked to give my opinion of the coalition forces performance last night I would say, "Pathetic."

I said to Mohammed, "Mohammed you need to understand that I'm sick. I need water, Pepsi and chocolate. I gave dollars for these items, you also took $100 US Dollars from me, you said if I good I would get my things, you say you are good and I'm safe, so I want my items you said I can." Sure, I was pushing my luck but I needed this stuff now. He replied, "I will get your items today, yes you have been good, remember we have busy last night so how can buy your items?"

The house was quiet for now, I dozed off but woke up just before 1000 hrs. The television and activity in the corridor were alive again, the door to my room widened, in walked my four babysitters once more and to my surprise they walked in with smiles all over their faces. Mr. Sudanese walked over to me, put his hand out to shake my hand, I was in shock to be honest. Was he honestly happy to see me or was it his way to take the piss of knowing I would not be leaving here anytime soon? A good time for charades and from what I learned from him was that Muqtada Al Sadr had given orders for his Mehdi Army to take as many hostages as they can, fight the coalition forces in Nasiriyah, Najaf, Basra and other locations. I started to think that this Al Sadr geezer held something special with his Army, what was so special about him and why would these men fight for him?

Just before brunch I was given some old rags and water to clean up my waste in the corner, not a great problem to do to be honest and it was a shame that the smell could not be erased, saying that I'm not too sure my body could smell any better.

Today we were going to have brunch, which was new, but the menu was still the same, no need to list the items. The jug of water was placed down, Gazza fuck it, go for it, so I sank the whole jug of water, bollocks to the shits, I can deal with the shits now, I just didn't want to dehydrate, I needed to keep up my energy levels. The jug was filled again, I enjoyed another few cups with the food and for some reason the salad seemed to be fresh, maybe the boss had given them perks for the battle performance.

After the scoff I sat back in my corner and my captors joined me. Chilling on the mattress, sharing their cigarettes but they would not take mine, Ishtar definitely separates the men from the boys in smoking terms. I took out the nickels, dimes I had and started to stack them on my elbow, then dropped my hand quick, to catch the coins. This went on for about two hours, it created some fun. Another part of my plan to get closer to their personal side, time well spent and it was not like I had anything else to do. It was quite funny watching them all trying to get the knack of it but most of the time they were scattering the coins all over the room but as I said it created some fun.

Ok enough of that one, let us move onto the next game and I have played this a few times over the years and made money from it but I don't suggest you play the game, it's brainless if I'm honest. I took out a one-dollar bill, wrapped it tight around my left wrist. I lit up a cigarette and after puffing away to produce a nice red-hot tip, I placed the point of it on the bank note and held it there for around twenty seconds. They could not hack this one at all, their barrier for pain was low and it surprised me. If I was in their shoes, no way would I allow them to beat me, no chance. They were all pointing their fingers at their foreheads and shaking their heads, I think they were suggesting I was not all there, an element of truth.

Early afternoon kicked, a reality check. I had been held for just over forty-eight hours. How much longer will all this go on? Is the result being shot or even more gruesome? Will I be staying here at this location or do they plan to move me? I hope that I stay in Nasiriyah, at least I know the place to a certain degree and that made a big difference to me. Having the same babysitters was also good for me, I was getting to know them and there was a connection, even small connections are better than having someone who hates your face and just wants to shoot you. I never let my guard down, to trust them one hundred percent was never on the agenda, they are my enemy, make no bones about it but I must be smart. The fear never left my side, anyone of these lot could have a bad day, just walk in, and put a bullet in my head. It's not like they are going to get into trouble for topping me. On top of that, my mind was always drifting back home to the family, to think too much what they are thinking and going through, I tried hard to wipe it out of my mind. I have to stick to the priority, deal with what is going on here, so far Gazza son you are playing a blinder, stay with it.

The three Iraqis left the room which left me and Mr. Sudani in the room.

He came a little closer to me, gave a smile and sat down. He looked over at the door, then back at me, shuffled his eyes and then said, "You want Pepsi, chocolate yes, good water in bottle, I can get if you like?' I replied, "Is this problem if you do, what happens if boss man can see this?" He replied, "No problem, Gerry." I took out a one-hundred-dollar bill and handed it over, the smallest note I had. He took it so fast, left the room, locked the door. He returned so quick, maybe only five minutes. He passed me a sleeve of cigarettes, a bottle of Pepsi and a chocolate bar and said, "Gerry eats fast, make fast eat." Mr. Sudani was taking a chance, anyway I got these sugars in me, not the best of sugars in the world but now is not the time to complain. Mr. Sudani binned my trash, came back in the room, as he sat down, I said, "Where is my water, where my change, my dollars?" He replied with a six toothed smile, "Dollar for me, no water, happy for Pepsi."

Son of a bitch! That cost no more than three dollars and you want my change? I cannot explain the humiliation of this, greedy backstabbing fuck! Take thirty dollars fair one, now all I have is another one-hundred-dollar bill shoved in my mattress, how am I going to get my fags again and pass over that note? If I have no money, how can I get my fags? I cannot be without a smoke, no fucking way, that is why I'm pissed, he has given me no change. For sure he didn't want me telling his mates he had taken all that money from me, you must remember, he has just taken the average monthly salary in this country from me, he has earned that in five minutes flat, without drawing sweat, fucker! He carried on where he left off with me, "Gerry name, my name is Bizu." The barrier was coming down for sure and so it should the robbing fucker!

Anyway, I thought I need to push the boundaries with him, maybe he knows my outcome. This is going to be the biggest game of charades so far and you need to nail it Gazza. I said, "Bizu, take Gerry to British soldiers, go tell soldiers where Gerry is, I give many dollars to you, come Bizu lets do this, can get car, I drive car, you and Gerry like brothers, I have much money for Bizu family." He replied, "Gerry no, not good for Gerry or Bizu, its ok Gerry inshallah you see babies soon, boss man good." I tried once more with him but he was having none of it, all he wanted to do is play the coin game, so that is what we did to keep him in happy mode.

I knew he was from Sudan but I wanted to know what brought him to Iraq. He started to talk about camels and I thought it was going to be some weird story that I had heard a few times before. He had explained he has no wife, no kids, he did not like Bush, Blair or Saddam Hussein but he loved Mr. Muqtada Al Sadr, he said he would die for him which is bad news. I explained my opinion of the world and politicians; he was hand signalling with the good old ok signal, I thought I would wind my neck in at this stage, now was not the time to make a true speech.

Television told me it was just after 1800 hrs and the three Iraqis returned, plus a new face. Mr. Newbie walked straight over to me, kicked out at my legs, drew his weapon and pointed the nozzle in my face.

Oh fuck, fuck no not the guns! I did not have this shit for a while and now it is back. I froze and was tightening up, fuck I hated this. He looked mingy, a scar to his right cheek and one on his neck. He put scar face in the shade, I moved my feet and attempted to cross them, I lasted about ten seconds as my joints were killing me where they were so stiff. Bizu came in between us and spoke to him calmly, with his hands ushering the gun away from me, thank fuck.

I looked at Bizu, gave a small smile so he knew I was thankful for his intervention and Mr. Newbie left the room. I stood up, walked around the room to try and loosen up, did some stretching for about half an hour, I thought they may stop me but I was allowed to crack on. I had learned something, it is best to have a small workout, it will help release endorphins for sure, I will do anything to try and keep my mind in a good place, good call Gazza. I had built up a sweat but I'm sure that will dry off, no worries.

Mr. Newbie came back in, he sat with his back against the wall with his AK47 on his lap. He caught a glance from me, he felt the need to pick up his weapon and point it directly in my direction. He turned his head to one side and spoke to his friend, which tickled them enough to have a laugh at my expense, yes fair one Mr. Newbie. It had been a while since a gun had been pointed at me, they were always with them in the room but a gun leaning against the wall is a different ball game to having one pointed in your direction, any fuck up could happen, especially with how old these damn things looked. I fucking hate the feeling when they are pointed at me, I cannot explain the feeling, my heart goes from a relatively low rate to off the scale. Bizu stood up, pointed at scar faces direction and raised his voice at him. Scar face placed the gun on his lap, Bizu is coming good for me, I need to get him alone again, I'm sure he can change.

Mohammed came into the room, came over to me and said, "Gerry come here." I followed him out of the room, turned left and into a room on my left. He stopped just before walking out to the front door and said, "You were not stupid, you were good, so tonight is your choice what can see on the television." A thought dropped in my mind about my birthday, was I going to share this with my captors? No fucking way!!

The last visit to the shop by Mr. Sudani cost me one hundred bucks, I will wait until I'm back in my own backyard before I have a blowout and I pity the poor fuckers who will watch me get pissed. Mohammed continued, "Gerry tomorrow you are move from here, go another place, we go in the morning." I replied, "Ok, so where am I going too, I will be released as a free man?" He Said, "Gerry I don't know where we going until tomorrow and I don't know what big bosses do, inshallah I hope good for us all." I did not waste my words, I just came away from him and said, "Thank you." And nodded at him with a half-smile. My birthday gift was going to be a new holiday location, I just hope that I keep my babysitters, I wouldn't like to change that, at least I know these lot and they know me, last thing I need is a set of nut jobs who want to climb the ranks.

Mohammed had brought my cigarettes; I had a good stash of them now. It was quite amazing how I was smoking; my body had obviously got so use to a high level of nicotine and was not going to drop anytime soon. Even with the atmosphere of just sitting around with a calm about the place, I could never relax. My impatience and frustrations were getting the better of me for sure and it was not possible to be laid back. For me, the unknown mixed with my imagination and fear was the daily challenge, on top of that my diet was fucked, I was shacked up in the same room and on the hygiene side that was in a shit state.

It had now been fifty-five hours since I had been taken, word is out I know, to what level I'm not sure? Time will tell for me, to see who has the balls to come and find me but who is going to take these fuckers on? Blair is not going to pay any money, Margaret Thatcher made that rule some years ago which I agreed with at the time, how times have changed!

After thanking Mohammed, we went back to the room, I sat down and thought about his words. It's good, it looks good for me, hopefully helps them relax, maybe they would switch off a little, leave a door unlocked or maybe more.

Could I have taken on Mr. Sudani when the others were asleep? Yes sure. Could I have overpowered him? Yes very possible but then I have to take on the other three when they wake up and then I have the outside to take on in the hours of daylight, this is not Hollywood here, so I think I had made the right call, Gazza you are still alive.

Since my boxer shorts came off, I have been suffering. My jeans rubbing in areas I don't like, so I was chaffing around the groin and also suffering with stubble on my neck, it kept pulling on my polo shirt and was annoying me, I had to do something about it but what?

Dinner had arrived, for once I was happy to see the oil in the pan, a great thought had come into my head. After the food was finished, I picked up the pan and poured the oil in to a plastic bag that they used to put the cucumber in. Bizu gave me a stare and said, "What you do?" Pointing my finger towards my head and playing with my hair I replied, "My hair is a problem, I need make oil on my hair so is better, I can do?" Bizu said, "No problem, welcome."

I walked out to the toilet and took my bag with me. I stripped off and started to lather the oil around my balls and crotch, not a pretty sight or smell but I had to do something. Not as bad as wiping your ass with your hand, so I will take the positive. Time to wipe it around my neck to create some lubrication, hopefully this will help me and stop my stubble from pulling so often. Here is a man who shaves daily because I don't like any growth and now, I have not shaved for over fifty hours. Back to the cell, I sat down and lit a fag up. I could not help but have a laugh to myself, I could just see my mates catching me rubbing vegetable oil over my bollocks, "Oy oy Gazza!" that put a smile on my face.

I started to feel a little more comfortable, let's hope that this oil does not dry out to quick. I did not smell too good but at least it keeps them away from me, the remote for the tv is mine shortly, I just need the popcorn. Not a lot on this television, some news and stuff but not a lot else. The stubble pulling was definitely better and the crotch was not so sore, it had calmed down, not perfect but better.

Muqtada Al Sadr was the star of each news channel, I wish I knew more about this man, especially understanding his past and what his mentality was like. If these lot do work for him, they have to have a chain of command, there would be the senior decision makers in Nasiriyah and they would report to Muqtada in Najaf, that is a given. I continued to flick through the channels, hoping for a miracle and find something that would make my evening and on the eve of my birthday. Can you believe it?! Arsenal vs Chelsea, 2nd Leg of the Champions League, Quarter Final, under the circumstance this was a blinding result! As I started to watch the game, something popped in my mind about the weekend coming. It is Easter weekend and there will be two games as usual and West Ham are in the playoff positions. I'm sure they are playing Friday and Monday; how can I find out the results? Not possible, bastard. I knew that we had Palace and Derby but because of the last few days I was not sure in which order and if they were home or away games. Will I ever be able to see West Ham play again? I hope so, yeah sure we lose more than we should but that is all part of being a West Ham lad, we are what we are, makes us so different to any other fan base. A love and a passion that has never left my side, wish they were on the television now but I guess the 'gooners' and 'plastics' will have to do.

Midway through the second half, scar face stood up and turned the television off, turned on the radio, then it was turned off as the prayer mats came in, ten minutes later the television was turned back on. Sheer intimidation from that cunt, just so he can pray he needs to show his power by turning the television off, just to have a pop at me, prick! I decided to give up the remote, passed it to Bizu, he smiled and seemed happy to take control of it. He flicked the channel and the news was back on, I resumed my normal program, laying down, lighting up a fag. They all seemed happy to listen to the news and were not unsettling me, scar face was well away from me, so that suited me. Mohammed and scar face stood up and put their sandals on, turned to the door as they were leaving, Mohammed stopped and said, "Gerry be good more, see you tomorrow." Scar face thought he would check out by a grimace on his face with a hardened smirk, his gun always favouring to look my way, I'm sure if it was up to him, he would have shot me by now.

The television was telling me that midnight was here, there had been no more gunshots during the day, the last being heard around 0700 hrs this morning. I had tried to reflect on the battle, who had actually won or gained any ground or bragging rights and would the battle have instrumental consequences to my plight. I also had to think of some kind of celebration for my 37th Birthday or should I be thinking about that? I have more priorities surely but is it wrong for me to be thinking this? Why all the thinking? It shouldn't be rocket science. To be honest I was never a big birthday person but saying that it would be nice to at least be in the place where I want to be, which is anywhere apart from here. For sure it is going to be another reminder to those at home thinking deeper of the situation knowing of my birthday, what can I do? The best gift I can hope for is to make sure I see thirty-seven years old.

The night was going to be like the nights before, ten minutes sleep here and there, nothing special, sleep, wake up, smoke a fag and then doze off again. The night, for some reason chose to drag on and on and a distinct smell had been lingering for some time now. As a non-expert on this subject, I cannot quote the actual reason for the smell, I could only put it down to the fact that the air was still infected with the smell of eggs, again. Maybe the smell was on my captors' clothes and skin, I can't say I have smelt anything like it before, I only know that it was lodged in my nose.

The morning came, as usual I was the first one awake, never knowingly slept for longer than one hour at a time. As breakfast was being made, I went to the toilet to enjoy the luxurious toiletries we had on display. We now had two jugs instead of one. Hey, don't knock it Gazza but it did make me smile, at least you still have your sense of humour, carry on son, you are not going down just yet. Consistency was one thing that you could not take away from these lads but hang on a minute, we have raised the stakes, boiled eggs today and cheese slices on the menu, OMG!

I was not going to miss the onions and eggs; I still had my bag of oil in case I needed to lather up again. I guess my mates thought fuck this, no more onions, he fucking stinks!! I would like to think that I had pissed them off but there again I would have to go some way to override the smell of the toilet area. I never thought that your nose could start to go numb and block out a stench but I was coming around to the idea, nearly. Wednesday came and went. On reflection my best day so far, an omen to take into my birthday, could the ultimate gift come my way, fucking come on, let me go.

18 ON THE MOVE FOR MY BIRTHDAY

Thursday the 8th of April, thirty-seven years old, made it! I got there and I wonder if I will get my gift of freedom, my new life?

For some reason Paul came into my mind as the sun was coming up, probably because we joked about the fact that I was going to have to try and celebrate my birthday without getting drunk or a little drunk. Where was he now? What was he doing and what is his next move? Does he have guilt knowing he should be sat in my shoes and would he have got as far, as I have now? The main reason I came back was the fact Paul could go and see his newborn son Donald and relax knowing that I would not let him down but at the moment I have let him down. Hopefully Paul will use common sense and not do anything stupid? Questions were going to be asked on the ground, that should be normal, I just hope he does not think he can go around Nasiriyah and piss others off and make it worse for me.

I wish I could take a shower, use some soap to freshen myself up and have a shave. I have never gone three full days without shaving and fuck knows how I'm going to get the shit off my face when I get the chance to shave. Change of clothes? Yes please, I was minging! Grease and grime all over me, my hair was in a shit state but the onion oil was doing its job, I must have stunk to high heaven. Parts of me dry, parts of me oily, my guts were not clever but I had no stomach pains. My downloading was not at the total water stage, I just hoped that I could stay that way as long as I could. If I get sick, I'm fucked. My scalp began to itch more than normal, fleas would not be ideal, mind you at this stage anything could be growing in there. For the first time in my life, I wanted a number one all over. I scrubbed up as best as I could in the toilet, the fucking stink inside was no better. I cleaned my hands and face but kept the water away from my balls, crotch and neck, so far, the oil had done the trick. I had a bar of soap to wash my hair with. I felt a lot better but no way was the soap working overtime trying to nullify the smell of stale urine and shit; that would be mission impossible.

I lay back down on the mattress having had my bit part wash but had to put dirty clothes back on. I lit up a cigarette, had a long sip of water, oh the joys of life today. Hey, I wonder where my clothes are, I guess they have taken all my stuff, wankers! My passport was in my case, but how am I getting it back? How the fuck could I travel anywhere? Why can't these bastards bring my stuff to me? I brought two West Ham shirts with me; I could wear one for the day and then put it back. Bring me my items, fuckers!

Breakfast was served with a cup of tea; fuck me did they know it was my birthday? Tea; well black tea with heaps of sugar which I would never normally have, but it was good for some energy.

19 JUST KILL ME

Thursday the 8th of April, a day that will go down in living memory for me and the toughest in my life without a shadow of doubt and an experience the world's elite soldiers would struggle to handle.

It was around 1100 hrs and Mohammed came into my room, joined by four others who were all new to me. Mohammed sat down and said to me, "Gerry you are moving now, I have these items you need to put on your body, is dish dash and shoe." I asked, "I'm being freed today?" He said, "Gerry you are being taken somewhere that is a safe house for you, always you will go where is safe for you."

I took hold of the dish dash, my instant reaction was that it was a heavy wool and not your typical polyester type, plus the shoes as he called them were sandals and they looked like they belonged to some geezer with flipper like feet. If it was hot outside, I would suffer in this dish dash (a dish dash looks like a dress, all the way down to your ankles), plus it was so tight against my legs, if I wanted to open up these legs to sprint, I needed freedom to move.

I said to Mohammed, "Mohammed I go by car or walking, why I have to put these items?" He replied, "Gerry you are walking to next location, to go by the car is dangerous for you, so we walk in the streets with the people and also not good we carry guns for your protection." No guns, I have a chance here, so I need my trainers on my feet and the freedom of just my jeans so I can power up my legs and sprint away. "Mohammed, I need to put trainers, not easy to walk in this shoe you give me, too much big, I will fall down all the time and this robe is not good, to hot?" Mohammed replied, "Gerry you have to put them on, you have to look like Arab man, same as us, I am telling you for your own safety."

Fuck it! I could sense a golden opportunity but everything again was out of my control. I had to roll up my jeans over my knees, my polo shirt stayed on and they would carry my trainers. A ghutra was placed over my head before we left the house and Mohammed said, "Gerry listens good to me, you walk with us and you keep your head down, be good again and we don't want any problems." I had just clocked up seventy-two hours since leaving the world with some sanity in it and we were going to have a walk in the midday sun! It is going to be 40 degrees celsius outside for sure; I wonder how far we are going to walk? The walk will be nice, I hope that many people will see us and report this to the military, a gift in disguise.

We were out of the front door, down the steps, over the open drain and then taking a right down this street, the ground beneath my sandals, uneven sand and rock. I raised my head without my friends seeing my left and right head movements, I was walking freely with nobody holding me. Within fifteen meters I could sense a crossroads, to my right was a corner house which was next door to the house I had been staying, we carried straight on. Mohammed was to my right and approximately ten meters in front of us were two others and then ten meters in front of them were another two. Why were we walking, why no car? Maybe the military had too many mobile units now and had pushed these fuckers back and started taking control? Maybe it made more sense to take a chance and walk me through the streets rather than the car? The pace was quite fast, my jeans started to roll down my legs but I was not going to speak up about it, fuck it, it was up to them to notice and its good for me as I stick out like a sore thumb. I hope! We carried on straight down this street, not too many buildings huddled together, quite a lot of space between them. I didn't notice anything that came to mind that I had seen in the past but then again, I did not venture out too much in the back streets.

I saw some locals dotted around the front of their houses, they took the time to look over at us but not one of them chose to come over and ask why these men were walking down the street with a European man but why would they? We had walked for about a kilometre when we came to a T-junction, Mohammed paused with me and noticed my jeans, "Gerry make your jeans up now!" so I bent down to roll them back up. He continued, "Gerry you must start walk fast now." We turned left, then walked straight for a while, the gaps between the three groups were expanding, by the looks of things they were looking for a clear and safe route in front of us. We came to some waste land, carried on straight, then to the left as I continued tripping up in these fucking sandals! Mohammed's tone picked up, "Gerry you will walk fast now! Yella fast now and keep your head down!" I snapped back, "You give me my trainers I can walk fast!" He came back, "Gerry no trainers! You will walk, no running away for you today, move Gerry!"

I was sweating buckets; the midday sun was taking its toll with all these clothes on. The woollen dish dash not helping matters and this fucking ghutra preventing fresh air flowing freely. We started to drift over to the left more and more over this wasteland. We hit some good flat ground and I noticed a solid three-inch white line, I looked around as much as I could and when I see the goal posts, I knew where I was.

To my left, about a quarter mile away was the first villa we ever stayed in. I could see all the new build villas that were going up for the start of the new 'property boom', yeah whatever! But I knew I was walking on one of four football pitches. Myself and the famous five had agreed we would play there one day and they drove by these pitches to show me, I remember being surprised how good they were. Now I was more pissed about not having my trainers. I knew they would not have a chance to catch me, no fucking way, my adrenalin also would come in to play and within four hundred meters I would have enough distance to be out of sight. I would have been able to evade them, hidden until dark, before making the twenty-kilometre journey to Tallil Air Base. I tried one more time, "Mohammed these shoes are hurting my feet, give me my own shoes so I can walk fast and no pain?" He retorted, "No shoes for you Gerry, now we are close to arrive, just walk fast now."

We moved to our right, aiming for a tree line. Fuck we are aiming towards the Euphrates River, to the right of the bridge. We came off at some low-lying ground and then onto high ground, the river then came into my view. There are no houses around here, surely, we are not crossing the river! How the fuck would we do this?

As we got closer to the riverbank I looked to my left where the bridge was, it was about three hundred meters away. Is the military back in control of the bridge? Maybe they have someone with binoculars now and can see us by the river? As I looked at the river, I could see a makeshift bridge and it looked a sorry excuse to say the least. What the fuck is that?! I could see what looked like polystyrene blocks, a meter deep and wide all attached to each other, then every now and then, old boats on their sides and then huddled in between all of these other pieces of wooden rubble. Surely, we are not going to walk across here. I was not sure how deep this water was but the flow of the water looked fast. I stepped out and focused on stability, it is not like I have the best safety footwear on. The water was splashing all over the dish dash and quite quickly became heavier due to the saturation.

Luckily, my sandals were cheap and made of rubber, which made them nonslip for now but the main thing was keeping my balance.

Mohammed and his men surrounded me; I wonder if they can swim? This river has taken many a life I know. How fast is it? What is the under currents like? We were wobbling all over the place trying to keep our feet steady, it was tough and slow going, my head was dripping with hot sweat and my legs were piss wet with cold water, the dish dash was soaked! After approximately twenty minutes we reached the other side of the river, walked up to the roadside then began to dewater the dish dash. Moments later we crossed the road, turned left, I knew where I was going and I was not happy.

We carried on down this road for another three hundred meters, two left turns and then we walked through the set of solid metal gates, I was back at the first place where I was taken after the raid on the villa. I was led around the back of the building, through a doorway, along a corridor and then into a room first on the left, opposite this doorway the stairs to the roof, where I had been before. As I walked into this room I was welcomed by a swarm of flies and I mean a swarm! It was crazy and I stood flinging my arms around trying to keep them off my face, I fucking hate flies at the best of times.

There was waste food everywhere! In front of me were about five large dustbins, they were just full of waste food; the perfect home for these flies, I was in the garbage room.

The dish dash was removed from me along with the ghutra. I put my socks and trainers on, the sweat was pouring down my face and the rest of my body from the midday sun. Fuck I was as sticky as anything, add to this these fucking flies! Mohammed ushered me against the wall, positioning me about two meters from the door. They all left the room, Mohammed being the last and he gave me a rather weird stare, raised his right hand to face level, gave a wave, come salute but said nothing. Why were there no words as the door closed?

A hot flush came over me, there was a deadly silence. I had left my cell where things were quiet for the last 48 hours, we have walked here rather than drive which I can't work out and now I have been dumped back in this room, alone and there is this silence. Before, when I came to this house it was all hustle and bustle, now it is completely silent. Where had they all gone? The occupants who were here before where have they gone? Maybe out and about trying to find other foreign nationals like me. It was pointless trying to move away from the wall. Everywhere in this room was shit, flies all over me and every other surface and the smell was disgusting. Five meters in front of me was a solid wall and two openings with no glass that was positioned

107

near the top of that wall. Beyond that I could see a perimeter wall, we had walked an alleyway to get into this room, outside it was so quiet, very eerie.

A few moments later, a pair of eyes appeared at one of the openings, eyes behind a face covering and a gun pointed towards the sky, I gulped as I did not know what was coming. It had been quite a few hours where I did not have to face masked men and guns. Another two faces appeared, one of which was covered, the other was open and I could not believe what I was looking at. I recognised him immediately, my heart rate went through the ceiling, my stomach turned and I could feel my fists clenching slightly, my body heat was already up and now horrific fear. It was the fearsome looking fucker I had met when I was taken to the roof. I could not forget those stares of such hatred; our initial meeting told me he wanted me to suffer and now he is in my face again. They moved away from my view. Fuck where have they gone? Where are they going? I just hope away from me... Gazza, switch on, control the breathing.

The door started to open; I did not move an inch. I kept my eyes facing forwards, legs slightly apart, hands behind my back and taking controlled breaths, I stood like I was on duty. The door was fully opened and I could see bodies entering from the corner of my eye, I didn't want to look at them. I thought they would feel that I'm being respectful, better that I'm the small man and they are the men in power, which is a fact at this stage. One of them let out a roar in my direction, I calmly turned my head slowly, slightly lowering my head to show I'm a tired, normal man and is asking for them to show sympathy. Four of them now, three dressed in black and Mr. Fearsome in white all heavily armed and wearing stocked up webbing; 'Rambo's' on steroids, this does not look good. They all started to remove face masks, all was open to see, they just stood staring and snarling. For fucks sake something has to happen. Big black boots were the order of the day and by the looks of things they had been on the parade square but forgot to bull up the toe caps.

Then out of the blue, "Fucking Jew Bastard!... "Americi fucker!" I did not move, just threw back my shoulders and breathed. A flying kick caught my left leg with the main contact made to the outside of my knee but also connecting the back of it, I went to ground! As soon as I went down, they were all over me, raining down with elbows and punches. They were catching me all over my head, neck, upper body and I could feel their saliva and breath as they came in close. Keeping me on my knees they began to rape my pockets and I felt my wallet come out the back pocket. One of them was shoving some paper in front of my face, he ripped them up in front of me, spitting on them for good measure, photos of my kids. Off came my wedding ring and my two necklaces. Fucking crooked cunts! Fuck you!

Mr. Fearsome stood in front of me, his weapon fell to the floor, he gave me an almighty bitch slap to my face that took me to my left, I tried to balance myself to come back; there was no pain as the adrenalin was taking over. My arms were being forced behind my body and pinned back as far as they would go, they began to bind me up with what felt like cable ties that were biting into my skin. Fuck me! The pain was shooting up my arms, I automatically went into shaking mode because of the sheer stress on my shoulders. My heart raced and I could hardly breathe as my body was fully encircled by these fuckers, I tried to find some slack on my shoulders and attempted to wriggle my wrists. There was no give at all, one of them must have sensed I was trying to fight my way out of the situation, a punch came in to take me to the floor; no way can I pull myself back. I was pulled back to my knees; my left knee was still throbbing from the initial side kick.

Fucking hell! I'm sure there is a breakage there, there has to be. I can hardly put weight on it, this is madness, I have pain shooting around my knee, wrists and shoulders. For fucks sake! Mr. Fearsome still in front of me, started to shout and froth at his mouth. Fuck me he will go into a convulsion soon.

He was fiddling with a length of cloth in between his looks of, "I'm going to slice you open you fucker!" He is so pissed with me, a complete fucking nut case. He stood there ranting and raving in my face which he followed with another two full blooded slaps to my face and shaking his hands about frantically. What the fuck did he want from me? Finally, I got it, he wanted me to close my eyes. I closed my eyes and he swooped to get the cloth across my eye line. I could feel him fumbling and the fucking thing pinched into my scalp. Fuck me that is tight! The light was gone, not even a pin prick of light could be seen. My knee continued to throb, I couldn't stop shaking, I was trying to shift more weight to my right knee and by doing so, my shoulder pain kicked in. The kick to the knee was pinpoint, how did this fucker know my old football injury, he could not of picked a better spot.

Hands came away from me and for just a moment I had no hands on me but I knew they were there. Then all of a sudden, I could feel sharp objects pushing against my head; two at the front and two at the back. Oh, my fucking God, these cunts have gun nozzles pointed at my head, are you fucking serious?! My body locked up, I could feel my whole being going into a huge muscle freeze, my eyes squeezed so tight, my lips followed suit as I held back the breath and puffed my cheeks. Fuck this! Is it coming down the barrel? Fuck I beg you don't let me feel it, has to be no feeling at all.

Fuck! No! No! Ok, ok fucking do this then, come on, fucking come on!

The nozzles came away, my mouth opened and it was like a kettle releasing the steam at boiling point. These fuckers let out fits of laughter whilst I knelt fighting for my breath. Sweat was pissing down my forehead on to my face, my clothes were saturated all over with the heat from my body, my whole body shaking. Fuck, I know I'm going to have a heart attack, I can't breathe, I can't get any rhythm to my breathing, I'm hyperventilating I'm sure of it. Gaz! I can't control this now, are you going under mate, are you giving up, maybe best you give up now son. Have you got anything else left in the locker? Fuck I don't think I have, I'm just trying to breathe now, my pain has to wait, I need air for fucks sake.

The nozzles came back along with more snarling and hollering in my face, more saliva as they were offloading their rhetoric at me. My muscles are going into spasm I'm sure, squeezing my eyes so tight. The shouting is off the scale, these lot are losing it and one of them is going to fill my head with lead. Come on you fuckers, lets fucking do this! Come on, come on! Do it, arrgghhhhh!

They came away again, pressure released. I'm calling for air, this is relentless, I'm truly fucked! I can't do this no more, this is beyond funny, I'm going into another world. I just want to fall to the ground... just fall Gazza. Easier said than done. How do I move to the side when I have this pain all over? Which side is less painful and how do I try and move my body to get there?

Then... One nozzle to my head, dead centre! Fuck here it is, straight to the middle of my brain, don't let it hurt, please no pain, just do it now! I'm ready to go now, yeah, I'm ready, son of a bitch just fucking pull, FUCKING PULL! The nozzle came away again, my head fell forwards but quickly back up so I could fight for breath and then, "Arrrggghhhhh!" My wrists had been grabbed and they pulled my hands upwards. Fucking hell, how the fuck have my shoulder joints not just snapped? I'm being held in midair, taking all of my own weight on my toes! 'SCHMACK'... the fuckers let go and I came crashing down, landing on my left shoulder which took the hit. Fucking excruciating. I was picked up by the scruff of my collar/shoulder and dragged out the room. Fuck me my arms are going to snap away from my shoulders. My right shoulder thudded into the door frame. I let out a scream, are you off your fucking heads? Fuck you!

As we came into the corridor, I was flipped over on to my back but quickly grabbed to the left and right of me, dragged by two of them by my underarms. I felt my trainers being dragged over a gravel like surface and I could feel a combination of a slight breeze but a twist of instant heat. Where the fuck are we going? As I was dragged along, I tried to arch my back to keep my hands away from the sharp surface, I was then dropped to the ground, falling again to my left side. I was then dragged back up to my feet, heavy hands pushing me to the chest, throwing me backwards, waiting to hit the floor. Instead, I hit a solid surface, smacked the back of my head on it but managed to correct my feet to stop me falling further. I could see nothing around me, I knew I was outside but the cloth over my eyes was so tight so no light could creep in. I stood there sweating like fuck. I was so hot. Fucking hell Gazza, wake up son, breathe and get your senses back. I'm against a wall, this is the end, I'm fucking sure of it.

I could feel hands playing with the cloth at the back of my head. The cloth was pulled away and my eyes were free but I could not open them. Two heavy, back handed slaps connected with my cheeks but still no pain. Saliva spraying my face as one of them screamed and snarled inches away. I'm not sure what I'm expected to do? I tried to open my eyes to allow the light in, trying to lock on to something to get my eyes switched on to my surroundings but it was so fucking bright stars appeared. The sweat in my hair ran down my forehead and into my eyes, stinging like fuck, with no chance of wiping them. I managed to see what the solid surface was that I was pushed on to, it was a wall. I was just staggering around trying to make sense of where I was supposed to walk to. I could see these fucking jokers about 5 meters in front of me and could make out some laughter from them. Wankers!!

As I started to adjust my vision, it was clear to see Mr. Fearsome in his all white was moving about in a weird stance, he seemed to be playing with his webbing. They all started to make some rather weird noises and before I knew it, two objects were thrown near my feet and they all ran away from me. I instantly fell to the ground and curled up… "Fucking aarrrghhhh!" A few seconds went by and nothing. Dust and gravel were thrown up and my throat gave way, I was coughing like crazy, trying to correct my breathing. They were kicking this shit in my direction then two of them reached down, picking me up, the pain shot through both arms again. Why the fuck can my arms not just go numb? No breaks or maybe there is?

They all came close to me and then kicks rained in all over me. I brought my knees up as far as they would come to protect my crotch. Thank fuck these pricks are stupid, they were kicking each other's feet which was helping me but they were still connecting. I was grabbed and the blindfold was put back on. They began pushing and propelling me forwards and after a few meters I felt the sun off my body, are we back inside again? I'm back in the shit room, no way of confusing that stench. I was pushed to the floor, on to my knees, automatically trying to balance on the one good knee but these fuckers forced me down.

I was back with a nozzle on my head with high velocity Arabic raining into my ears, snot and saliva filling my ear cavity. My muscles froze again, this is the final, no semi – final for me! I'm fucked, fucking pull please! You spineless fuckers! Why cover my eyes? Give me the right to see it coming, look at the whites of my eyes and then crack on! Is this bravado now? For me it is the inevitable, my luck cannot last, so just fucking do it! My whole body was on fire and my head was full of steam, I just wanted to explode. I was physically shaking from my shoulders down to my wrists, I could not stop, the throbbing was constant, why can I not be numb? I was still trying to get my weight onto my right knee but now my right knee is struggling because I have been putting too much pressure on it. Have I given up? The combination of the physical and mental torture has taken its toll. Sooner or later the games will finish and I will be killed, these fuckers are just having fun with my mind and mental state.

The door was closed and locked and the room went silent. I stood still, was the coast clear? Could I be free to move as I like? About five minutes, and I decided to take the chance to move and relieve my pain. I sat on the floor, keeping my hands away from the wall, stretching my legs out, pushing my toes forwards, bringing my knees up slowly and then out again. I got onto my front and tried to rest each arm on my back, one minute at a time for each arm.

A noise came from just outside the door. I sat up, the pain relief although short was bliss. The door was unlocked and I could hear footsteps enter the room. I immediately tensed up, it is decision time for sure, they have given me five minutes of hope only to finally finish me. Is it going to be Mr. Fearsome who is going to get his wish or is he under orders to allow someone else? Has he been given orders to keep me alive? If so, he could also just kill me and then make up an excuse that he had to kill me because I grabbed a gun, so he had to shoot. This fucker would kill anyone in cold blood, he just had that look about him. I had never been looked at in the way this peace of shit looked at me. I could hear at least two voices and I hated the fact that I could not see anything, it infuriated me that these bastards were spineless and gutless. Yes, you are so fucking hard with a gun! Wankers! Just fucking end this, I'm fucked, I know that bullet will come, stop the mind games.

Over the next couple of hours, I was left to my own devices. I was shuffling around on the floor in this stinking room trying to gain the best position to comfort my injuries but all the time blindfolded. The door was kept open, I know this as I could hear the voices in the busier corridor. It seemed that others had joined the crazed morons that had enjoyed their sessions with me and in typical Arabic style, the talk was loud and borderline hysterical. The main pain barrier I had now came from my shoulders. The pain was now a profound ache, continuous throbbing, thousands of heartbeats all over me. The cable ties had really had a go at my wrists but my body heat mixed with humidity made my wrists sweaty, so the moisture had helped. The heart had taken a big pounding over the last few hours, so the last hour it had slowed up and been given a little relief but I could still feel it beating more than normal and for the first time the swarm of flies meant nothing to me. I wondered what my family are doing. Christian will not know anything as he is still a baby but Lisa will hopefully be home with family around her. Well, I hope so? I should think my Dad will have the lads from the village to keep him company and keep his sense of humour going. Irchester Sports Club will keep him on track, of that I am sure, great lads and mates! I wondered how much Jake, Alice, Charlie and Elizabeth will know? Charlie just passed seven years old now, I wonder what he got for his birthday on the 7th of March. Too old now for a 'Bob the Builder' outfit. Jake will have his head in a book, Alice will be nicking goodies from the fridge and Elizabeth, I hope she is having a tea party with her dollies. Mum... if you can hear me, I'm sorry. I know I keep saying sorry but I really am and I know I have taken things to far now. I know there is not a lot I can say now to change what you are feeling and only a hug will put things right but I can't just yet. Hang in there because this fight is still going on.

Just then I was grabbed by the arms and brought to my feet. Again, the pain shooting through my frame, I let out a cry of pain. I was motioned forward but my legs did not want to know as my left leg gave way. Arms and hands came in to help me walk but that was worse for the pain in my arms, no winning at all with this movement. I was being forced forwards down the corridor, not able to see where I was walking, for all I know I could be walking into a door frame, what would they care? Fuck all, they would get a kick from it. We had turned right out the shit room, along the small corridor, to a door that led outside, we turned left and towards the courtyard again. Arms released; hands grabbed again... 'WHACK!'... Hands up towards the sky, the pain once more shooting through my shoulders as I was instantly dropped to the ground. This time my chest took the brunt of the fall, as dust kicked up into my face. How my arms had not snapped away from my shoulders or no dislocation had taken place, I really do not know. In the future I'm going to have problems as it is not possible to come out of this injury free, unless I'm shot and killed, and by then it does not matter.

Picked up by the arms again, then pushed to the middle of the back which sent me forwards. Although unbalanced I kept my footing, stumbling to correct myself but not falling. We came to a halt as my head was pushed downwards and forwards. My backside touched a soft padding, followed by the smell of leather, that old leather smell, I was inside a car. I tried to shuffle to keep pressure off my arms and shoulders but was restricted from doing so as I knew I had a guard to the left and right of me. I heard the engine start and within a few seconds we were moving, turning left out of the gate, my body bounced to my left uncontrolled, I was forced upright and head pushed forwards. My focus was keeping the tension off my shoulders, which pissed me off because I wanted to try and understand which way we were going just in case the opportunity came up to get out of this shit. Where are we going now? I'm sure these pricks had not arranged a surprise party for me. What a memorable day so far for my birthday, with the best gift so far... staying alive. How I have got through all that shit I will never know.

20 LOCATION NUMBER 3 – BIRTHDAY GIFT

The vehicle came to a stop, the engine was switched off and I was quickly taken out of the vehicle and forced forwards. Within a few steps I knew I was on uneven ground; I couldn't keep my footing and as my weight moved to my left, I felt foliage on my face. The chill in the air was met by the voices of children and a distinct female voice. Am I heading to a family home or am I in an open area where families are in the streets? I was led through a doorway and made to stand still; my company had multiplied for sure. Did I still have the same company from my beating?

I could feel hands around the back of my neck and the blindfold was released, at last I could see. I began to go through the motions of opening and closing my eyes, the stars were back as I was guided to the floor. My blindfold went back on, fuck it! A young voice came into my ear, "You want water?" I replied, "Yes please I want water and also cigarette would be so nice." I could feel something pushing up to my lips and then the wet feel of the water as it started to flow in gently which was good for me, I was as dry as a bone but did not want to take the water in too fast. The young voice came back, "Mouth open is cigarette." I started to draw on the cigarette and it stayed in my mouth without taking it out, how could I? My hands were tied.

Halfway down, the fag was removed and a new voice came into the room. A woman's voice and it was quite loud but that is normal in this part of the world, for us it is shouting but to them it is normality. The tempo of the conversation calmed down and then I could not hear the female anymore. Just after she left the room the blindfold was removed. Hopefully it will remain off, the feeling was great and it made me feel better to see what was going on around me. I decided to just keep my eyes looking forward and to wait until the time arose that I could start to have a better look of the room and who was with me.

The room was rectangular, approximately six by four meters, the four walls were all lined with cushions and mattresses. The walls were plastered with pictures of Muqtada Al Sadr and his father. His father I would learn about later. The wall to the left of me housed a big sword, like a samurai sword with dress knives either side. The samurai blade was about one and a half meters long, a scary looking thing. I did not pay too much attention to it; I didn't want to put ideas into their heads. To my right in the corner were my four new best mates who had given me a birthday I would never forget and they had been joined by two new morons, the good thing is that I had distance between them.

To my left, sitting quite close to me was a young lad. As I looked at him, he offered me a smile and said, "Are you American or British?" I wanted to reply that I was English but thought it is best to keep it simple, "I'm British man, my name is Gary and your English is very good. My Arabic bad." He replied, "My name Omar, my English not good, inshallah Gerry you eat food soon and have water, ok?" Another Omar in my life, he looked the same age as my little friend Omar on Massirah Island but I think his father was going to be different. I looked at Omar with puppy eyes, "Omar can you put your hand in my pocket? I have cigarettes, can put in my mouth for me?" Omar went to the men and came back to me, "Is ok I can get from you and will help you." Omar pulled out the packet from my pocket and to my luck the packet had survived. The cigarettes, although crooked could be smoked, a miracle. Omar helped me smoke the cigarette.

During him hand feeding me, he had so many questions, wanting to know about London. Had Gary been to London? Have Gary been to see David Beckham or Michael Owen play football? He told me how he liked Alan Shearer; he went on and on how he liked English football and I thought it's not best to talk to him about West Ham, I had been tortured enough and not good to torture the poor kid in turn. Omar told me that I was in his house and he was happy that he had a British man in his home. There was so much I wanted to ask my newfound friend but thought I would take it slowly with him. The adults in the room seemed to be ok with Omar sitting with me and talking, maybe they thought they could play the soft man routine, maybe get Omar to make me talk.

The door opened and in walked a man in his mid-forties, he was carrying plates of food. The food was put in front of me then within a few minutes more food came in. You know, you think I joke but it is amazing the foods they eat. It never changes. I'm not going to list the foods again as you know what it is. I like routine in my life but this is insane. Oh, go on then, rice, chicken, tomatoes, cucumber and Arabic bread.

My server gestured his hands to me to eat but how can I? I said, "Omar my hands are tied up, I'm tied up my friend, cut me free so I can eat." The server went to the morons then he walked out the room only to come back with a knife in his hands. Thankfully, the kitchen knife went to the back of me and the cable ties were cut free, finally. On release, I froze slightly, motioned my arms forwards slowly, bringing them in front of me and I began to move my hands and wrists. Everything felt like lead and to be honest I did not feel hungry, I just wanted to fill up on water and cigarettes but rest was also on my menu, I was shattered. Do I take the food now? Maybe this is the last chance to eat for a while and it looked quite fresh. I decided to take some chicken, break it up and make a salad wrap in the bread, that was enough. The water jug told me that tap water was on the beverage list but I guess my guts were getting used to this.

I turned to Omar, "If I give you some money, can go shop for Ishtar cigarettes, I buy you some candy, you do for me?" Omar replied, "We have shop here is good one, not same London but is good for me." I had my slush fund; thank fuck they were stupid and never thought to search me properly. In my small one-inch pocket at the top of my jeans I had stashed a five-dollar bill, so I gave it to Omar and ordered my five packs of cigarettes as my others had been taken away from me.

Omar went, came back and he came up trumps with my five packs of Ishtar. As he passed my packs to me one of the pricks came over to find out what was happening. He picked up my cigarettes, spoke to Omar, threw them back at me and then walked away. Thank fuck for that, I thought I was losing them again but the amazing thing is, he did not ask me where or how I paid for them. They had taken my wallet before, so they had all my personal shit. Mr. Fearsome walked over, raised his gun, bent down to my face and said out loud, "If you are problem fucker, bang bang, ok?" He must be the thickest prick on the planet. Six geezers in the room, all with guns and he thinks that an unarmed man with his arms fucked up is going to be able to take them on. What pissed me off, is that I wanted a one on one with this fucker so much, it was making my piss boil that I could not have that wish come true.

Omar came close again, "Gerry you have children?" I replied, "Yes, I have Jake he ten, Alice she eight, Charlie he seven, Elizabeth she is three and Christian he is a baby and I hope soon I can see them, hug them and play games with them. Omar, do you think I can see my children again soon, what do you think?" Omar just shrugged his shoulders. I went on, "Is Gary sleeping at Omar house tonight?" Omar came back, "Gerry I not know but I can play the cards, you like to play the cards?" I replied, "Yes Omar, no problem, we play cards is good."

I was so desperate to find out what was going to happen. Should I involve Omar now as my translator? Maybe not as it might piss them off because I was involving a child? I plucked up the courage to ask Omar some questions. "Omar you are very big boy now, do you think I am bad man? Do you think I should be dead man? Do you think these men will kill me?" Omar looked at me, "Gerry why says like this, I like the British man is good, same Muqtada Al Sadr, he also good man, so both is good Gerry, he not shoots Gerry."

As I thanked Omar, I sat there just looking around the room, the words made me feel better of course but who knows what the final outcome will be. This was the ultimate killer eating away at me, the unknown. My babysitters all stood up and walked out of the room. One of them reappeared, walked over to me and Omar and then Omar said, "Gerry this is my brother his name Sameer, before he was soldier Iraq army and now, he has no work to do, he is twenty years old." They spoke a little then Omar stood up and said, "Goodnight Gerry." and he left the room.

Sameer, who remained, walked around the room then made his way to the wall where the samurai was, took it from the hooks it was rested on and began to walk up and down the room, swinging the blade from left to right. He turned towards me with a grin on his face. I decided to take a fifty-fifty approach to this new game, looking down, then looking up at him, always with the look of pity and not arrogance. He stood directly in front of me, legs slightly apart and said, "This my fathers, you like it?" I replied, "Yes, it is nice, you must be proud of your father." A few moments later, he walked away, placed the sword back on the wall and walked out of the room. Sameer returned within minutes with Omar who had a glass of water for me and a clean ash tray. Omar said to me, "I have message for you, need to tell you to sleep, can smoke cigarettes and I will bring jug water for you." The jug arrived and the door was closed behind them, I heard the door being locked. Was this a proper goodnight or just some kind of break for them and for me? Little Omar has been my birthday gift for sure, thank you little Omar.

So now on my own, first things first, I needed to chill, which basically meant I needed to find how to lay down. After a few minutes, it felt best to lay the cushion just behind the back of my neck and not lay my head on it as I needed to shift the weight away from my shoulders. As I lit up a cigarette,

I kept my hands laid out on my chest, I wanted to restrict my arm movements just for now, minimal effort. You know, the choice of Ishtar was a good one, good job I looked into changing from the Gitane that were not easy to get. Both of these cigarette brands had no filter and the extra strength was just what the doctor ordered for now. I would have to work out how to keep my supplies up as the money had finally gone. Good thing is, they are cheap as chips. I was going through the baby steps of keeping the joints moving, can I get back to normal? Is that going to be possible? The shoulders were an issue for sure, I could hardly move them, shooting pains all around the rotary cuff. Keep the small movements going Gazza, you don't want to seize up.

I dropped off for about thirty minutes but the throbbing in the shoulders prevented me from falling in to a deep asleep. I sat up and started to take stock of my situation, lit up a fag, pushed my legs out with my back against the wall. I can't believe I have got through all that bollocks today. How have I got through the shit? It seemed like a lifetime, the differences between my first babysitters to my birthday crowd was chalk and cheese.

If I remain with these fuckers I'm not going to be around for long, that is for sure. My heart rate was all over the place, my body temperature high since Monday. If a doctor was in the room and checked my blood pressure, I'm sure I would have been put on tablets to get it down. The myth of the cigarettes keeping it down is a load of bollocks but I need them.

Mentally I'm still hanging on and I'm learning things about me I never knew before. I have never had any military or hostage training in my life, the only thing I can compare it to was riot training at Police College with live scenarios.

I don't need someone to try and convince me that I'm emotional and competitive. There is nothing I like more than a fifty- fifty tackle on the football pitch, nine times out of ten coming out the winner, an all too often a let's have it attitude. Every game is a cup final, that's the way I have always been. To come second you get nothing. Gazza you have to keep that mentality, that is what this is, this is the comparison. It is a fifty-fifty geez, so go through them all, come out with chest pumping and clenched fists! You've got this son, fucking come on!

The lights in the room had been switched off which was fine by me. I lit up yet another fag and just looked around the room. The wall in front of me had a large window, two meters by two meters and the wall to the right also had a window about the same size. The bottom of each window was 30 centimetres from the floor and at the top they were fitted with the old-style farmhouse glass slats, the ones that you can remove as the window had been fitted with a lever to create a wave effect. On the other side of these windows, I could see a wall that looked about two meters high. On top was a flat concrete finish, I could see an alleyway between the window and wall.

As I sat, I noticed that every now and then a body walked from the far right of me and to the extreme left, going out of eye shot. I started to count in my head the time between each walk past, from his starting point on the far right and then his return journey. It was only thirty seconds one way and then he would make his return journey every seven to eight minutes.

I stood and walked to the window. Stepping up on to the small ledge at the base of the window, I tried to lever the top window but it was welded. Fuck it! I came back down, nursed the pain shooting through my shoulder. Some air would have been nice but hey ho.

The lights in my room came back on. I opened my eyes to the brightness of the light and slowly raised my frame so I could see. I was helped to my feet but that created pain; fuck please don't touch my arms! Two meters in front of me stood four individuals, one of which was a very large-framed man, wearing a pin striped suit, head and face covered with a red and white ghutra. He walked towards me slowly with his hand held out in front of him removing his ghutra as he moved to show a well-groomed beard. A small smile appeared as he said, "No problems from me, my hand is here, as a British man is good to shake it." I kept my hand to my side and returned a smile. He placed the ghutra over my face to show my eyes only, came to the side of me and began to guide me forwards but with no force. We stopped so I could put my trainers back on and he helped me because he could see my movements were painful for me. We then continued to walk.

He walked me passed the idiots, spoke a few words in their direction, continued to lead me forwards through a doorway and then into darkness, which was accompanied with a chill in the air. I was led by the foliage once more and over the uneven ground. I was taken to a car that was parked up ten meters or so away, the door was opened and I was guided into the back of the car, joined by a guard either side of me. As we pulled away, I saw that the driver had a passenger beside him, so I'm one of five in the car and the big man is to my right. The immediate area was slightly lit by the lights of the street and quite built up. I was trying to motion my head to my left and right without wanting to cause any kind of alarm bells to them.

Mr. Big Man tapped my arm, "You are British, yes?" I replied, "Yes Sir I am British." (get the Sir bit in early Gazza, start how you mean to go on). He said, "I'm pleased to meet you, my name is Mr. H, would you like water and cigarette?" I replied, "Yes Sir I would like very much." Mr. H passed me a small plastic bottle and a cigarette that was lit. I took the bottle and said, "Shukran (which means thank you in Arabic) the bottle is good but I have my own cigarette in my pockets of my jeans, you have my jeans I think?" He replied, "Yes your trousers I have here, you want?" I replied, "Yes my cigarette inside."

I took out my cigarettes, placed one in my mouth and lit it. As I twisted the top of the bottle, I could not believe my luck, fucking hell, happy birthday Gazza, your gift is clean fresh water, amazing and I necked it all, straight down. Mr. H said, "Here have another bottle, I think you sick and I not shocked you sick. How you smoke this Ishtar cigarette? It's not good for you, too much strong and is bad for you." That tickled me. I think there are quite a few other things my friend that could kill me before these fags do. Funny to hear though and the Iraqis could not handle the Ishtar brand, they simply do not appreciate a good smoke.

The weapons were all too familiar by now, AK47's, some with short stock and others long but the good thing for now they are not in my face. I moved the ghutra away from my eyes, I wanted to try and get a panoramic view but a few moments later the babysitter to my left had seen the movement and said, "No move this, make no problems and if you not good then is problem."

As the car made its way out of the city the talk was mainly coming from Mr. H. The general mood of the car was quiet, which suited me after the events of my day. I noticed when Mr. H spoke the others seemed to really pay attention to him with complete eye contact, he clearly showed that he demanded respect from them, fair play. Mr. H definitely had aftershave on of some kind, this is a first for sure, I don't think he would have liked the smell coming from me, ha-ha, I still had my Eau De Onion oil on. Mr. H had a well-groomed beard, maybe two millimetres in length, the same as his hair style and a very clean man which was hopefully going to be portrayed in his general mannerisms. I would say he was in his early thirties, must be eighteen stone, six feet four inches tall and spoke in broken English which is better than none at all, but the best part has to be the fact that he is smiling every now and then which made a big difference. I turned to Mr. H and said, "Now I will go home to be with wife and my babies? "He replied, "Inshallah soon go home, no problems but for now not good time talking."

As our journey continued, I noticed that the buildings were becoming less, not a lot of activity on the roads and then I saw a check point ahead and a shower of excitement came over me, the Police have to see me. If they see me in the back of the car, what will happen? Hopefully, simple talk and I will be carefully handed over to them with no gun fire. I can only hope. The car drew closer and my heart rate picked up further, I could see they were Iraqi Police. The driver's window came down and we came to a stop. The Policeman looked into the car, he could see me clearly and I puffed my face out with a big frown, he remained calm, a few words were spoken and then waved us on! Fucking Iraqi Police, son of a bitch! You can clearly see my face, you can see my reaction and you have waved us on, like it is normal to have an Englishman in a car at this time of night with four armed Iraqi nationals. Not! It just goes to shows you how fucked up this country is, old bill who are bent as a two-bob bit and simply do not want to change, total waste of time, I would probably be worse off with them on my side, they would sell me to the highest bidder.

The car carried on into the darkness of the desert roads. I did not have a clue in which direction we are headed and all I ask is for a miracle to happen now. You read many times that special forces soldiers are normally in remote places, places where you least expect to find them, it would be great if they were out here now and they need to ambush a car as they need transport. I should be so lucky.

21 LOCATION NUMBER 4 – VIDEO TIME

The surface of the road changed, we went from tarmac to a dirt track, then lights started to appear from small buildings and the number of stone buildings increased, it looks like we are in a desert village. The car came to a halt and the engine was switched off, it seemed like we had been travelling for ninety minutes but not at excessive speed. I was allowed to get out of the car by my own steam and then guided up a few steps, through a gateway, into a courtyard and then led into a house.

After negotiating some corridors, I was taken into a room which was approximately five by eight meters. The lights were on and I could see the carpet was wall to wall and one side of the room had large cushions propped up against the wall. I was joined in the room by Mr. H and he moved his head in a forward motion, suggesting I should go and sit down against the cushions, I did not disappoint. I sat down, lit up a cigarette, why ask? No need as Mr. H then passed me an ashtray. A man walked into the room who looked about five feet tall, a small dude with short black hair, short cut beard, dressed in a brown thobe and brown dress jacket with sandals.

He walked over to me, I stood up, he smiled and held out his hand, we shook hands. He said, "This is your house, we will eat and then make a video, my name is Mr. A, welcome." I replied, "Shukran Mr. A nice house you have." and gave a smile in return before sitting back down. Video? What video do they want? Fucks sake, just as things were starting to look better and they are talking about making a video. I have seen some of these 'videos'! What type of video are we doing?

My friends from the car all came into the room and sat down with Mr. H. Mr. A was busy bringing in a large plastic sheet to place on the floor, then oh

123

my goodness! Fresh as fresh salad and cheese! Yes cheese! There was also cooked chicken that looked to have an amazing crispy skin. I took a little of each, the salt was amazing to see, orange juice and bottled water, this is a banquet for sure, a birthday tea party after all! I couldn't get the food down my throat quick enough. It tasted so good and the salt made it even better, I never thought I would see the day when I'm having an orgasm over salt. Every single last crumb went. Great food and definitely the best I have had since being back here.

I sat back, lit up a cigarette or two after such a feast, it all went down so well but the video was yet to come, how will that go? Mr. H allowed his food to digest and after a cup of tea he came over to me, sat down and took my hand in both of his shovel like hands and said, "Mr. Gerry, we now make film with you, this to tell your wife no problems and that everything is ok with us, ok?" I replied, "Are you sure that is what I have to do, you only want show my face on video to explain to people that I'm ok, you don't want to kill me on the video?" He sat up very quickly and said, "Mr. Gerry, we are very good men, this house is your house, you are invited here as special guest to Mr. A but we have to make the special video to show your family in real about you, you very safe with me and my brother Mr. A. I want you sit down or kneel and speak words that we write for you to speak, if we not do then maybe can have problem."

All the banquet items were removed from the room and then two other men came in, both early forties and dressed in white thobes, again I have to say looking very different and clean. These two men had brought in some baggage with them and as they unpacked, I could see a video camera, tripod and lighting systems, fuck me they had their own camera crew. Mr. H came over to me, "Mr. Gerry, now I need you go with this man and make hair washing, ok?" I did not need to be asked twice, I was taken outside by a young lad and we walked into a small shed. He poured water over my hair which was freezing cold and I was given a bar of soap. Fucking hell, soap as well now! I smashed that soap all over my head, neck and face. It wasn't the best of smells in the world but it was going to knock spots off my situation, not sure if I wanted to have my neck oil removed but let us see. I rinsed all the lather off, had a pee and then returned to the room, sat down, lit up a cigarette and waited for the camera to role.

Mr. H came beside me, "Mr. Gerry finish smoke quick and then we make video fast, after we leave here." I replied, "No, why leave here, I like here with you and Mr. A, it feels good for me." He said, "We go somewhere else, is close by, quick Mr. Gerry." I explained to Mr. H that my knee had a problem, also my wrists to my shoulders were also a problem. He agreed that I could be on one knee, so I decided that I would kneel on my right only.

I went down on my right knee, to my left were two men and to my right was Mr. H and Mr. A. I was told that I would be counted in by the cameraman. He would give me a countdown with three fingers and as he got to number two for some reason, I looked to Mr. H and saw his face uncovered and that Mr. A was covered. I turned to Mr. H and he looked down at me. He turned his head to the side and frowned, "Mr. Gerry you need speak now, speak!" I replied, "Mr. H, you do not have your face covered, is not good they will be able to recognise you, where is your mask?" He began to shake his head and then broke out into laughter. I could see Mr. A asking Mr. H what was going on? After some mixed talk around the room, the whole room was laughing.

Mr. H composed himself, "Mr. Gerry thank you for telling me, I know my face not covered, this is practice video to make sure we do correctly, ok?" I replied, "Ah ok, I understand, I'm sorry I did not know, ok I will start to read, sorry for that." I propped the paper up on the book in front of me, it was not too hard to remember, so I started, "I would like you to know that I am very well as you can see. My friends are looking after me very well, they are very nice people, just like back home in the UK. I don't want my countries soldiers here anymore; we should all return back to our own homes and allow these nice people to be alone."

I sat back down to my place, Mr. H walked to his camera crew, they were obviously looking over the recording, they were stood there for about fifteen minutes. Mr. H came over to me, "Mr. Gerry we are ok with video, thank you for smile a little is good, people will see you are happy with us and can see we are good men." His cheeks cracked with his usual small smile.

The video passed, of course it ran through my mind that it was going to be a farewell video to family and friends, I had heard about them before, luckily at the moment it has not happened to me. I was dying to stretch out but did not want to compromise my good vibe with them, so I chose to just sit quietly. I fell into a world of my own for a while. I kind of felt relaxed, which sounds silly to say but no one could blame me for that because earlier I was in a place that the world's elite soldiers would have struggled with, let alone Mr. Ordinary. If I can get through that kind of shit, I'm sure I can manage other stuff that may come my way but the guns held to the head again.

To get through that again could be dangerous, how I didn't have a heart attack or just break down, I will never know. For a man like me this cannot be possible to achieve without some kind of training. These lot are different beyond all belief but why? Gazza, don't fall into any traps, you still have to keep switched on, this could be the soft man plot now after the hard man routine, do not fall into a false sense of security. Mr. H came to me, "Mr. Gerry we have to go now, we cannot stay here any longer, we will go to my brother's house." I was given a white thobe to place over me, ghutra around my head and I had my trainers on. Mr. H said, "Mr. Gerry, when in car you have to keep down because now this journey is dangerous for you and for me, ok?" I nodded in acceptance; we exchanged looks but this time his look was far more serious but why? Mr. H and the others had a conversation, the looks between them showed a lot of uncertainty, so what dangers are they facing? Maybe they fear the coalition forces or other factions that are also interested in me.

22 LOCATION NUMBER 5 – FLY FURY

We were ready to move. Mr. H walked out to join Mr. A and then came back to me. We stood silently for a couple of minutes, I then heard the distinctive crackle of gunfire and it sounded like it was nearby. Mr. H was looking at me, he must have seen the concern on my face, he said, "Mr. Gerry is no problem for you, I think is one crazy man in village." The gunfire had finished within a few minutes and Mr. H was leading me outside. He stopped, checked for a while and then briskly got me in to the car, we were on the move and heading out of the village.

Mr. H was easing my back downwards from the back of my neck, "Mr. Gerry keep low, quiet, no noise, quiet I say!" The car was traveling very slow, maybe just twenty kilometres per hour, the windows were down, I could feel the night air around me, slightly chilly, it had to be midnight or just after. I was trying to push back up to take the stress off my body but Mr. H was pushing me back down, not realising that he was hurting me. The car stopped; I could then hear Mr. H talking to someone. Doors were opening and closing all over the place, conversations continued, Mr. H held me down, he eased me up as I was guided out.

Mr. A walked in front of me, underfoot it was boggy, I could smell farm animals, I hope this is only boggy mud I'm walking in and not something else? It was now up to my ankles; all you could hear was the slurping of the mud. Mr. H was trying to guide me but he was the one losing his footing, not me. We finally got to solid ground and I started to stamp my feet to lose the shit around my trainers. As we came through a doorway, there was a porch, Mr. H and I stood there. Mr. H said, "Gerry, take off the shoes now, leave them here and we will go into this room." We walked in and I was met with the typical surroundings, carpet wall to wall, cushions decorating the

127

side walls, the room was probably 6 by 4 meters. I took the chance to sit down and make myself comfortable, Mr. H joined me sitting to my right. Mr. H came closer, "Mr. Gerry, this is my brother's house, he has babies so must be very quiet, he will allow us to stay here, so is very good and safe for you." I said to him, "What do you mean we will be safe here, who are you and who do you work for please?" No reply. I lit up a fag and offered one to Mr. H, he declined an Ishtar, the look on his face was the same as the others, always funny to see.

The air was cold now, it had to be about 0100 hrs and there was a definite chill kicking in from the desert. I had been in the Middle East near on three years now and I never really had been able to experience the desert that much, Iraq can be bitterly cold for sure, I remember back in December on the Iraq – Syria border, that wind was freezing.

I could hear activity from inside the building, the door opened and a man greeted Mr. H with a hug and a few words. As he walked into the room, it was more or less in darkness, just a glimmer of light. Mr. H was blocking my view. We were being joined by others and I could see that it was the two passengers in the car but I could not see Mr. A at this stage. Everyone in the room went into a group huddle. They sat around and the main voice was Mr. H, no high-pitched tones, quite calm which is quite rare to see. Again, it was obvious that they all had so much respect for Mr. H.

As they were talking, I could hear gunfire, what the fuck? This time of the morning in the desert with these villagers and there is gunfire. Mr. H stood up, walked back slightly from them, held up his right index finger, spoke two sentences and did so with such calm and authority. Mr. H walked over to me with the man who greeted him at the door, "Mr. Gerry, this is my brother, this is his house, he is my blood brother, you will be very safe here with him. Now I go from here and then I will be back after some time. I need you to be good for my brother, he is my best friend and he is good man like us, ok?"

Mr. H turned away from me, waved his arms at two men and they huddled around to talk. At the same time a man walked into the room with glasses of sulaimani tea and some other goodies by the looks of things. Mr. H's brother waved and motioned for me to join him on a small mattress, so I sat down without hesitation. Gunfire could still be heard, Mr. H's brother could see that I was not comfortable with the sound, he said, "Mr. Gerry no problem, my brother back soon, I'm Ahmed, welcome to my home, is same your home." I replied with a smile, "Shukran Mr. Ahmed for allowing me to share your home."

The sulaimani was very much welcomed, ultra-sweet but I did not care for now. I needed some energy and the goodies on the tray, some Arabic sweets, saturated with sugar but a nice treat. Ahmed had a friend serve the tea.

Now I'm not the best-looking man in the world but this geezer had scars all over his face, neck, hands and I could clearly see burn marks. I was not going to ask Ahmed why this man had all these injuries, I didn't want to really know the nasty stories but he looked like he had a story to tell for sure, plus I didn't want to piss anyone off. He seemed happy with filling my glass, offering the sweets. His smile made me feel at ease with him, so I took advantage of the situation and smiled when I had the chance to interact with him, I never stopped looking for the sympathy vote.

The room we were in was like most you see here, family pictures on the walls, large cushions with various rugs dotted here and there. My 'mate' Muqtada Al Sadr was once more a prominent figure in the room along with his father. I had to find out more about the past of the Al Sadr family, for now he was not on my Christmas card list but I want to know more.

A young man walked into the room, he looked at me, nodded his head and smiled. He sat down opposite me, was served some tea and started to talk to Ahmed who had joined him. It was interesting that Ahmed brought out the first gun, he placed it beside the young man. You would think that by now I should be used to the guns? It was amazing how these guns were calling the shots with my general mood and body temperature; my heart would instantly change and a quick intake of breath was never far behind.

One thing is for sure, I will never be a gun man. I guess you either like them or you don't? Many Americans have this fascination about guns, it is an integral part of their life, their gun culture is huge. I'm glad the Brits are very different to them. I wonder why they think it makes them look so hard. The 'Big guy look'? … 'Look how big I am'? What is so hard about pulling a trigger and taking a life? How do you get a buzz from holding a lump of metal that holds so much misery to others? From my time in the Middle East, I had many a conversation with some Yanks, I just don't get the mindset with the gun culture? Many get weird and ultra-protective when you suggest their laws on guns are a bad thing, then in the next sentence, they say the Brits are nuts and crazy for fighting at a football match… Oh well.

I understood the gun in the room. I'm a stranger in his house and he has to protect his family, I get that, not sure I would take the same choice but there again this is Iraq. Everyone in the room was just sat chilling, not a lot of talking. The looks from the tea man and young boy were sheepish, I guess it was a new one for having an Englishman sat in their family home. I looked over at Ahmed and said, "Mr. Ahmed, I want sleep is ok?" I cupped my hands to one cheek to suggest I wanted to sleep, he replied, "No problem sleep Mr. Gerry welcome." Good news, light up a cig, drink some hot tea and get some relief to my body. How I will feel over the coming hours I'm not sure.

How was I still awake? Technically I should just fall into a deep sleep, what is keeping me awake? I cannot be certain, for me it's the uncertainty of my future and has been like that for the past eighty-six hours. Gazza, don't think too much, drop the guilt with the family, you have to be selfish more than ever, you have to keep it together.

The day's events had thrown everything at me, apart from the kitchen sink as we say, so I had taken my fair share of abuse but hey ho it could have been worse. I should feel lucky, they could have really gone to town on me, kicking the fuck out of me. If they wanted to, they could have made me even more ugly and had a real good go at my face, at least no blades were used on me. Most of the hits on me felt like back handers rather than full blooded punches. Trouble with that is the stinging sensation but then it goes numb, which is the lucky part, perhaps the adrenalin cancels the pain, I'm not too sure. Full blooded punches could have broken bones, so I should be thankful. It had only been a few hours ago, my body was aching all over and I had a lot of pain in various areas, mainly my shoulders and left knee. My face was swollen and I'm not surprised, those knuckles are probably responsible for that one.

As I lay there the gunfire was still going on, it wasn't heavy but it was continuous. I wonder if Mr. H is there and involved, is this tribal stuff going on? I don't think it is coalition forces, I could be wrong but if it is tribal, I'm not too sure I would want the wrong type of characters being in this room right now. The most amazing thing I have overcome today is the controlling of adrenalin and hyperventilating. How on earth I never had a heart attack I do not know? My blood pressure would not be one of the lowest in the country right now, not with one hundred Ishtar a day on top of that experience. I tried to understand how long I had been in the company of those fucking wankers, it had to be between five to six hours. That is some workout my friend and you have come through it but I know I was so close to going down or being killed by those pricks.

The tears broke, finally I had given way. It was so hard to hold back but why no tears earlier? I know how close I had come to losing my life but my thirty seventh birthday gift was the reality of how strong I was. Will I ever question again if I'm able to take shit, stress and physical pain again in my life? I believe it will teach me so much in my new life, I just have to get out this mess I'm in to put it into practice. My birthday gifts, young Omar bringing me cigarettes, my food at Mr. A's house, the use of soap and the simple pleasure of bottled water. It is kind of surprising what can make us happy and the ultimate gift is that I'm still alive.

I drifted off to sleep, I'm not sure for how long but I was woken up by noise in the room. Mr. H had returned with the two others who had shared my car journey. I sat up slowly, made my way to the tray where the pot of tea was, poured myself some sulaimani, sat down and lit up a fag. My movements were slow with my body was stiffening up from the beating and injuries. What I wouldn't pay for a hot 'Radox' bath, followed by a cool swimming pool right now.

Mr. Tea man brought in a large bowl of hot water and Mr. H and the others washed their hands and faces with a bar of soap. In came a plastic sheet, ready for the food to come out. Wow! A good spread was coming out, boiled eggs, fried eggs, cheese, soft Arabic bread and breakfast cream with honey! Shit me, my favourite! As I looked out of the window, I could see the dark passing us as the light came up, I'm sure we were at 0530 hrs and now I see prayer mats coming out.

When the prayers finished, Mr. H walked over to me and brought out a smile in me, "Mr. Gerry now we eat good breakfast and then we talk, no smoking now also because my brother has made sure we eat good foods for you, I want you eat much now." I just nodded and started to tuck into the breakfast cream, honey and Arabic bread.

The food I have to say was amazing, I could not believe how much I had but of course I was so happy that I had found my appetite, such freshness but that breakfast cream with honey was something else, the Arabic bread was soft and warm and hot off the press.

The one thing that had been bothering me from day one of being taken, was why have I not heard more fierce battles between the locals and the coalition forces? How on earth did this even happen? How did they lose control of Nasiriyah? How the fuck can a western military power lose control with such power at their disposal? Unreal. At some stage they would have had their ass kicked but when? Surely to gain control you have to fight for it and I had not heard anything before being taken, just goes to show you how much presence they had, obviously not enough.

What is the point of having tanks and not using them for sucks sake? This local lot are not going to be able to hold off 20 tanks coming at them, so fucking use them! To the best of my knowledge, there is not a large British military presence in Nasiriyah. Only small pockets on Tallil and I only know that as they were coming into the laundry. Are they are not going to organise some special army to come and get me? No chance and I get that to be honest as they have better things to do than come to try and find some Brit who has a personal problem here in Iraq. Special Forces, will they come? Do they know where I am and they are just waiting for the right time to strike?

Mr. H suggested that I wash my hands, so I took the opportunity and asked for the toilet. Mr. H walked me out of the room and said, "Ok Gerry when I open this door you will see small house of brick, go in fast and come back, need talk to you." I nodded and walked on; Mr. H went back to the room. As I walked out, I was greeted by sunlight which kind of took my eyes by surprise as I had not seen clean open sunlight for some time, strange to say but a new experience to handle, the brightness was difficult to deal with. Oh well onwards. As I opened the door to this brick built shed… fuck me! I was greeted by a swarm of flies and I mean a swarm! It must have looked like I was in some kind of frenzy as my arms attempted to be flung around me but easier said than done with my injuries. The damn things were all over my ears, nose, mouth and head!

Gazza, get your business done! So, I straddled the hole in the ground trying to concentrate my weight over to my right once more but not easy whilst fighting these flies off my meat and two veg! Oh my God this is outrageous and the best part is that I have diarrhoea! I was in a time trap, everything seemed to go to slow at the wrong time, just get me out of this room please! I had soap again and a good supply of water, a hose pipe connected to a waterline, so I could wash my bits properly with soap and cleanish water, then wash my hands. I had finished and as I came out, I could breathe in properly, fuck that was awful. It is just amazing how they live like this, at least try and do something about it, clean the damn place.

I made my way back to the room but thought I would take my chance to try and look around. I could see it was a farm for sure, no neighbours around them, so just a standalone building. Mr. H came out and snapped, "Mr. Gerry what you doing? Yella come now!" When we got into the room Mr. H said, "Mr. Gerry what are you doing standing looking outside like that, this not good if someone see you, this is bad for you and for me, plus my brothers' family." As we sat down, I said, "Mr. H I walk out from toilet and the sun catch my eyes, I could not see properly, I think the other building the right way." He nodded at me and smiled in such a way that he seemed to believe me.

Mr. H reclined himself down on the floor, he lit up a cigarette, smoked it and then stretched out, only to fall asleep. Why is he sleeping now? He has been awake for most of the night but what has he been doing? I don't think he had been involved in the gunfire last night, his clothes did not look like he had been involved in dirty work. The only people in the room now were Mr. H and one of the guards, I thought it would be a good time to get some shut eye myself. I'm now approaching the start of day five and Mr. H has made me feel the safest since being taken but still I could not turn my back to the room, not possible. I could only but try and fall into a deep sleep. What I wouldn't give to sleep for a week right now, I must have bags on bags under my eyes. I was dozing off for ten minutes, then waking up, having a cigarette and then dozing off again, this went on for at least three hours.

In my head, today was my release day, it had to be today, why the delay? Is there ever going to be a release date? Mr. H just seems too nice to be a bad guy or unless this is the soft man routine, as I have had the hard man routine far too often but why would they be thinking down that line? It's not like I know things and they want to question me. Oh my God there is a thought, maybe they think that from working on the base I know things and they want me to eventually speak about it? My head would not stop thinking of the permutations, I was going crazy by the day.

I wish I could switch off the guilt for what I was doing to my family and friends. What were they all going through? I cannot dwell on this for too long as I'm going to fuck myself up, that is what I had maintained from day one. It keeps coming back to haunt me, sure I know I'm going mad, I should just shut it out and that's it but I can't, why? I have always maintained in my life for one reason or another, there should always be a focus on something and that number one factor is survival. I needed to get back on track with the plan, sympathy vote and many questions. Now is the ideal time to do that through Mr. H. He has to know but can I get him to give way and spill the beans to me? Do I want to know the real answers? Can I take the bad news if it is going to be the worst scenario?

I realised; it is Good Friday. Hey, wait a minute, I'm sure today or tomorrow West Ham have a game and another on Monday? We have! And I know the two games are Crystal Palace and Derby but in what order I don't know. How weird that I should be thinking about this at such a time, not good to be honest as I know they were in the play-off spots, I also know that they have Coventry at home next weekend at Upton Park, minimum is to get to play off final and get back to the Premier League. They have let me down so many times over the years but wouldn't have changed a thing, never.

I wonder why I have been moved around so much. Since Monday I have been moved five times and had different teams looking after me, why all the changes? I'm guessing they all work for Mr. Al Sadr and I'm assuming Mr. H and Mr. A do also, I'm also starting to think that Mr. H is high up in the pecking order. The video, what is the video all about? Mr. H was adamant that the video was made. From the time I set foot in Mr. A's house, the good food, the set-up of the camera men, not just the equipment, they had but even their style of dress and how they presented themselves, cut from different cloth. Where has the video been sent to? Who has seen it? Are they expecting some feedback from the UK Government or my family, thinking they can demand a ransom for me? I know UK Government will not pay, especially the lamb, Mr. Blair. That has to be it, the delay is because of a stalemate, they will wait to see if someone is going to come forward and pay.

Ok, time to up the ante then. I stood up and started to pace the room. Pack of cigarettes in hand, I will just pace about, one of them will have to wake up. I want answers now, I have to know. I didn't go over the top with the noise I was making as I didn't want to startle or shock any of them. I didn't want panic to set in and have them reach for their weapons and discharge them on me. The exercise was good for me, the pacing let off steam in a controlled way but the more I paced the more I was thinking about wanting to know about the future, the more I wanted Mr. H to wake up and get it off my chest.

Finally, Mr. H stirred. I don't think he saw me as his movements were initially slow and then he moved quite quick, "Gerry what you do, why like this? Now is sleep time for us all, we tired from the work." I replied, "Mr. H I cannot sleep good, I think is good now that you tell me when I will see my babies in UK, you are a powerful man, I'm sure you know." He turned over and went back to sleep, what the fuck?! Now I'm in different territory again, I'm in danger of having him turn against me. I should not take it for granted that he is my new best mate, he is not going to bow down and listen to my plea. Back to boredom and frustration. Smoke, sleep and no answers, the silence is pissing me off and is out of my control.

I had been asleep for a while; the room was quite hot and I couldn't see Mr. H but his brother and others were spring cleaning. They were rolling up rugs, taking them out of the room and bringing in new clean ones in plastic bags. Mr. H's brother Ahmed was in the room with two young lads, one of which I had seen before, they were sat opposite me, huddled around in conversation and the odd look over to me. The young lads were quite shy, when I returned a smile to them, they gazed away from me but why?

I got Ahmed's attention, "Ahmed, these boys are your sons?" A smile appeared on his face as he said, "Yes my sons, they good boys, they shy for you but happy that an Englishman is in their house." I said, "Do they speak any English or maybe have books for reading?" I used my hands to gesture the opening of a book and Ahmed spoke with his sons briefly as they disappeared, only to return with a pile of books. As I looked through them, I could see they were all in Arabic, except one. The book's title was, 'Ships of the World', great news, I can read about ships all day.

I tried to interact with his sons but their English ability was very little, they both got a little frustrated with themselves, it seems their smiles were indicating they wanted to learn more but was hard for them. Ahmed came over and explained to me, "Mr. Gerry, I allow them to come and be in the room with you because I feel that you would not make problems. My wife she did not want me to involve them but I know they were excited to know an Englishman is here, I hope is ok, they want to learn with you but not easy, thank you for smiles for them."

It was just before lunchtime, Mr. H came back with two others. He was carrying a radio which he gave to his brother. Not sure if the radio would be good for me as everything is in Arabic but there again, the silence in the room can be a killer, at least some noise is good, breaks the boredom and helps prevent my mind wandering. Mr. H got into a huddle with the two other guards from the car last night. What were they talking about? I don't know but they were not involving me with it. I needed to get time with Mr. H, he cannot keep up this silence. He kept a gaze my way and I made sure my face read a picture of anxiety, he has to come and speak.

The huddle broke and Mr. H came over and sat down, "Mr. Gerry, I understand you have been very kind to my brother and his sons, I thank you for doing this, you are good man so everything is good." I cut in, "Mr. H I need to know what is going to happen to me, I have the right to know and I know you have information, so tell now please?" He looked at me, took hold of my hand in both his hands, "Mr. Gerry you need to listen, inshallah tomorrow can go see babies but I not sure, Muqtada is good man for Gerry and Sheikh Ouse is good, hopefully speak more soon, now I eat with you now, I like to see you eat good, keep you strong and healthy." I replied, "Mr. H I know you good man, I not want problems for you and family, take me two kilometres from Tallil Air Base, take me when dark and then I run to the base, nobody can see you then, you have no danger and I can find my way." He came back at me, "Mr. Gerry, what you ask not easy, is problem for Gerry and Mr. H and is a dangerous way to do, maybe some peoples will be looking to follow, we will see later but now have to eat."

Food arrived and I was taken back by another new addition. I could see a whole fish on a plate! I hope the damn thing is not out of the Euphrates, mind you I don't have to eat it. There were potatoes also with some fresh yoghurt, Mr. H's brother was spoiling us all. When you consider the monthly salary here in Iraq, he is treating me special. Why all the special treatment? Is it because they like me or are they fattening me up like they would a goat before they slaughter it? I waited until I was invited to eat and as they tucked in, I came forward, took my food and returned to my position to start eating.

Mr. H looked at me and said, "Mr. Gerry please the fish, my brother phone his friend for special order for you and only you." I was looking at Mr. H and Ahmed to see their reactions, I'm thinking, oh no, I hope this damn fish is not full of oil from the river. Mr. H said, "Mr. Gerry, this fish is from Basra you know this? One time each week his friend goes Basra, he has big truck and he bring many things, so my brother asks him for this fish for you, please come." It was from Basra. Ok then maybe I might be in luck, I hope the damn thing does not taste like shit, I don't want to offend him. Back I came to take some fish, I said, "Ahmed please enjoy with me, eat with me, maybe your sons will enjoy to share with me?" Ahmed replied, "Mr. Gerry please, is special for you, you know Basra number one for this fish, please enjoy my gift." I put half of the fish on my plate, I couldn't see any bones which is great and for now I can only see the white flesh of the fish, no discoloration and no bad smells. I cut into it, the flesh fell away, very soft. I scooped up some flakes on my fork and in it went, all eyes were on me looking for my appreciation and feedback. Relief, it was a fresh fish from Basra out of the sea, for me I could taste the brine, tasted very nice actually.

I must have spent the next hour thanking Mr. H and Ahmed for the great food and it was followed up by an Arabic sweet treat and sulaimani tea, a sugar fest. For good measure I was given breakfast cream, honey and Arabic bread again, I can't explain how much I love this stuff. With all the chicken you see in Iraq I was always curious where it all came from? I didn't see it being processed in Iraq and if it was, what was the process? I dread to think!

Four cigarettes later the toilet was calling me for the second time. Oh cigarettes! Ahmed had brought in a full carton of Ishtar for me, two hundred fags on him. When I gestured to pass money Mr. H looked surprised, I could not help but to see his facial reaction. "Sorry Mr. H what is wrong, I do something wrong?" He replied, "No no Mr. Gerry but I surprised you have money, how you keep for yourself, where keeping?" I showed him my small secret pocket, well not that secret because you can see it, it is just that nobody thought to search it, lucky for me because it kept the supplies coming to me. Good job he just laughed and thought no more of it.

Back out to the toilet and I knew what was coming, not nice at all but I have to go. I opened the door; the swarm was still there. Fuck my luck. What made it worse this time was that there was a piece of shit that wasn't even aimed to the hole… for fucks sake! Now I will need to try and move the wayward poo so I'm able to straddle the hole without standing in it! These flies, what do I see and get those others don't? At least if they kept the place clean then they would see that the flies would not come here so much because of the smell of the chlorine or other cleaning fluid, but to just leave it and let the smell ferment made no sense at all to me.

I got back to the room and I was allowed a bowl of warm water and a bar of soap but unfortunately no razor for shaving. I really needed a shave. I asked for some cooking oil to use. I was given it but not explaining what I wanted it for and it brought a smile and laugh. Five days growth of stubble and I hated it. The irritation did not help at all, it was just another frustration and another item out of my control. We take it for granted when we are in control of things, we don't stop and think what it would be like if we didn't have a choice. Being dictated to is not nice I can assure you; it totally pissed me off.

My skin in general was bone dry, for all the heat and sweat you think I would be greased up to the eyeballs but it was the opposite, only exception was my neck and crotch… how lovely. This dish dash (thobe) I had on was so heavy. I'm sure it had been made from potato sacks which would be ok for the winter months but for now, not good.

Mr. H was up and about putting his jacket and shoes on, he walked over to me and said, "Mr. Gerry, now I go out for some time, you can read the book, you have many cigarettes and drinks, be good again for my brother, I will see you soon." He made no comments about when or how I will be going home; he didn't want that conversation with me again today, his intentions were not clear, only time will tell. I was left with Ahmed and Mr. Tea man. The radio was banging out some local tunes, whether they liked it or not I'm not sure, maybe they were persevering just for me and it was better than the silence of the room. I wondered how Ahmed feels about me being here. Maybe he is just keeping the smile on his face and playing the nice man because his brother has told him to or maybe he is under orders? From what I have seen, he has been relaxed with me and he has only been absent for small periods, I'm sure he has the farm to run also. I think it makes sense that I go and talk with him, get closer to him, maybe I will need his friendship later, the more people I have onside, the better it is for me.

I stood up, made my way over to the other side of the room, stopped halfway and said, "Is ok Gary sit?" He sat up straight, moved his weapon, "No problem Mr. Gerry, please come." Over the course of the next thirty minutes, we both got through many questions and answers, we did this by using a mixture of broken languages, amazing what you can achieve with hand and body movements.

Ahmed wanted me to give my opinion of Mr. Bush, Mr. Blair and in the USA, 9/11. I gave my account of what I honestly felt and he looked like he understood and agreed with me. He explained that he hated Saddam Hussein, he was thankful that he had been removed but wanted the soldiers to leave so they can make their own choices in life. Anywhere in the world, any man would want to have freedom of choice for his own country and not want outsiders to make the choices for him. A worthwhile conversation, it was an icebreaker with Ahmed and I felt it brought us closer together but when I spoke to him about being released back to my normal life I was greeted with, "Inshallah soon Mr. Gerry."

Ahmed had asked me about my general treatment and when I explained what had happened yesterday, he reacted in shock, he even involved Mr. Tea man at this stage, he also looked perplexed and shocked at what had happened. Whether their reactions were credible or not is another thing. For now, I can only assume that their apologies for their fellow countrymen are sincere, the shock factor was a little over the top, I'm sure they have heard worse.

Ahmed as a non-smoker could not understand why I was smoking so much. I tried to explain to him that of course I'm worried about my situation and my family's situation. I said, "Ahmed try and put yourself in my situation, what would be going on in your mind? Do you think it is acceptable that a good man like me should be held by force and treated in this way?" Ahmed gave no response, he sat and smiled at me with a shrug of the shoulders, what could he say to defend the indefensible? Between Ahmed and Mr. Tea man, I dodged the bullet of family, two Gulf wars, plus the war with Iran on top of that and all the normal shit that goes on in this country, I'm sure one of them had experienced fatalities with family or close friends. Both had been in the Iraqi army and Ahmed left to take up farming away from the city life.

Mr. Tea man like so many others in the Army were dismissed from the Army.

This put many men out of work. No money, no food to feed the family and too much time on their hands doing nothing, a recipe for disaster. How can any man accept this? Not easy at all, take away the emotion of the war and who is on whose side, these men have to find something to do to earn a living.

Ahmed's son walked into the room, he walked over to me and handed me some mint flavoured sweets, nice one. I received them giving a warm smile to him, bowing my head and thanking him, mint flavours to clean my pallet and taste something else, not just fags.

The most I had ever smoked in any given day of my life would have been two packets and that would have been an away day with West Ham, going to the game somewhere in the UK and then after the game, hitting the town on a bender till the wee small hours of the morning. My body is so use to all this nicotine now and it just wants to keep topping up to its newly found level. For now, I will just have to live with the fact that it is ok and if I ever get out of this shit, I will just have to learn to readjust, not more I can do.

It had been about fourteen hours since I parted company with the nut jobs who had their fun on my birthday, my new sitters were so different. Too different to be honest and that also worried me because it was chalk and cheese. I had asked Ahmed if I was allowed to change my clothes, why do I need this thick robe on? Every time I mentioned it a smile and hand gesture were the reply, no big talks about it and again I'm confused why they want me to have it on? I'm not too sure the purpose it is serving. A control thing which would make it hard for me to run in or maybe help to disguise me if and when I'm outside?

I spent the afternoon reading about the world's ships, smoking and getting sick on sulaimani tea. I was totally pissed off that I could not fall asleep with by back turned away from them. I was so desperate to drop off asleep and not have to worry about anything, where is my Mum when I really need her the most?

My knee was getting tighter by the hour, it started to lock up, it was like it was freezing in a position, I had to push and force it to go straight. My arms and shoulders had definitely found new pulses, I'm sure I will have these aches and pains for weeks to come. I'm constantly moving from one position to another, it seems that moving around is my best option for now. The pains in my shoulders felt similar to the feeling of when you have not been in the gym for one month and you start again on the heaviest weights and push for one hour, realising the next day that you cannot even move and if someone even brushes your skin you freak out.

My mind went to Paul again, he would have known on Monday about the situation, so I wondered where he was now and what was going through his mind and what were his plans. He would have to make flight plans and of course people will be talking to Paul, concerned of what he has in his mind. Paul could be a loose cannon and make the situation worse for me, maybe get himself taken as a hostage or even killed.

It was Good Friday and the kids would be looking for the Easter bunny in a couple of days. It's not right, I should be there with Christian and having fun on his first bunny rabbit hunt for chocolate eggs and sharing the chocolate, lol!

My eyes opened, I woke up to a little hustle and bustle in the room. I looked at Ahmed as he was placing some food on the floor, I pointed at my wrist to try and understand the time, Ahmed said, "Now is six." Wow, I had been asleep for like three hours and I felt great that I could do that. It had to come, a time where my body was going to give way and go into some kind of lockdown for a while, I was shattered. I have banked three hours sleep and now I will be eating, nice news coming all at once but I was not super hungry, my appetite was off. I sat down to eat that was placed by Mr. Tea man, he looked at me and said, "I Sameer". I replied, "Oh, shukran Sameer, arfwan" (arfwan means you are welcome). So now I know the name of the sulaimani maker, nice that he said that. All this bad luck he had in his life I feel sorry for him. He had never put his business in my face which was good for me, he stayed away and just felt happy to pour me a drink and I'm sure he was the go for this and go for that man around the place.

We sat there for some time eating our way through the invitingly fresh produce in front of me, I wonder if Ahmed's farm was supplying it. The door opened, two men walked in, no guns, both looked to be in their forties, looked quite clean and stood with smiles as they went about embracing everyone in the room. I felt the need to stand, standby waiting to shake hands, you never know who they are and where they are in the food chain. They could be important players, my mind was still telling me to sell myself, keep the standards. Play the sympathy cards when you can mate, has to be my ticket out of here. I sense a soft side to Mr. H. so I need to try and take this to the next level. I have kept the tears out of this so far but I believe if I open the floodgates that could seal the closure of the deal.

They moved forward to me, hands out ready to shake for sure and smiles, I did not hesitate, took a good grip and shook hands with them both, "As-salaam alaikum, keefer hal." One of them replied, "Arabic is good, is good, alaikum salaam" (As– salaam alaikum means "peace to you" and keefer hal means, "how are you"). I'm sure these men were aware why I was there, whether they found it weird or it was a normal circumstance I'm not sure, the main thing is the meet and greet went fine. They all sat around in a huddle to eat, as usual I could not join in, I just could not bend that left knee in, kneel or sit crossed leg is impossible. As usual they were hand-picking foods from the plates, whereas me I had a plate and put my food on it. I have seen this many times in the Middle East, they like to eat from plates with the hands, very different from us.

I have experienced a feast where they cook a whole sheep or half of it and place it on a silver tray, which is just over one meter in length, surround the meat with an ocean of rice, salad, pickles, a gravy and Arabic bread. They just pull of a lump of meat, mix it in with some rice, form a ball and then down the hatch.

It was lovely food and now it was time to enjoy a few fags. As I lit up an Ishtar, one of our visitors picked up the packet and started to share his intrigue with the others. He looked at me, shared a warm laugh. I offered him one but he kindly shook his hand and head side to side, I was not surprised.

These guys blended into this new group, groomed beards and clean clothes, yeah sure it is Friday, the Holy day of the week and they make more of an effort. They also seemed to make an effort to have cleaned themselves, unless they just sprayed aftershave on without a shower first but they had a better smell to them compared to me, I'm surprised they are so close.

One of them could speak English like Mr. H, on the same level, so he started to open up more with me. He was giving it the full twenty questions and they all seemed very interested to know about me, my past and general life. Where I was from? How many children do I have? Where do my family live? What is my work and normal job? Why did I come to Iraq? What do I think of Bush and Blair? What is the base like? We sat through question time for about two hours, I was starting to feel tired from talking so much. I was making sure to be careful about what information I gave, this could all be part of the plan and they are not going to get to much from me. My new friend told me that they all liked the fact that Saddam had been removed and this is not the first time I heard this, Mr. Saddam had really pissed of thousands in the south.

The other subject where they all seemed to be in the same boat was work. Over the years many worked in the Police and military and so many just been thrown out onto the scrap heap. Yeah, sure you had the street market traders, a vast number of small shops selling electrical goods and other hardware essentials but thousands were in the Police, military and the Americans sacked the majority of them. Goods were streaming over the Iraqi border from Jordan and Kuwait. The laws had changed since the regime had been toppled, so goods flowed into the country and many were trying to jump on the band wagon.

The coalition forces needed supplies of all kinds, money was everywhere to be made, the market has become saturated. I always thought of Iraq as a third world country but when you consider the volumes of oil they have, where is all the money? Before the coalition forces came here, I was told that it had not changed much, a shit hole is the word I'm looking for, Saddam was not too keen to share it and infrastructure is desperately needed. I guess over the years a lot of money found its way out of the country, there would be a few Iraqis with fat bank accounts outside of Iraq. If Saddam was such a great man and leader, why did he leave his people to suffer and allow this shithole to fall apart?

Thousands are happy that the coalition have rid them of Saddam but now it is time to give them jobs, work on the infrastructure for reliable electric and water supply, deal with new drainage and sanitation. They believe it is time for their families to start their new life, allow them to prosper and grow, deprived for many years, now they say is their time, well noted and agreed.

Sameer brought in some fresh sulaimani and as I lit up another cigarette, I moved slightly away from them and thankfully they gave me my space. The talk had gone on for long enough, it brought smiles at the end of it and I wanted to stop whilst I was winning.

I asked Ahmed the time. It was just past 2100 hrs so I asked the room, "What time will Mr. H come back?" Ahmed replied, "Inshallah two hours' time." Mr. H had been out the best part of last night and for the large part of today, so what is he doing? What is his job exactly? I wonder if I can get this information from anyone. I looked across at Ahmed and said, "Mr. Ahmed can I ask you please?" Ahmed walked over to me and sat down. "Yes Mr. Gerry what you want to ask me?" I replied, "Mr. H, what is his work please, why he always working?" Ahmed replied, "Mr. H he has big job, he always busy, he is big man in Nasiriyah and other places, he is the best man who help us so much." I said, "Ok he has big job, does he work for Muqtada

Al Sadr?" Ahmed said, "Mr. Gerry he works as good man, he likes Al Sadr, we all like him and I also think you will like him." I thought I would leave it at that, I should not press him anymore, that is good enough to know. I'm sure Mr. H is one of Muqtada's players, I'm not too sure that I like him just yet, after all his men have fucked with my mind and made me this wreck. I thanked Ahmed for talking to me and let him go on his way back to the crowd, it was time for me to settle down for the rest of the evening.

The past twenty-four hours had gone with no particular reason for me to worry. How they fit into this whole system I'm not sure. If they were as good as they say they, I would be a free man and allowed to go on my way. They are not all doing this free of charge, someone is fronting them. The tribal element forever tells me that many different groups could be involved and I think for now I'm with one of the better groups but they cannot hide me forever, something has to give but when?

I need to loosen up, I had been sat around for too long. The others were doing their own thing and looked happy to sit and talk. Ahmed's friends had been with us for a few hours now, maybe they are waiting for Mr. H or just didn't want to go home to the wife and kids? I paced the room at a snail's pace and tried to raise my damaged knee and bend it as quick as I could but it was not having any of it. Stretching out my shoulders was nice but I could not do it for too long, still the pain was shooting through the arm. I did this for about twenty minutes and that was enough, if I can do this every day at least for ten minutes, I will not seize up.

After sitting back down and having a smoke, I fell asleep for a while but was woken by a chill around me. It was Mr. H, he still had his jacket on, he reached down to me and held out his hand to shake mine; I shook his hand as my eyes were still adjusting, his hands were cold. Mr. H said, "Sorry wake up, I hope today is good, tomorrow could be good day, inshallah could go see baby", his hands spanned out like he was playing the aeroplane game. In one swift movement I was upright and trembling with emotion, I was overcome, "Oh my God, tomorrow sure can go home, you think so Mr. H, so where have you been? You will drop me near military base? What has been said? How I will I be handed over?" He brought his hands out in front of him, waved them up and down in an attempt to calm me down and then took my hands with his hands, "Gerry inshallah if you are good still, I'm hoping can happen." He moved over to the large bowl to wash, this was prayer time for them all, so the mats came out.

The night was going to be very slow; Ahmed's friends had left the room after eating, Mr. H had fallen asleep as soon as his head hit the floor, which left Ahmed, Sameer and I. A few moments later the door opened and in walked two strangers, I did not like the sight of new faces I would rather the same calm routine. Ahmed moved to Mr. H, woke him up as these two men wanted to talk with him. When they started to talk Ahmed and Sameer left the room. All seemed to be ok with their body language, one of the new men made a smile in my direction and the other showed no emotion. Mr. H looked over at me, "Gerry, these two men are looking after you now, I need to go to sleep now, these men are my men and are good men, so please be same good person you are." I said to Mr. H, "Will I ever see those men again from yesterday?" He raised his finger in the air and said, "Woolah Mr. Gerry, you will never see this man again, you are with Mr. H." He looked pretty pissed at me for the fact I thought I could be sent back to those wankers, he looked slightly angry with me.

I needed the bathroom; it was moving towards midnight and one of my new friends decided to walk with me. I was allowed to open the door and go inside. The flies had made the best decision of the day, they had fucked off which was great news but the stench had accumulated and due to the extra visitors using the damn thing and it had been overloaded. Why can they not use the basic toilet skills? I had never paid much attention in my past to breathe only through my mouth, not a natural skill for us but I had mastered it for now and you try doing it for five minutes, not easy.

I was led back into the room by the man mountain, he was heavier than Mr. H for sure, had to be twenty stones hanging from his bones so I did not fancy trying to shoulder barge this lad, mind you I wouldn't be capable at the minute of barging a two-year-old. The night was cold, the weather had turned for sure, luckily the room was warmer and Mr. H had given me an extra blanket but I had decided that the blanket would become my new pillow, the other pillow was so hard for me. I folded the blanket, placed it where my neck would lay on it and found instant success, this will be less stress on my shoulders and arms. I put my other blanket around me and I have to say it was the best I have felt in sleep mode since Sunday last week, I felt good and maybe this will help me sleep for four or five hours. The radio was on low and there was a mix of slow music and talk. I wish I had been able to understand more, maybe the news would help me understand what is going on in the country.

There had definitely been action between the coalition forces and Muqtada Al Sadr's Mehdi Army all over Iraq. From what I saw on the news the other day, on the Wednesday, Muqtada's lads had got brave across the country in an uprising. His following is in the thousands and I guess the coalition did not want to bring in the big guns just yet, which pissed me off.

As far as I was concerned, I wanted them to go to war against my captors.

In the morning I hope Mr. H has a plan to go to town and when he comes back, he has a plan to drop me on the road towards the base. If he drops me in the daylight hours it is easier for me, I can just proceed to the entrance of the base. In the dark it could be more difficult as I know there will be security that will have eyes on the surrounding areas if they see a body moving around, they could fire on me and our friends across the pond don't have a great track record when it comes to friendly fire. At nighttime, random bad fuckers could be lurking and hiding in wait; the desert leading to the base is an eerie big space.

I wonder if Mr. H does know what is going to happen but is keeping it hush hush for now? Why should he come back and say, "Inshallah you are going home?'" It simply does not make sense, what would he get out of it? Maybe he thinks it will make me happier and I will sleep more? Maybe he thinks I will remain good and not be a pain in the ass to anyone? He could be waiting for the green light from Sheikh Ouse or Mr. Al Sadr. I would love to know who he actually works for; I know Mr. H and Co are with a different set up, another tribe and yes, they are all linked to Muqtada Al Sadr. I will try again when he wakes up, I'm going to cross examine him a little more on this subject. If I can get him to open up and spill the beans, I know I would feel better knowing either way.

The night was doing its own thing, one minute I was asleep, then awake smoking excessively as I could not stop thinking that I could be really on my way out of here, is this going to happen today? It would be a dream to get out of this situation, all I want is the time to go so quick and for Mr. H to get up and leave the house. Time was standing still. It's always the same way, when you want it to go slow it will go quick and vice versa. To sit and wait for potential death was a killer mentally.

Mr. H and his lads had been amazing to me compared to the others, better food, more smiles, fed me drinks and no signs that someone was going to give me a beating or play extra time with mind games. The mind games will always be there, that can never go away. Any of these lot could turn in minutes, if money came into play, money just changes everything, that concept applies to anywhere in the world and these people have no money. It all seemed too good to be true but the last twenty-four hours and twists and turns are not welcome, unless it is my route out of here but I knew there would be even more twists, I just knew.

I could not turn my back to any of them though and this had been the case from Monday the 5th of April. I could not even close my eyes for too long. Trust is a funny thing for sure, every minute you are waiting to die, I couldn't even trust the quiet ones, we always say watch the quiet ones. The sun had just started to come out to play and Mr. H stirred and finally got to his feet. He picked up the large bowl used for washing and walked outside with it. Returning with clean water he had a wash and he ushered others to do the same. After their prayers Mr. H came to me and sat down. He said, "Good morning, Gerry, how are you?" I replied, "Yes, good morning I'm ok not to bad but…" He cut in, "Mr. Gerry, sorry I want ask you, I not see you pray, why don't you pray?" I replied, "Mr. H I have nothing to pray to, so how can I pray? I don't want to talk about that if it is ok, thank you. What I do want to talk about is this, I think you know what is going to happen but you are not telling me and I don't think this is good from you. You have been good man, your brother and other men have also been good but you must remember that I have my own life to live, I should be a free man. Many men ask me about my opinions of Bush, Blair and Saddam, I tell the truth that I think you should all be free men and make your own choices, so if I think you should be a free man, why can you not think the same as me?" He stood up and said, "Mr. Gerry, go and get clean water in bowl for cleaning yourself, I think will be good for you, yella go now for me please." I walked outside to get clean water, he was right, it was nice to have a full wash down but I still did not get my answers.

Breakfast was served and it was the real deal today. Nectar straight from a hive, now that is cool! I shit you not, if you have never experienced eating the solid part of the honeycomb you don't know what you are missing. It's a shame that a fly cannot make honey like a bee can. If they could, Iraq would be very rich. The fucking flies get on my nerves, mind you, they did add to some sport sometimes to pass the time but an annoying sport of swatting.

Mr. H went out of the room and returned thirty minutes later with a clean shirt, groomed beard and the same suit which still looked well finished. He said, "Mr. Gerry, today I very busy, inshallah I get good news for you. Ahmed will now come with Sameer and sit with you again to make sure you are ok?" I replied, "Mr. H, now I want to know who you work for, tell me, is it Muqtada Al Sadr?" He retorted back, "Gerry, I not tell you and I say this before; Muqtada is a good man, Gerry is a good man and so is Mr. H." I came back to him, "Ok, if I not go home, who I stay with Mr. H or I go with those other bad people from before?" He looked deep and longing, paused and said, "Mr. Gerry, you are now my brother, you be good for Mr. H and you can stay with me." I just nodded and smiled back; I was not going to get the full story. For some reason he was still holding back on me, not being up front and I'm not too sure how much more pressure I can put on him? I sense that he lost it a little with me then, I guess he is not use to others questioning him.

The unknown and the waiting game was going to be the ultimate killer for me, my gut feeling was that I was involved in a game of Poker. I was in the middle of the pot, there were many players and each one was trying to win the pot but for what reason I don't know. It's not good Gazza, Mr. H is playing one group off with another, waiting for the best bid to come in before you're released, who wants to pay the most?

Mr. H left the room. So that's him gone for the best part of the day, so now it was me and Ahmed again, who didn't look so happy to babysit me again. Sameer came over to me, sat down and was happy to share a cup of sulaimani and smoke ourselves senseless. Sameer was such a simple man, he just went about his day doing the same thing, motionless nearly but I'm sure he felt that he was contributing to the cause for Mr. H and Ahmed. Apparently, Sameer had many stories about his military career, one of which, how he escaped death from the coalition forces. He was cool with me.

The rest of the day would drag on. Lunch arrived which was well prepared, so no complaints there and my ships book came into play again for the best part of the afternoon. Funny thing with that book, as I was reading, I felt sleepy each time but still could not fully fall into a deep sleep. If someone had said to me in the past that the human body can go for ninety plus hours without too much sleep, I would not believe them.

Some years before when I worked for myself in the UK, I used to work forty-eight hours nonstop. Yes, it is true but that is when you have something to do, not just sitting around. The gremlins were preventing it and it could only be one thing, I was simply afraid all the time. Gazza, you can dress it up as much as you like but the answer is fear, being afraid of what is going to happen… I just hope that fear keeps me alive.

I was up pacing the room, then back to the book, then laying down, then up pacing again, I just couldn't settle. I was waiting for my departure details and I don't have the most patience in the world at the best of times! Then it was my first visit to the toilet of the day and it was not good news!… everything dripped out of the rear of me… maybe the fresh food was flushing out the bad food? But I had no pain which was the good thing.

Panic started to set in, it was about 1500 hrs and still no sign of Mr. H. If he was going to have good news for me it should have happened by now because the hours of darkness are closing in shortly. He has to come here first to collect me, then drop me off near the base whilst it was still light, unless they feel they have to do this in the dark in case they get lifted by the military? What if Mr. H can't get the confirmation of my release today and who is he taking that information from? Maybe it is more difficult than he anticipated? Maybe the deal on the table is with the Italians? If that was the case, I hoped the negotiations were nothing like, "You Italians have to leave Nasiriyah before he is released!" Any kind of heavy terms like that I'm fucked, I would have a long wait, I could be brown bread!

Ahmed and Sameer were looking at me differently, Ahmed said, "Mr. Gerry walk to much not good and not look good face, what happened'? I tried to explain to him that Mr. H said I could be released soon, so the waiting is making my mind go crazy. By the looks of his face, he seemed to understand, Sameer said in broken English, "Gerry sit Ishtar and sulaimani, come." I must have been getting on their tits also, they must have far more better things to be getting on with, not sat around babysitting me and slurping tea all day, but their again maybe this was the normal for them. I would imagine that Ahmed is normally working on his farm with his sons helping him, Sameer is the right-hand man for him, so I guess it is down to his sons. Sameer had signalled that it was just after 1900 hrs and dinner was served. It was the normal stuff as usual but at least I still had some kind of appetite, more than I thought I would have, the cigarettes were suppressing a lot of the hunger and on top of that I had this cloud of being released hanging over my head.

If nothing happens in the next hour with Mr. H coming home, I cannot see me realising my dream of freedom and I want to know! I sat, lit one fag up after the other, no patience whatsoever, I was borderline getting angry which is not good but I have never liked anyone bullshitting me, just be straight and come out and say it, stop fucking about. Yes, I have not had beatings from you lot, I have had great food and generally nothing of great concern but now you are taking the piss with stretching it out. I fear the worst because I can't get a straight answer, it is all, "Inshallah inshallah", that is the same as maybe to me, no more!

I wished that my mind would stop having all the different permutations buzzing around it, I know I have found my imagination and learned so many things about myself. Having been through many experiences, I only hope I experience only one more and that is the experience of being released to freedom. The same old things just kept on happening, lighting a fag, pacing around, back down on the mattress! The news has to come tonight or at first light. Eventually I dropped off to sleep, I was shattered, my mind just gave up, I was over tired, I was exhausted from it all, everything going around in the same circles in my mind and the boredom of it all.

I finally woke up to a chill coming near me, Mr. H was back, he walked over to the far side of the room. He was talking to Ahmed, Sameer and the two others he had walked into the room with. Looks came my way but with no smiles and I could see some fear and confusion in them all, so what is going on?

They all washed themselves, had a group prayer on the mats, sat down and food was taken in. I was spitting feathers but couldn't interfere with their routine. I was pissed that he did not update me as soon as he came in, he knew how I was and obviously didn't give a fuck.

Something has changed with him and I don't like it, he has more or less blanked me since coming in the room. I'll leave him alone, no good to piss him off, after all he may have some good news, so I will give him the benefit of doubt but I hope it has a positive spin.

Mr. H walked over to me, he sat down near me with a glass of sulaimani and lit up a fag, he just sat there and had his moment. Talk for fucks sake! Eventually he turned to me and made his usual approach, taking hold of my hand and said, "Mr. Gerry no go home now but inshallah tomorrow I think but we have big problem." I closed my eyes, bit my top lip and dropped my shoulders. I fucking knew it would not be today and so did he, so why oh fucking why did you not say? Why is he lying to me? tell me the fucking truth! He carried on, "Mr. Gerry you know Ali Baba men who take your ring and other things, they are looking for you, many of them are searching for you." I replied, "Why are they looking for me now, you have me now and I think you are the same group of people yes?" He came back, "Mr. Gerry these men are very bad men, things have changed and we have to move you, if they find you this is a big problem for me and you, ok so let's go now, we have to move fast." I wanted to know more, "Mr. H, how many men are looking for me and if they find me, they will kill me? What will happen you have to tell me now?" Mr. H looked me bolt right in the eyes, "Gerry, if they find you, they will kill you or sell you to more bad men, we have to go another place that is ten minutes away, they will come search my brother's house, I'm sure. Gerry there are many now in Nasiriyah look for you, maybe around five hundred men, they will look day and night to get you."

I was up on my feet, I was allowed to have my white polo shirt on, with jeans and trainers, I would be back to my normal dress. My heart started to pound big time. Just as I thought this was all coming to an end, I'm getting involved in deep political shit. Someone wants to kill me or trade me to some sad fucker who wants to parade me on television in his cowardly fashion. My body heat turned up within seconds, I'm fucking shit scared, I can't get out of this mess and I can't take any more. I'm not going home; I can feel it and I have nowhere to turn.

23 LOCATION NUMBER 5 – WHAT A MESS

My big dish dash was draped over me followed by an over jacket that looked similar to a donkey jacket. My head covered with a ghutra, Mr. H and the others had also decided to put a ghutra on so we all blended in and I wasn't going to be the sore thumb. Mr. H guided me out of the door and said to me, "Mr. Gerry you stay close to me, I cannot hold you because I need to carry my weapon, keep your head facing down and I will protect you." In front of us were three men and behind us another two men, so I had six of them to protect me.

The early morning air was cold, the ground was solid under my feet and we are clearly walking across the desert because of the cambers in the surface, this was not even a dirt track. I could see they were all carrying AK47's and also had handguns in holsters, webbing packed with grenades, which told me that they are taking this seriously. Mr. H and his men cannot be the same group as the others if he is saying these words. If these others came and found me by a setup, Mr. H can say what he wants to cover his shame, what would he care if he is paid thousands of dollars? Oh my God I sense a setup now, it was all too easy for Mr. H to take me in, the bad fuckers handed me over Mr. H for what reason? Just to have a break from me? What is the link between these tribes and who was Sheikh Ouse protecting?

We were moving quietly but at a fair pace across this land, it was pitch black, the night sky was not giving much light and the surface under my feet was undulated. I could hear dogs barking in the distance, hopefully their noise was not being made because they could hear or smell us. My personal radar was working overtime, anticipating a group coming our way but then again it is about 0200 hrs. I don't think they would be out at this time looking for us, maybe after first light when prayers and breakfast has been consumed.

We were staying quite close which is not good but what can I do at this stage? I can't exactly call for a recce point and suggest that I'm advising them but, in my opinion, it was not good being so close to one another. Mr. H started to come in front of me, every step I took to his left or right he was dead in front of me, protection at its highest I guess to him, protecting an asset of good or bad. The cold air started to find its way through me and I was trying to counterbalance the heat inside me. My steps tried to quicken hoping that we were very close to our destination but my injured knee simply would not have it and I was finding it difficult to walk now.

We had been walking for about twenty minutes, the men in front stopped as Mr. H and I caught up with them. Mr. H said, "Gerry waits here now, I need go and see something to make sure is safe for all of us, so be quiet and wait." Mr. H set off with two others and within thirty seconds I could not see him, I hoped that he would return to us quickly. Maybe if we can get to this new location, hopefully by first light, Mr. H would finally agree it is time for me to be dropped off at the base. Mr. H returned after ten minutes, spoke to his men and me, "Gerry stays close to me, stay just behind me, do not walk anywhere, just follow my steps now, yella." We moved forwards to our right and the surface under my feet changed to a flatter ground which was better for my knee. I could now see some streetlights in front of me. As we moved on, I started to see the outline of a few houses and from what I could make out it just looked like a random desert village. The lights were now shining down on us but luckily, they were very dull but there was still enough light to be picked out by any onlookers. Mr. H stopped at a solid iron gate on our left, he knocked twice, the gate opened immediately. Mr. H grabbed for me quickly and before I could blink the gate was locked. As we got through the gate, I took an immediate left turn through a doorway and into a room. As we entered this room Mr. H was pointing at my trainers, I removed them and waited. Mr. H said, "Gerry go in the corner please, you see mattress, blanket and pillow is for you, now go, shukran."

Mr. H was chatting to my new host and the odd glance was afforded in my direction but what were they discussing and what was going to be the plan? I was passed a few packets of Ishtar and I placed them in my small plastic bag. I kind of feel lucky that I have always had the cigarettes, I even find it quite amusing that even the fuckers who had 'fun' on my birthday allowed me to keep my fags but I'm not complaining.

They both walked over to me and Mr. H said, "Mr. Gerry this is my brother Mohammed, this is his house, he lives here with his wife and children. He said is also your house for now and you will be safe here. Gerry you must be so quiet, you will be safe here. If the children come in the room just be

152

Mr. Gerry, be the good man same before. I will stay here all the time now, I cannot go anywhere and my men also stay here, so many of us here together." I held out my hand to shake his brother's hand, I said, "Thank you Mohammed for welcoming me into your home." I looked at Mr. H and said, "So you and your men staying because the bad men who are looking for me?" He nodded downwards to signal a yes to me. I continued, "Mr. H you say this is a safe place? Do these men know you have brothers and know where they live?" He replied, "Gerry I don't know but I don't think they will know but we still have to be very careful." I asked Mr. H to explain to his brother that I'm very grateful, that I will just sit quietly and of course I will respect his family if they come into the room, I promise. Mr. H spoke to his brother, we shook hands once more, my normal covering of my heart with my right hand, expressing my heart felt sincerity and thankfulness.

I went back to the corner of the room, away from anyone else so I could just try and reflect. I lit up a cigarette and tried to assess the reality of events. Technically I have everything stacked against me, the only hope I have is what my eyes have told me since I have been with Mr. H and yes there could be a flip side to this. The odds are simple now, I have a fifty-fifty chance of being released. My mind was in exactly the same place it was on my birthday in that kneeling position, every noise and movement I was waiting for, hoping that it's not going to work against me. Damn you Teeley and your imagination, for fucks sake switch off from it, stop the permutations and just sit this one out.

I had tried so many times to block out emotions, thinking about my family but it was easier said than done. I thought I knew myself and my mind but how wrong was I? This shit can make a human go crazy. For a lot of the time, I had done well to keep my focus but the demons would always sneak back in and it was hard not to fold. It wasn't good to have the guilt now, I can face the guilt later on, my emotions have better things to deal with, I have to remain switched on and sell yourself towards the ultimate target, survival!

A plastic sheet came into the room to signal we were eating. How and why are we eating at 0300 hrs? It does not really make sense, what have they got planned? I caught the eyeline of Mr. H and said, "Mr. H why are we eating at 3am?" He replied, "My brother always eats his breakfast at this time of the morning, he is a farmer and has to start his work early, we also have to make plan for Gerry." I came back, "Make plans for what, what is happening?" Mr. H walked back over to me, "Mr. Gerry, the plan today is that we hope you can go home." My eyes filled with excitement, my body raised slightly, Mr. H could see this in my eyes, he stepped in and he said, "Mr. Gerry wait, it is very difficult to do in the daytime and so many are looking for you, as I tell you, they want you back to much." I left it at that.

I was ushered to wash my hands in a bowl of cold water with a nice smelling bar of soap. I ran the water through my greasy tangled mop of hair, I felt the soap lather up on my whiskers, disgusting to feel. The towel I was given had a nice smell to it too and was very soft to the touch, crazy how small things like this mean so much to me now, we do take so much for granted, we really do.

The food came into the room and it was a very good spread plus it looked fresh. It is best to try and eat a little of each I thought, I need to get as much energy in me as I can. My physical condition I can't do a lot about as I have no medicines, I can only try and reduce the pain by my positioning. What was draining was the mental torture and I need to liven my brain up. I asked Mr. H what type of farm his brother had, I was told that he had a very good farm and had people working for him, that is why he eats good food. It was near perfection. The salad was crunchy, the yolk of my fried egg was nice and runny for dipping in, the chicken was very soft and the chips were nice and crispy.

After eating I retired to the corner of the room. Lit up a fag, sat back as best as I could with a cup of sulaimani. I was able to sit out with straight legs. Mr. H had given permission for me to do so but I kept sliding down the wall, then readjusting every five minutes. To stay in one spot for too long was too painful still, but moving and stretching helped me.

Contemplation mode. How is this day going to end? Will it drag on? I hope the day is quiet, it has to be quiet with not too much activity around me, silence will be key for me today, I'm on tenterhooks without a shadow of doubt. Please let the wait be short. I hope they have worked on the best place to drop me off and made sure the location is not being watched by others. The last thing I needed was to be so close to a base and then caught at the last hurdle. The weight of my eyelids got the better of me, I drifted off and then woke up again, the same as usual but it was better than nothing. At least when I'm asleep the time is ticking away and hopefully towards the time my transport takes me to dreamland.

'BANG BANG!' A loud noise thundered out from the front gate, that seemed to shake it to its core. I was up like a shot from under my blanket, instant heart race! Fuck me a search party or something? My heart was pumping like fuck. Who the fuck can that be banging so hard this time of the day? It can only be someone who is pissed off to knock so hard. Mohammed stepped out of the room to check. Mr. H was the only other person in the room with me, the others had left after breakfast. I hoped that Mr. H had them sat up at different points around our location, so they had eyes on any bad fucks that want to ruin my day, that is what I would have done. Mohammed returned to the room and spoke with Mr. H. Mr. H turned to me and said, "Is one man who works for Mohammed, he come to collect keys from him because my brother not working today." Mr. H could see how I had looked at him, I could also see in Mr. H face the same feeling, which can only be a good sign if he is sharing similar fear for the day. I lit up a cigarette as more voices came from outside, not just one voice. I was amazed how close the voices were to the room. Mohammed and Mr. H looked over to me and gestured their hands to say calm down its ok. Easy for them to say they are not in my shoes; they may be used to this shit but I'm not. I laid down with the back of my head on the pillow, to sleep on my side and cover one ear would not be a great idea, I needed A1 listening capability however I wished that I would not hear any more voices or noise. These villagers in general wake up early and go to bed early which is not good as activity will be greater in these early hours.

I can never remember a time in my life where I had no control of anything and that had to be the worst part of all of this drama. I was never a big fan of authority if I'm honest and this last week has proved that without a shadow of doubt. I have had to learn to suck up everything to stay alive and if it was not to keep me alive, I would never of toed the line, bastards! I dropped off a little but not for long. Activity had picked up outside in the small courtyard, Mohammed's children were up and about, playing by the sounds of it. He had warned me about his many children and there would be quite a bit of noise. Not good at all.

'BANG BANG!' For fucks sake oh no please! Please let it be a friend, this is unbearable, I'm tensing up, this waiting game is not a fucking joke now, I'm a wreck.

Mohammed left the room, walked back in with two men and as they walked in. I was up, looking at Mr. H as if to say, "Who the fuck are they and what is happening?" Mr. H walked over to me, "Mr. Gerry this is our friends, they come to sit with us for some time, they are like brothers to me and have come to help Mr. H and Gerry, that is all." I just looked back and nodded, what else could I do? This wait is a killer and now I'm entering panic mode again. I reached my hand out, shook their hands and returned to my corner. I just carried on trying to make each minute tick away, to arrive at some stage for my goal and I sensed that I was not going to have an easy route.

How many twists and turns have I had since Monday? Too many for my liking but I sense so many more. The frustrations today though are agonizing and still I'm unsure of Mr. H. I remember closing my eyes and thought to play a game. I wonder if it really is true, that you can be thinking about someone at the same time they are thinking about you? Nothing to lose, so I tried to speak out to my Mum and say how sorry I was to put her through this. I convinced myself that she could hear me, our Mum to son telepathic love. Does it mean that I love everybody else less? Not at all, I just know that my Mum would take it worse than anyone else.

For an area that is so far out in the desert with nothing or nobody around I could not understand why there was so much noise? I just wanted to hear nothing, just silence and then at some stage get up and leave this room to my freedom. Children were coming and going continuously from the courtyard, that big solid metal gate was being banged, knocked, opened, closed and I really started to understand what some prisoners say that when they go prison for the first time and hear the cell door close, its fucking chilling. I was playing with pictures of home inside my head and my school days in Irchester. Time was standing still, the activity outside was playing with my heart and mind, I'm drained. We are just sitting ducks, waiting here for these fuckers to find us. Why the fuck don't we take the lead and initiative? Just get in a car, drive to near Tallil Air Base now, let us take the chance as we have nothing to lose.

I fell asleep, maybe for an hour. How did that happen? Shit don't question it. Mr. H said I was only asleep for thirty minutes; it seemed the smell of food had woken me up. Mr. H explained that it was just after 0800 hrs so it was like dinner time for his brother because he started eating so early at 0300 hrs every day. This time his children joined in to eat. It was like a mini feast for the children. Mohammed had five kids, three boys and two girls. I had a mixture of smiles, shy looks but nothing bad as they just carried on filling their faces. I couldn't eat, I explained to Mr. H that I was sick and no way could I eat. I told him that I was just not hungry and asked him to respect my feelings, he understood. The Ishtar had suppressed my diet, my nicotine intake in the last ten hours had increased. It was one in, put it out, another in. That food that was on display looked very inviting I have to say and I did join them all in the washing of hands after. The children seemed happy to help me wash my hands; it was a little humour with them.

I went back to sitting, lounging about for the rest of the morning but the never-ending activity was an issue of course. I found it a little ironic that today I continued to fall in and out of sleep, more so than any other time and for longer periods it seemed. Maybe my mind had given up on this day, it's not going to be my happiest day and maybe through all the bangs and voices I thought, "Fuck it, it is only a matter of time before it gets bad again." My fear had kept me alive, so why should I throw the towel in now? I think it was the fact that I had heard the words, 'Inshallah go home tomorrow' too often and now it was just the easiest thing to say to appease me.

It had to be nearing midday and once again I'm thinking that the next few hours were going to be a defining time if there was ever going to be a miracle release for me. I had got it into my mind that they would have to take me near to a base for my security but as I previously said for the safety of both parties it can't be too close to the base.

Mr. H stood up, walked over to the door to the room and put his shoes on. Standing near the door he looked at me and said, "Mr. Gerry I shall not be too long, you will be fine, many men here for you in the room and outside, yes I have men outside also." He smiled at me, nodded and walked out. His reactions did not make me think or feel anything was wrong but I would feel better if he was here, just in case the shit hit the fan. I tried to settle for the afternoon and as the time ticked by, I was getting more and more pissed off beyond all belief. I have had enough of this shit, I'm just as well to say, "Mr. H fuck it I'm going now with or without you and it is up to you what you want to do! Let me walk or choose to shoot me but do fucking something either way, I want to know! Why all the stories and lies I don't know, be man enough to at least tell me... I sounded like a broken record.

I must have dropped off for a while but I was suddenly woken up by the voice of Mr. H coming back to the room and followed by Mr. A. Oh, what is he doing here? I had last seen Mr. A on the Thursday night, my birthday when we made the video at his house. He stopped and said, "Hi Mr. Gerry." I replied, "Mr. A is nice see you." he brightened me up for a warm smile. Mr. A stood still, looked directly at me, raised his arms to the side of him, started to move around and said, "Mr. Gerry I come to you again for good taxi, now aeroplane for you, you now go home see babies and family!' I jumped up, ran over to Mr. A and Mr. H. I grabbed Mr. A to hug him! "Mr. A, sure is real, is true I go home now?!" He replied, "Now we go Nasiriyah City to see Sheikh."

I grabbed my trainers, slipped them on my feet, I kept the dish dash on and placed a ghutra over my head. Now is not the time to be seen, now for the first time I want to be seen in the Arabic dress code. I was ready to go but not too sure how to be. I needed to be calm about it, now was the time to raise my game further.

The right thing to do was to say goodbye to Mohammed and the others, "Mohammed my good friend, thank you so much." covering my heart and giving a quick hug of my appreciation. I asked Mr. H to translate my words, Mohammed had some water in his eyes. I shook hands with the other two men, gestured my respect and thanks to them, smiles were exchanged. I was ready to leave the room.

24 SO CLOSE TO FREEDOM

Mr. A and Mr. H led the way out of the courtyard, opened the gate on to the street. Mr. H had signalled for me to stay then moments later he came back in the courtyard. He led me out of the gate and straight into the back of a car. Mr. A was driving and Mr. H sat to the right of me, I could see that both of them were armed as usual. I had the ghutra over my head but could still see if I raised my head more. Mr. H just sat there looking around everywhere as we made our way through the quiet streets of the village and then into some open ground. So just the three of us in the car, I was happy that we did not have more in the car and no other cars in front or behind us. The less attention we could bring on ourselves is best, good call Mr. H!

The sun was definitely up and running. There was a lot of heat in the car and no air conditioning! The heavy dish dash was making me sweat like crazy plus underneath I had my polo shirt and jeans. We were on a dirt track, heading into Nasiriyah city but I did not recognise anything around us, I had never been this far out in the desert before.

After about five minutes, straight ahead of us in the distance I could see people, maybe a street market? As we drove closer, I could see a large group of individuals, it was a march, a procession with everyone dressed in black and holding many different flags. Black and green flags! This is a tribal group; we have driven into a hornet's nest! What the fuck? No! I turned to Mr. H, "Mr. H stop the car, do something, turn around you cannot drive that way!" Mr. H pulled me gently so he was face to face, brought up his shovel like hand, waved his finger in my face and said, "Woolah Mr. Gerry, woolah is ok, these people are not problem and I tell you, if any man want to come to you, he has to go through me, now I promise you on my own life, you go see your babies, this I do for you." I had never seen him look this way before,

I was looking at a man possessed, his eyes said it all, I could feel his emotion.

We were now ten meters away from the crowd, they were all chanting and punching the air in some form of defiance. They were all over the road, there had to be at least a hundred people. Mr. A drove the car off the road around them and as we came through, the noise was deafening. We skipped past them all, moments later we were good to go, away from them. Oh wow! Fuck me that was close, fuck I'm riding my luck here!

We hit a good tarmac road and we were going down a highway into Nasiriyah. I could not help but keep looking behind us, I was expecting the inevitable twist. It still didn't seem possible I was getting out of this.

Then, behind us, a white pickup with people in the back of it all dressed in the black and green clothes of the group we had just left behind us! I tapped the shoulder of Mr. H and pointed at the pickup. Mr. H said, "Gerry is ok this people not like that, they are not concerned for us, they shout angry because of politics only, not us." Mr. H spoke in Mr. A's ear, he put his foot on the gas, I guess Mr. H had told him how nervous I was and to get the fuck out of there.

I tried to look for a landmark I could recognise, that would make me feel better about the situation. At least then I would be aware of where we were and maybe where we were going, nobody had mentioned where we were actually going. I got a fix of a railway line to the left of me, the only railway lines I had ever seen were near the main road to Tallil Air Base, near the villa. The lines continued in the same direction as we were pointing and it was making me feel good. Oh please, please drop me half a kilometre from the base! This would be a gift.

Straight ahead was the route, not a lot of other traffic around us. My observation went into overdrive, in my mind I was driving the car, willing it to be steered in a particular direction. Up ahead, buildings started to appear more frequently, the railway lines peeled off to the left. I'm sure the base is over that way. We are going to the right where it looks more built up, fuck we are going into the centre of Nasiriyah. Within minutes we had the full view of the centre in front of us, cars, trucks and people were everywhere. The food markets were busy with shoppers but the good thing was that there was not too much activity around our car and nobody staring at me.

Mr. A was making steady progress but not too fast. The hustle and bustle of the street continued to ignore us, I was scanning like crazy looking for any scum or dickers looking out for me. This situation took me back to when

Paul and I travelled from Baghdad to Nasiriyah. We were stuck in that traffic jam for thirty minutes plus, now I just need to reach a place where I have security, simple. We started to move out and away from the crowds, I could see a group of official looking men to the right of us all standing around some 4 x 4's that were parked up on the side of the road, next to a large building. The building had quite a few Iraqi flags perched on top of the roof, definitely a government building but I'm not entirely sure what they did there, I had never been down this part before.

Mr. A pulled into the right side and as he did so a group of five or six armed men were making a beeline for our car. I said, "Go! Go! Don't stop here Mr. H I don't want to stop, go please!" Mr. H grabbed for my head with two hands, "Mr. Gerry now quiet, these men work for Sheikh, this man now protect you from all bad things, also I'm here to look after you, I know all the good men, I tell you many times I know only good for you, when we get out from the car I have you." Mr. H stepped out from the car, "Mr. Gerry come to me please, walk beside me, hold on to my jacket and don't let go, I will also hold you by the back of you to push you inside these doors, so walk fast as you can for me."

I stepped out of the car and latched onto Mr. H jacket; his left hand grabbed the back of my neck as he held his weapon in his right hand. Many Arabic men were close by, their dress code was the same as private security, combat trousers, denim shirts and bullet proof jackets. All of them carrying Heckler & Koch MP5's. These men seemed to be circling us and walked in the same direction, heading towards a double door, as we arrived at the entrance they open automatically. As we continued walking, once more I was back in Wellingborough train station, old wooden floors benches everywhere and seated on them, older looking men dressed in local dress, each one of them had eyes for me. Mr. H walked over to the benches, began to shake hands and greet by typical Arabic male affection. Mr. H seemed to be the most popular man in the building, I wasn't too sure who he was meeting but they are all in different coloured thobes and ghutra, a mix match of colours.

Mr. H brought me forward and said, "Mr. Gerry, these three men are here for you, they are all local Sheikhs, please greet with them?" I instinctively held my hand out to shake their hands, "Shukran jazeelan" (which means thank you so much). There were lots of head nodding, warm smiles being exchanged but I was wondering why were we here and what were these Sheikhs going to do for me? What is going to happen now?

I was looking around this busy room trying to locate a western looking face or maybe someone who could translate for me (no disrespect to Mr. H).

The room was huge with many wooden benches strategically placed against all the walls; the space must have been 10 x 10 meters. I thought is best to take a seat to see what was going to happen as Mr. H and Mr. A were talking to so many people but Mr. H stayed right beside me, so I sensed I was far from safe. The activity was calm though and the tone was quiet, which was pleasing to see and feel, it was so good to be around so many quiet people.

Mr. H held out his hand and gestured for me to stand up. I was led forward, through a door and on entering to the other side we walked into a wide corridor space. Mr. H said, "Mr. Gerry, now I need you to wash your hands, face and hair, right now, just here. Here is a towel that Mr. A bring for you, I want you make yourself look good as much as you can, need to be quick." Off came the dish dash and my greasy white polo shirt which had the QIT logo on it. I went to work, washing from my waist up to my head, got a good lather, rinsed it all off. I decided to fully wet my hair, get this bar of soap to lather and clean this matted shit on my head. I could only do as good as the tools I had been given. As I finished, I turned around and there stood in front of me was Abu Haider! I could not believe it; I had not seen him since the day I sacked him as one of the guards! Why is he here? I walked to him, slung my arms around his massive frame and I started to let out a cry of relief, now it is game on for release, it has to be.

As I stood back, Abu Haider looked at Mr. H and Mr. A and said, "How can any of those men be so bad to my English son, he so good man, best man in Nasiriyah is Mr. Gerry." Abu Haider said to me, "Mr. Gerry now we have to go to another building to meet the Governor of Nasiriyah, the Sheikhs will come with us, we have to say many thank you." I replied, "I'm confused little, why are you here for me, where is everybody else?" He replied, "Mr. Gerry I wanted to be here for my English son, I have not stopped looking for you, Mr. Paul wanted me to be here for you, finish."

I was moved back to the other room, and was seated on a bench while Mr. H, Mr. A and Abu Haider were talking to the Sheikhs. I stayed where I was, minding my own business. Mr. H came over to me, sat down and said, "Mr. Gerry my brother, now you are going to see the Governor, I cannot come with you, this is where I say goodbye to you." I then saw his eyes water. He continued, "Gerry I am so sorry this happened to you, please try and forgive them in your heart. I could never give you 100% to speak of everything. Many things had to be talked about and I had to make sure that I tell you only the truth. Many times, I looked at your eyes, you as a man, all I could see and feel the goodness in you. I was told of the story that you give work to all Iraqi man. This you know work good for you because man know you think like a true man, you think the right way to think for Iraq. The night in Mr. A house when we make video, why did this come in your head that my face not covered? I think I know why and I feel that your smart man to say like this, this I will always remember in my future." Mr. H being the giant he is, hugged me, patted my head, water filling in his eyes. Wow, this is heavy and I need to move on. Mr. A was next up, he did not speak but also chose to give a bear hug, on release Mr. A had water welling up and so did I. I'm looking at two grown men who are crying for my happiness, I thought they were part of the nutters I had on my birthday, turns out I was so wrong and they were very different for some reason.

Abu Haider put his hand on my shoulder; he wanted me to walk to the double doors. He said, "Mr. Gerry we have to go." We moved forwards and stopped just before the doors; Abu Haider was talking to a group of men, all of whom seem to surround me. Abu Haider was the man in control of these, who they were I don't know. Abu Haider turned to me and said, "You stay behind me now, only hold my thobe very strong, we go in special car for you now, do not move from me, ok?" I nodded to him and said, "OK but what about Mr. A and Mr. H, they are coming?" Abu Haider called Mr. H over and spoke to him. Mr. H then called Mr. A to join us. As he came in Mr. H said, "Gerry now is goodbye we cannot come with you now, now you will go see Governor with Sheikhs, these men help to release you, my work is done and so is Mr. A, is not easy to explain but you have to go, don't think about us now, look after yourself Gerry my brother, you good man." Tears streamed out of me and they do now as I type these words, how can I repay them? Abu Haider said nothing and neither did I as we walked away. I looked back and waved to them, once more covering my heart to them. It was so emotional for me.

The double doors opened and as we stepped forwards there was a black 4 x 4 immediately in front of the doors, I was moved inside the car beside Abu Haider. There was quite a lot of activity going on in the car, Abu Haider stepped out of the car, shouted at the top of his voice and signalled one man to be beside me, "Mr. Gerry boss wait, don't be afraid now, this man my cousin, his life is for you." Abu Haider was a big-framed man, a good eighteen stone. I could see him organising men in front of the car and could hear him from behind. What he was doing I was not quite sure, it looked like he had assembled a small army for me, I was overwhelmed to say the least. Abu Haider came back into the car, moved his cousin out and sat beside me. I felt the car pull off, we were underway, to go and meet the Governor of Nasiriyah.

There was a total of eight men packed into the car and each man was armed. Abu Haider said to me, "Mr. Gerry I have two cars in front and three cars behind us for you, now is forty men protect you my friend." I was not out of the woods just yet but was closer for sure. It had not really sunk in yet that I was free and safe. When will I feel complete safety? I know this journey is not finished yet. We were travelling quite fast considering we were in a built-up area. People outside in the streets would not know what was going on with our six-car procession. The six cars told me that they were taking nothing for granted.

Abu Haider had moved his body around so he was facing me, his back to the door, so his left arm rested around my shoulder and he organised the man to my left to do the same, I felt like a VIP for the first time in my life. We came out of the town and onto the carriageway. We picked up more speed and the sand was flying up everywhere which was good. If anyone was out there and wanted to try an attack, they would have to be a crack shot or very lucky to connect. Within five minutes we started to move into a built-up area once more and I recognised where we were! We were by the roundabout where the big hangar was, I glanced over to my right and as I thought I could see a high wall with a line of trees. So over there was the first place they kidnapped me! Ok Gazza move on, forget it.

I took out a cigarette from my bag and lit it up, as I did this the man in the front passenger seat said, "No smoking, you wait!" I looked at Abu Haider to say why I cannot smoke. Abu Haider spoke a few words and then I heard, "Ok no problem, can smoke quick but only one now." The air conditioning was on full blast, so it would be able to deal with thinning the smoke out, no dramas. Moments later the car pulled into a narrow street and I could see a large group of bodies standing by a sand-coloured building; a clean looking building for Nasiriyah and again the Iraqi national flag was flying high on the roof top.

The car came to a stop, the door to my right was opened, Abu Haider stepped out of the vehicle and the noise of the crowds was quite intense. Abu Haider said to me, "Stay with me, only follow no stop." As I stepped out, I felt like I had the worlds media on me! There were cameras, men carrying video cameras and notepads everywhere and microphones being pushed in my direction. I just ignored the activity and followed Abu Haider towards the building entrance. Abu Haider was going about his business in a controlled way and he led me to the front doors. As we entered, those inside were not allowing everybody in so our movements became easier.

It dawned on me that this shit must be quite big news now. How did they all know that I was coming to this building today? For them to be here now tells me that Mr. H and Mr. A should have told me earlier than they did.

164

Unless, they had to get the word from their boss, which I'm sure was going to be one of the Sheikhs and their boss would have spilt the news to the media. That way it looked like good news on the propaganda side!

We made our way through some wide winding corridors and then up a large flight of stairs. I had to slow up as the four flights took my damaged knee by surprise. After dealing with the stairs, the winding corridors continued then Abu Haider stopped me as we came to a group of people. Two men stepped forward from the group, both dressed in suits and ties with massive smiles on their faces. I tried to drum up my best smile, knowing the camera crews were filming. The man to my left introduced himself as the Assistant Governor of Nasiriyah and then introduced me to the man on his right, the Governor himself. I must have been stood there for a good two minutes so the media could take their pictures for the history books. To be honest I just wanted to be out of there, in a safer place with those who I trust more but I guess this had to be done as it would look good for PR and people's CV's.

Eventually I was invited to go into a room and as I walked in, I was greeted by the faces of Ali and Bassim, two of the famous five! I could not believe it, more friendlier faces, especially Bassim. We were in the Governor's office and what an office it was! Ten meters by thirty meters, the floor dressed in the finest rugs, curtains draped all around the walls. The place was full of chairs, the kind you would see at a banquet for a King, antique tables and the biggest table of all for the Governor. I shit you not his table had to be four by two meters. The assistant to the Governor ushered me to a chair at the desk of the Governor with Ali and Bassim sat to my right. I looked for Abu Haider; he was sat behind me on a chair by a small table.

I turned to Abu Haider and said to him, "I need cigarette can I smoke in here?" Abu Haider spoke to the assistant Governor; I was given an ashtray and so I lit up. Those around me were talking with some laughter mixed in, Bassim could see that I was looking to try and understand what was being said, Bassim said to me, "You know before, all of us joke with you because you smoke Ishtar? The Governor is now asking if they are yours? We tell him that you always smoke Ishtar." I nodded at the Governor, smiled to say it is true, yes. I then offered my packet to him, he raised his hand and smiled to kindly turn me down, no problems. I did ask him for the record.

The room was quite full, the media was still around us filming and clicking away with cameras. The Sheikhs had joined us, the Governor walked over to them, they all embraced and welcomed one another. I knew I had the worlds media on me, so I felt a certain level of respect had to be shown but easier said than done when you are still going through an ordeal. It was a lot to take in, I don't know why I was being so kind. The fact that my knee was throbbing like fuck and any sudden movements or people grabbing me around my arms, neck and shoulders was a problem for me.

I got the attention of Ali, "Ali how much longer I have to be here and when am I going to the base?" Ali replied, "Gerry please, you have to stay with Governor for a while, you are going to another room with them all to have lunch, then after will go to the base." As I was looking at Ali, I could see Bassim beside him and he had a continuous grin on his face, he said to me, "I cannot believe I'm sitting looking at you, we have all be searching for you we not stop Gary, we knew you would be ok because you are a good man." I sat trying to keep smiling for the cameras, to make everyone who is watching anywhere in the world see that I was happy and that nothing really bad had happened. It was just a show and soon I would be on the base controlling my own world once more.

The Governor and Sheikhs were in their own bubbles from what I could see. I'm not sure what was being asked by the television interviewers and what the replies were given but everyone was smiling which was the main thing… let us all keep a positive vibe! Bassim said to me, "Gary my God what is wrong with you, you smoking one after the other man, chill is ok." I replied, "Bassim, if only you knew my friend. Yes, I'm smoking a lot but please, I'm ok, I feel good with this smoking, just make sure they don't take my cigarettes." I felt good being with Ali, Bassim and Abu Haider but I just wanted to be in the real world and in the full protection of the base, then I can really sort myself out.

A few minutes later the television camera was on me and a microphone was placed near my mouth. The man holding the microphone said, "Mr. Gerry how are you feeling now?" I paused, longer than most would take; I had to say what they wanted to hear. I said, "I would like to thank the Governor and the Assistant Governor from the bottom of my heart for such a warm welcome this afternoon. I would like to make a special thank you for the wonderful work the Sheikhs before me have done on behalf of me and my family, I cannot thank you enough. All of your tremendous work will now make sure I return back to the UK to see my family and friends. I also wish and hope the people of Iraq can really start to live good lives, make this great country a better place for all and thank you for allowing me to come here as a visitor, thank you." The camera came away and the interviewer moved onto the six Sheikhs who were huddled around the same area, this is their time to enjoy there moment for the hard efforts for my release.

I wanted another cigarette but the packet was gone. I stood up and looked around the floor. Ali said, "Gerry what is wrong where you going?" I replied, "I'm staying here but I can't see my cigarettes." Ali replied, "Gerry is here in my pocket." I snapped, "Ali do not touch my fags! Leave them alone, you just don't understand, don't touch them please they are mine! The last thing I need is for someone to take my fags!" After this Abu Haider decided to call time on me sitting in the chair. "Mr. Gerry please stand with me." As I got up Ali came forward to me and all of a sudden Abu Haider gestured his hand forwards in a sweeping motion to suggest Ali back off and muttered some select words. Ali didn't look too impressed. The look on Abu Haider's face said it all for me; he wanted to be in control of me from the minute he saw me today and I was very happy for that to happen, he was on a mission. Everything in the Governor's office had been completed so I finished my handshakes with the Governor and Sheikhs.

Abu Haider escorted me out of the room, down the stairs and through the maze of corridors to the main front door of the building. He gathered his troops together and my car arrived within seconds at the entrance. The media had stuck around hoping to get an interview and more photo shots but Abu Haider was having none of it; he even gave Ali and Bassim a severe ticking off as we got to the car. Abu Haider literally ended up bundling me in the vehicle and I caught my knee on the side of the door and landed on my shoulder! He had killed two birds with one stone. I let out a scream as it was so painful, no need for drama but it bloody hurt! I landed quite hard as he is a powerful unit. He could see I was having problems; so, he went to another level of hysteria with those around him. His cousin once more arranged my space in the car with Abu Haider barking out his orders on his telephone, shouting out to those at the front of us and at the back. Abu Haider then joined us in the car as we screeched off where he carried on his verbal attacks on everyone in the car and on his mobile. I had never seen this side of him but it made me think of his real true skills, he must have learned all of this when he was in the Iraqi army, how foolish was I for sacking him. I was told we now had extra guards, the Governor had approved ten of his personnel, which required two additional cars. We were a total convoy of eight vehicles and fifty men! Elvis Costello thought he had a good army (as in Oliver's Army) but I think Gazza's army was bigger today and so it should be!

I turned to Abu Haider and said, "I little confused with all this but I need ask you calm down, you so angry, I feel?" He placed his hand on the front of my shoulder and said, "Mr. Gerry my brother, this is all for you I swear, you don't understand me also. I look at you like my own son, you did something so special for me and my son, my blood son. I came to you and asked you to take chance for him, he was nothing, now he becoming a man for real working because of you, I tell you, my life I give for you." I replied, "Abu Haider, I know, I see this but also have to be calm little, your son needs you more than me but I surprise how you are today but thank you my friend." I nodded and smiled in recognition of his loyalty and emotion.

Ten minutes later after bobbing and weaving through all the back streets we finally came to my next port of call. The cars up front came to a stop. I could see a crowd of people in front of the leading car and the guards were piling out pretty quickly and drawing their weapons up. Oh my God no! Don't fucking tell me it is going to kick off?! I shrank in the seat and Abu Haider gathered what was in my head, "Mr. Gerry no no, not like that, they are under orders to do this, before attacks on this building when cars come, we make sure no problems now, is ok my brother." Abu Haider's phone rang, he spoke and then opened his door, "Mr. Gerry please come out and do same, hold my thobe."

He walked towards the front doors of the building which had all the hallmarks of the previous building. The media were the crowd that I saw and once more I was hurried into the building surrounded by guards. I held back from his steps; my knee was fucked and I just could not keep up that pace. Abu Haider stopped, looked down at the left leg limping and said, "You have problem in leg Mr. Gerry?" I replied, "I have bad problem in my left knee, also my shoulders, some men make big problems for me on Thursday, I have many pains, so please slow little and careful how you grab me." He could only look with sadness in his eyes and shake his head, he looked so pissed at the news. I just hope he does not completely fly off the handle, it would take quite a lot to stop this tank in its tracks.

As we moved further into the foyer area we came to a set of large wooden double doors, they were opened, people started to remove their shoes and began to fill the room. Abu Haider bent down and removed my trainers for me, took his own shoes off, then led me in the room and I was seated. I wanted a cigarette and could not see my bag. I looked over at Ali and Bassim. Fuck me! Ali had my bag again, I said, "Ali for fucks sake my friend, I told you stop taking my bag, my cigarettes are in there. I keep them there because is easy for me, don't control me now Ali, I have been controlled for the last one hundred and forty-seven hours, no more." I got a look from Ali that was bemusement. "What can I do?" Yeah, sure it sounds selfish but he needs to know, sure it is not right to lose the plot but I'm still in stress mode.

Shortly after this Bassim's satellite phone rang, it was Jassim Al Misnad,

Chairman of QIT. Bassim said to me, "Gary is Jassim for you", he passed me the phone. I said, "Hello Jassim how are you; you are in Qatar?" He replied, "Gerry I'm on Tallil air base please try and come here as soon as you can, I would like to see you." The conversation lasted for about one minute, Jassim was adamant I should leave the building I was in and get to the base. I explained that I will try my best but there is an order of play here. I turned to Abu Haider, explained what I wanted to happen. He went over to our other guests and explained the situation. Nobody was offended, it was fully understood, anyway after all they had entertained the media, their good work will be seen by millions, kudos to the Governors and Sheikhs. We were on our way out of the room, Abu Haider put my trainers back on my feet and I was shown out of the building by the Governor. He came to shake my hand once more, we stopped for some last photos for the family album and exchanged pleasantries.

As we moved out of the building the same car was waiting for me which Abu Haider got me in rapidly with his men seeming to be more proficient this time with less hollering from Abu Haider. For some reason there looked to be even more guards. Maybe it was just my imagination but the feeling was a good one. Ali and Bassim were trying to get in the same car as me but Abu Haider was having none of it and signalled a no to Ali. Ali did not look too happy that he did not have the centre of attention, Abu Haider was and that was cool by me. We had to sit and wait and I could see the Sheikhs coming out of the building, their cars were waiting for them as they had to follow me, wherever I was off to next. I whispered to Abu Haider, "Where we go now, go to the base now?" He replied, "No Mr. Gerry, now we go to Italian soldiers and then after you go to the base, I think the Italian soldiers are taking you there, ok?" I just nodded back and gave him a smile of acceptance. Inside I was ecstatic but felt I had to contain myself out of respect. It sounds bizarre I know but it is very hard to describe the emotion with Abu Haider during this last one hour or so. Having him by my side was a dream, I guess it made him feel that he has repaid me in his own way. Many would not be able to understand such loyalty and I would be the same if I had not experienced working in this country but it just goes to show how these people were made to suffer over the years in the south of Iraq and the job his son had was making him $200 US Dollars a month, double the average salary. I have to respect his wishes, to deny him his moment would not be memorable for him, let him have his time Gazza.

We pulled off, started to make our way through the sleepy traffic around and before long I knew where we were. All of a sudden, I saw a row of military personnel carriers, Italian flags flying on them, I counted at least three of them and a few jeeps with mounted guns. Fuck! Yes, yes, yes ! This can only mean they are back in control of the city. Surely now I cannot be compromised, it is sealed, has to be, not possible to be taken again? The car was driving down the road where we stayed in the first villa and the Italian compound was just a quarter of a mile away so I know where we are now for sure. Moments later we passed the top of the road of the villa I was taken from, my eyes stayed in the same place for a quick reflection of the last time I was on this road. I picked up the towers in the Italian compound and then caught the sight of the high walls, sand barriers and concrete. The same compound that was attacked and bombed when I was here before, eighteen Italian soldiers were killed in that attack.

The car pulled off the main drag, drove into a car parking area which was surrounded by a five-meter-high wall of sandbags. A group of people could be seen at the entrance to the compound, a different mix by the looks of things and I could clearly make out the Italian soldiers' uniforms. The media had also arrived before me and I could see men who looked to be of European decent but I could be wrong. The car stopped a few meters short of the sandbags and the barbed wire décor sat on top of it. As Abu Haider stepped out of the car, he offered me to get out. As I looked around the car park, I could see the Sheikhs arrive and they were led into the compound by their guards but all the other personnel stayed in the vehicles, including the car I was in. I was looking at Abu Haider as if to say, ok let's go or what are we doing? I was stood looking directly at him and smiling looking for him to speak.

Abu Haider stood silent, took a breath and placed his right hand on my shoulder as those at the compound entrance looked on, he paused and then said quietly but with a quivering in his voice, "Mr. Gerry, thanks to God you are alive, I am so happy to have known you, my God bring you to Iraq so that you could help many man, I wish you could stay here as my son but I know that cannot be, please say sorry to your family from me?" Tears flowed into his eyes. For me it was bad timing as again I had the worlds media to deal with and knowing my Mum would see my release, I didn't want her to see my tears. I had to be strong but that was easier said than done when you are faced with a man who idolises you and knowing the relief I will have once I get through that entrance. I looked at him and said, "Abu Haider, I'm also sorry that I sack you, I was also wrong to do this and I know this would not have happened if you were the man guarding me, I made you have no job with no money." He came back, "Mr. Gerry, no not like that, I have work now, I do many works now for security. The money my son gets for working we set up our own company for us and this is all because of my brother, my son Mr. Gerry, I can never say thank you enough for you." Bassim came over, "Mr. Gerry you know they wait you?" I replied, "Yes go tell them I'm coming but, on my choice, and speed." Bassim cut in, "Gary, I think has to be said now, the day you taken many people try look for you, including myself, when I not working but of course the life had to go on for QIT and the business. Paul ask me and Ali to run things because Gary cannot do. You have to know, Abu Haider not sleep, he looks for you twenty-four hours a day, he has these men turn every stone for you, he did for you, sorry is true." I had to close this conversation; I put out my hand to Abu Haider, "I know now is goodbye, I will go see your son tomorrow on the base. Please respect that I have to go now, I'm very emotional and need to be strong. I cannot repay you my good friend and will never forget what you have done for me, never forget." A few of the soldiers began to walk in my direction and I walked away from Abu Haider with my hand on my heart and took one last look at this great man. He returned the compliment to cover his own heart... enough said.

I started to walk towards the opening between the giant sandbags with the soldiers in a brick formation and there in the doorway stood a man dressed in a navy pin striped suit, shirt and desert boots and I do have to say it looked slightly strange to see. He greeted me with, "Gary it is great to see you, my name is Rory let's get inside?" I couldn't believe his accent, it was a truly well pitched English tone, it was your typical private school sound and looked so young, maybe around thirty years old. As he was speaking, I had every man and his dog trying to get me to speak into microphones and telephones were being pushed near my face.

I had to ask, "Is there any family on the phone for me?" Bassim spoke up, "Gary your mother is on the telephone, she wants to speak to you." Momentarily I froze, can I deal with this now? I took the phone, "Hello can you hear me? With the answer I knew it was Lisa's Mum Yvonne, she said, "Gary thank God you are safe I can't explain what..." I cut in, "Yvonne, you can hear me loud and clear?" She came back, "Yes I can hear you loud and clear." So, I asked, "Yvonne, how did West Ham get on yesterday, I mean Friday, did they win?" She replied, "I can't believe you just asked that?!" I said, "Don't you know then?" "No", she replied. In my mind I could not believe she did not know, "Yvonne try and turn on the teletext or try and find out for me please?" She responded, "Gary let's speak later as it is very noisy?" The line was closed and Rory said, "Gary let us go inside please?" I obliged and followed him with others following us into the building.

I was led through a corridor that was lined with Italian soldiers before walking into room that was dense with sofas and chairs, I was shown my place on a sofa. A plain clothed Italian came over to me, he was wearing a blue denim shirt and a pair of cream colour trousers and desert boots, well groomed, he turned and said to me "Gary can I get you a drink please?" I paused, I'm in the company of the Italians! I had lunch on the base with the Italian contracting office a few times, these boys have wine, beer and other choices, so maybe I can ask... I replied, "Do you have Peroni here at the compound?" He replied, "Yes we do have Gary but I will have to ask the Sheikhs if they are ok for you to drink alcohol in front of them." I said, "Sure ask them!" I was given a smile and a green light to drink. I nodded and smiled as I was thinking what to order, "You have Peroni then?" He came back, "Yes Gary we do" I said, "How much do you have please?" "How many or how much do you want Gary?" he said. No hesitation from me, "I would like one case please, it was my birthday on Thursday!" and kept a straight face as I looked at him. He did look slightly surprised but just walked away from me.

The Italian returned with my request, what a result! He opened a can for me and it did not touch the sides so I opened the second one and I let out a belch of relief... wow that feels amazing, ice cold also. Rory was in his world with the Sheikhs as I looked for my cigarettes, nowhere to be seen! I will kill Ali if he has my bag! My new Italian friend could see me looking around the room for something so he asked, "Gary can I help you, you are looking for?" I said, "Oh, sorry yes, I need some cigarettes please, do you smoke?" He replied, "I don't but I can get you some, what is your brand you have?" I replied, "Ishtar please, can you ask them buy me 200 cigarettes please and I will get the money to you." A soldier stepped forwards and gave me a packet for free and they were Ishtar! Haha, I had found another who smoked them or maybe he just had them, great timing. I lit up the fag and just sat there for about five minutes, drinking and smoking myself crazy. The combination was great, is this happening now? Ooooffff! That first beer is reacting quick on me and I was a little dizzy straight away. I was being left alone to do my own thing; Rory carried on talking to the Sheikhs and I'm sure they were polishing off the final terms of the deal that was made locally.

Moments later, Rory said, "Gary the Sheikhs are leaving now and I need to talk to you for five minutes, then you will be transported to Tallil Air Base, ok?" I just nodded and smiled back. A few moments later the Sheikhs stood up, it was time for them to depart. I got to my feet, walked over to them, shook each one of their hands as these men for sure had a huge part in my release, I'm very aware of that. I asked for a translator to relay my personal thoughts and fondness to what they have done for me and my family.

The Sheikhs had left, Rory came and sat by me, and said, "Gary I need to speak to you for five minutes or so and then you can go to the base. I don't think it would be a good idea to drink too much at this time as your body has probably not had the best food for the past week and the beer could make you worse?" I replied, "Rory I understand your words and you could be right, however I feel fine and I need my own space to decide what I will do, if I feel that I should stop then so be it but for now I'm drinking." Rory gave me a nod of the head, a confused smile but I'm sure he could understand where my mind was at the moment. We all react in different ways; I just want to try and forget as soon as I can and move on. He stood up and said, "Ok Gary let us go to another office?" I followed him out of the room and down the corridor. I was carrying my crate of beer but had no cigarettes. I said, "Rory I have no cigarettes and need some." He passed me a pack and said, "Gary give the beer to that man and he will carry it for you, he will also arrange to bring your cigarettes." To my side there was a young Iraqi lad, I handed over the crate and he followed us. Rory walked on, up a flight of stairs and then quickly into an office, I followed him in. As I turned to see where the Iraqi boy was and he was right there with me, then another man arrived just in time with a full carton of Ishtar! Top man, I am being well looked after.

Rory and I sat for just over five minutes, we spoke very briefly about how I was feeling in general, he asked did I need any urgent and special help. What the plan was in my mind what I wanted to do tomorrow. I was happy with what he was saying in general, who am I to be critical of his decisions. Let us see what happens up on Tallil Air Base, after all, I am a free man in a free country now. As we left his office, we were followed by my new friend who was carrying my urgent supplies, he was the most important man on the planet for me at this moment in time. As we came down the stairs my escorts were waiting for me, dressed as though they were going into battle, all armed up to the hilt, I did not know quite how to take it. You would think that I was now thinking like a free and safe man but I still had the journey to complete to the air base and I was in a military convoy which could be a target and with the recent events of losing control of this city it made me nervous. Surely nothing could go wrong now.

25 FREEDOM IS CALLING

As we got outside there were two military lads standing waiting for me by an ambulance and they had a stretcher, I was thinking, who is that for? As I walked towards the ambulance Rory said, "If you jump onto the stretcher, they will make you comfortable. I said, "Thank you but with all due respects I just need a helping hand getting in, I don't need a stretcher, I would prefer to sit up and be myself thank you." The boys did not have a problem with my request and helped me up; booze and cigarettes followed me in, waves of goodbye and thank you, I was on my way to Tallil Air base, finally!

As the ambulance pulled off, I said to my two mates, "Is it ok if I smoke, please?" Smiles all round, I opened a can of Peroni and lit up a fag, the journey to the base was going to be thirty minutes in all. Within minutes the driver was chucking us around all over the back of the vehicle, my new mates seemed to be ok with the moving around, so it must have been quite normal for them, maybe the driver had been on the vino! One of them spoke up, "This is quite normal for us, you need hospital care and we have to keep up with the other trucks in the convoy." I said, "How many vehicles we have in the convoy, three or four?" They looked at each other and one of them said, "Gary the ambulance is in between four vehicles in front and four behind us, there are one hundred soldiers in total, do you think we would take the chance for you to be taken again? The British who are waiting for you would go crazy for sure, if they know we only send a few men and small vehicles, not good way." Bloody hell, all for me? It did not seem real but if that was the case then fair play, why should I question it, I still had not completed my safety, not yet.

I couldn't see out of the ambulance but I knew we were on the straight road up to Tallil. We started to slow up and I felt the ambulance go over a big camber, I knew we were at the gates of the base. I tipped my can back and said, "Salut my friends." They smiled back as they knew what I meant; they knew I was aware that we were on the base. I was finally there, on the base. I sat back, trying to keep my back upright to the wall of the van, I looked up to the roof and said to myself speaking to the man in the sky, "I remember asking you for your help on the night of that battle and you did not come up trumps for me and now I have arrived at my destination, you let me down but I have succeeded."

The ambulance came to a halt, the doors opened and we were met by another mass of people. As I was guided down, many soldiers were walking up to me, big smiles, hugs and handshakes, it turns out the first man to shake my hand was the Colonel but I was not told who he was until a few minutes later. It was a party atmosphere, very nice and special, the Colonel came back to me, "Welcome Gary, let us go inside now I need to care for you." A wheelchair came out and I was asked to sit, I did as I was asked but looked over my shoulder for my 'goods', one of the ambulance soldiers was following me with a grin on his face, he knew I did not want to lose my beer and cigarettes, no way.

The journey to the hospital was a smooth one in the chair. I was wheeled into a room, then helped to my feet and lifted onto a bed in the middle of a theatre. Within seconds a big man walked towards me, introduced himself and then it was a free for all. Hands all over me, needles being injected into my body, left right and centre. The head man was actually a consultant, so I said to him, "I do not mean to be disrespectful but what are all the needles for?" He replied, "We are getting some good sugars and things in you, I want to try and flush you through a little and take a sample of your blood and urine." I said, "Ok I understand that Sir but over the last one hour or so I have had some other types of sugars from a can, the blood and urine, yes please test for sure." He came back to me, "Gary, yes, I was told you have been enjoying those types of sugars but to be honest, they are not good sugars." My blood was taken, the pipes and tubes were taken out from me, I was given a beaker to piss in and then I was taken to my room.

I was gagging for a proper, shit, shower and shave. I was told there had been a whip round for me, for some smelly stuff, a toothbrush, toothpaste and razor but no shaving foam. I looked at the new 'Bic' razor in the packet. Oh no you are fucking kidding me, a single blade 'Bic', no shaving gel or foam, no moisturizer that I could put on before to reduce the drag and pulling? This is going to be a killer; I hope they have a plastic surgeon here because I think I shall need one. I jumped into the shower and I cannot explain how it felt, the feel of the pressure of the water, the temperature, I just wanted to stand in there for an hour, it felt that good. I washed my hair four times, shampoo, scrub and rinse times four. I was able to get hold of a scouring pad and used that with a bar of soap to scrub my skin which made me slightly red but I wanted to be clean.

I came out of the shower and went to the sink, put the plug in and opened the tap, made a five-millimetre water level, perfect. I then began to agitate the bar of soap backwards and forwards against the surface of the sink basin. I was there for about five minutes making a foam as best as I could and enough of it, I was not going to be rushing this. I splashed water on my cheeks and neck, rubbed the bar of soap all over to create as much as a lather as I could and then topped it up from what I had in the sink. I turned the shower back on so I could keep rinsing the razor blade in the shower jet as it was clogging after every small part I was removing. It was painful, fuck me! It felt like a cat was scratching my sun burn from a hot summer's day. It took me a full thirty minutes to shave and once it was all off, I filled the sink up with cold water and just kept dunking my head in it trying to cool my face down, what a nightmare. I was not brave enough to attempt to put any smellies on my face so I thought I would brave that maybe tomorrow or after. I had no clean clothes, so they gave me a plastic jump suit; I looked like a forensic crime officer going to swab a murder scene, hood included.

I came back to the room I had been given. A single bed in a VIP room, no others around me. I walked in and a doctor was there waiting to see me, I was not too sure about the room but I would see what was going to develop. It was just a bed in a room with various medical equipment in there with me. I had spent the past seven days alone and isolated, I was not keen on that feeling anymore, I felt I wanted to be around people. I climbed onto the bed, got under the bed sheet and reached for the glass of water beside the bed. The consultant began to examine me again and as the consultant was going about his various checks, he was interrupted by a nurse. As they were talking, I looked to my left and saw one female and two males dressed in British military uniforms, all of whom smiled in my direction. The consultant invited them into the room, they started to talk between one another and after a couple of minutes the female soldier turned to talk to me and all eyes were now on me. "Gary good evening to you, my name is Major Sarah Anderson and these are my two colleagues, we are delighted with your release and welcome back." All of this delivered with big smiles from everyone.

She said, "Gary tonight you are welcome to come and stay with us, we have a small set up near here and you are welcome. Tomorrow morning, we will be leaving here at 0600 hrs on a Chinook, taking you down to Basra. You will be in Basra for a few days I would think and then we will arrange for you to be flown back to the UK to be repatriated." As I was laying there, I was calm and I was absorbing her polite words, but I was thinking so many other things and maybe she was not going to like what I have to say. An exchange of words took place between Major Sarah and the consultant who was looking after me, they were standing either side of the bed. The scenario I would describe as 'handbags at twenty paces', both seemed to be fighting for bragging rights and to be honest my neutral stance was with the consultant. Sure, I'm English but the Italians have been good enough to take me into their field hospital, free of charge and look after me, therefore the Brits should understand and respect that, plus the talks are going on in the backyard of the consultant.

I waited for the chance to cut in and politely give my opinion on what was being talked about. Here I had both sides telling each other my plans without asking me and they seemed to have forgotten what I had been through, that is the way I saw it. I interrupted, "For me, can I ask that both sides give me two minutes to explain what I want to do and then you can decide what you will be doing? I have decided that I will be staying in this hospital tonight but I will take a bed in the ward next door where I will not be alone. I will be having a party tonight with some Italian friends of mine as they have invited me to a barbeque and singalong for a belated birthday party from them to me as it was my birthday on the 8th of April. As it is my party you are all welcome to join us, no problems but I have to respect the effort they have made and this starts in an hour from now. Tomorrow morning, I will be going to work, my work here is not complete and I have to sign off some contracts and also understand various factors with my workers. Once I have completed my work, then I have no problems being taken down to Basra, no issues at all, but I need to try and sign off as best as possible." I took a pause and watched the different facial reactions, the consultant seemed to be happy with what I had said, Major Sarah Anderson was looking a little perplexed and then one of her male colleagues spoke up.

He was an Irishman, a good six foot four inches tall, red hair, so maybe a bit fiery. The 'maybe' was too light, he was fiery and not afraid to speak for his colleagues of the Royal Intelligence Corps. He began, "So you are saying that you want to go to work first and then when you are ready you will let us know when you want to fly in a military Chinook to Basra, have I heard you right?" I replied, "Yes that pretty much sums it up, why?" He replied, "Gary we have been on the ground for the past week working on how to try and find you, try and find out who has taken you and how we can look at ways of getting you released safely. If you had said before that you wanted to book a Chinook to take you to Basra when you were ready that would have made it easier... do you think we can just organise a Chinook when you say so?

177

I'm not sure what world you are living in but it does not work like that, plus we have better things to be doing than looking for British civilians who decide they want to come and work out here and maybe also have a holiday." I thought the best thing to do was to treat him and his comment with the contempt it deserved, "As I said, I, like you, have a job to do and I cannot be paid unless I sign things off, therefore whether you like it or not I'm going to work in the morning on Tallil Air Base. If you are not able to take me to Basra when I'm free then I will make arrangements myself. I think you should remember something here, I'm a free man in a free country for now, so I think I can decide what I do and when I do it. My invite still stands, if you wish to come this evening, let me know what you want to do, now if you can leave so I can get on with my evening, thank you."

The Brits left my room. A few moments later someone brought in my suitcase and briefcase, which was a little bit of a shock to me as I thought that everything would have been taken by the Alibaba gang. I got out of bed and opened my briefcase which was completely empty, so they had taken everything that was in there. On opening my suitcase, I had a great laugh to myself, all that was left in my case was one pair of socks, one pair of boxer shorts, my West Ham shirt and West Ham tracksuit, everything else had been taken. I shared my joke with the consultant and others in my room, the joke being that they took everything and then looked at the West Ham stuff and said, "Fuck that, who wants that?" What a result, I have something to wear and it was the best kit I could put on! I couldn't wait to share the joke with my mates, funny as fuck that is.

I took my items to the bathroom including my trainers. I gave them a good clean and put on my West Ham shirt and tracksuit bottoms, so I was all ready to go to the party. The consultant wanted to share more information with me, he said, "Gary, with your knee I don't believe there are any broken bones but I think that the injury you said you have from three years ago playing football, I think this kick was in exactly the same place and has caused an issue. Your shoulder muscles of course have been torn, that is for sure. It is just rest that you need and time. I will give you some pain killers to take with you and anti-inflammatory tablets. I will have the staff make a bed available for you to sleep in tonight in the main ward, so you are not alone and we will move your few items to that area. Once we know where the bed will be located, I will get someone to come and find you outside, tell you the bed number and show you quickly. Now I know your friends are waiting for you outside, so go and enjoy your late birthday and please do not drink too much because your stomach is not strong, thank you."

I thanked the consultant and left the room, heading for the party that awaited me outside and as I walked out of the huge hospital tent the barbeque smell hit my nose. The barbie was in full swing, many of the soldiers had come along to share the happiness of my release and I was told that my case of Peroni was in the fridge, well safe. The British visitors I that I had came over to have some food and have a chat but no booze for them, all T Total, but it was nice that they gave up their spare time to join in. The Italian lads did not let me down, they had arranged two guys to play guitars and being Italian they loved the idea of me singing Frank Sinatra and Dean Martin songs, they were even surprised that I could hold a tune. I sang songs during the early part because I knew as the time wore on, I would get a little worse for wear, that was definitely on the cards.

Major Sarah Anderson came over which was great, she had a satellite phone that I could use, so I thought ok, I best take the leap now and make some phone calls but keep them short and sweet, I did not want to be getting upset now, not with alcohol inside me. I phoned Lisa, she was good, a true tower of strength as usual which helped me a lot. Then I phoned my Mum and she was great to be honest, she had lots of questions but I only told her small amounts of information and only what she needed to know. I told her that I would see her very soon.

The night had to calm down at some stage and the numbers started to dwindle. Major Sarah Anderson came over to explain that they had to go back to their accommodation as they had to be up early and she suggested that I should do the same as I was being picked up at 0600 hrs by one of her drivers to take me to work. The Chinook would arrive later in that day. They could not really understand that I wanted to get straight back to work, they thought that I would want to get the fuck out of Iraq as quick as possible which is fair, but I wanted to get back to normality as soon as possible and I have a living to make. I sat with a few hangers on but then found myself with just my fags and Peroni at 0300 hrs.

My friends had suggested that I sleep but I had other ideas as it was not so easy to just switch off and sleep. I sat on my own, just casually drinking and smoking. The night air was warm but my body for some reason was still keeping a high temperature. I was sat on this comfortable cushioned chair, looked up to the stars and thought how lucky I was but also not to dwell on it and move on with my life. Thursday, my birthday, fucking hell, what a nightmare that had been, I don't think I want to analyse that too much again, how can you analyse it without being affected by it? I have to blank it now and just think not to trouble my mind with it.

The reality for me, was how on earth did I not get shot in the head by one of the four weapons that were being held to my head, anyone of those fucks could have seen red or just thought fuck it and blown me away. How am I going to see and understand fear again after this? It's not like a fight in a bar or night club would get me shaking when you compare this experience, none at all but it is also dangerous if I do not see or understand possible dangers in the future or be afraid if two or three men want to kick seven different shades out of me. As I said, I didn't want to think about it. When I have to in the future, I will just have to learn and decide how far I go in explaining the reality of what took place. If somebody asked me, "What did they do? Or how did it actually happen? How can I make them fully understand. The answer is, you cannot unless you arrange it for them and that could not happen unless it was a movie you were making for the big screen.

One of the night team in the hospital came over to me and said, "Gary, you said you are being picked up at 0600 hrs?" I said, "Yes that is true my friend but I'm ok thank you, I'm enjoying the night sky and I'm very relaxed." He said, "I understand and that is good but it is 0500 hrs now, I thought you would like to know." Once the information had sunken into my drunken head, I was up on my feet within a few seconds. Shit I better go shower at least, I have to go work! I stumbled to the tent, grabbed my plastic washbag and towel and made for the showers. Ok I will start with warm to hot water and then try to take the cold water for thirty seconds or so. I jumped in the shower and for some reason the control was not playing ball and it was cold only, no problems, I was a little braver than normal because the drunken part of me did not care. I took the plunge and once I surpassed the twenty second barrier, I got used to it. Next up was teeth, I thought I better brush for about five minutes and use extra toothpaste to drown the smell of beer, I pretty sure everyone will not want to share my stale beer scent. I slipped my clothes back on, went to find the nursing staff to see if they had any special meal in a bag which they did, the nurse had two of them! I put the kettle on and then scoff time! Spicy spaghetti and pasta breakfast, lots of energy for sure.

I went outside and stood waiting for my lift. I then saw the consultant walking towards me and instantly thought he was up and about early; I wonder what he wants? His opening line was, "Gary what are you doing, you have to sign out and take your medical papers with you, you need to give them to the doctors in Basra." I was looking at him but also looking into thin air as I was trying to stir up an excuse to take myself out of looking so stupid, I said, "Sir, I was coming back to see you before leaving, I'm only going to work now to see some contractors and my workers, then I will be back." He came back, "Gary this will only take a few minutes, ten at the most, it is only 0540 hrs so you have twenty minutes to spare, please come with me." We went into the tent and into his office. He made a few quick checks on me, established that I was drunk and said that I should make sure I drank a lot of water so I didn't dehydrate. He read me my rights actually, oh well. I said my thanks to all and left them in peace. I had my cases, washbag and papers so that's me, all my belongings.

As I came back outside there was a Land Rover waiting for me, the driver stepped out of the car, held his hand out to shake my hand and said, "My name is Tommy, I will assume you are Gary, I'm here to pick you up and fuck me look at the state of you!" I said, "Morning Tommy, what does that mean exactly?" He said, "Well you do look a bit pissed mate, are you alright?" I replied, "Tommy no probs for me, I need you to go down to the entrance of the main base so I can meet and greet my workers for my contracts here on the base, cheers mate." Tommy through my gear into the back of the car and we made our way down to the VCC where my lads would be coming through the security checks to get onto the base. After five minutes we arrived and Tommy parked the car up so I could walk into the building and meet my lads.

The VCC is a massive canvas tent that is surrounded by giant sandbags and it is the point of entry to the base, everyone has to be counted and documented when coming on and off the base. Sometimes it could be a nightmare to get onto the base but luckily for me I had a great relationship with the head shed plus there was also the fact that if my lads were delayed starting work there could be an issue for the soldiers not having their uniforms or personal clothes to wear, so we were seen as a priority service, thankfully. As I walked into the building, I managed to turn many heads and I spent the next fifteen minutes shaking many hands and sharing bear hugs, whether it was soldiers I knew and other contractors from companies such as KBR. It was a nice moment and the VCC was a happy place for everyone, even my American friends from KBR managed a chorus of three cheers and hip hip hooray for Gary. Many could not believe what I was doing back at work and most were saying that I should be on a plane back home by now.

There are two sides of the VCC tent, processed and unprocessed. Unprocessed workers are actually deemed to be in the civilian side, out in the car park. Every day my lads who worked in the laundry would have five guards with them, I was also classed as a guard and I had access to ninety five percent of the base with the badge I had. I started to make my way to the unprocessed side, which means I was walking out to the car park when Tommy looked at me and said, "Gary where are you going, that is the car park of the civilian side, anything can happen to you out there, don't you think you should stay this side, just in case?" I replied, "Tommy I will be fine, there is too much activity going on here right now and the chances of me being shot or blown up are very small, this is something I have to do."

Within five minutes I could see the bus in the distance making its way to the car park, Ram was on time which was good to see on my last day. The bus pulled into the car park and the automatic doors opened and my lads started to pile out. The first one out was Sameer, his reaction was a big smile and handshake, he was shouting out to all the lads in celebration that I was there. After a while I had to get them in, we completed the first stage very quickly and then it was onto the vehicle checkpoint to check the bus for any bad goods or any nasties. After all the checks the bus made its way to the location of the laundry. Ram would be at the laundry already I would guess, so I directed Tommy to go to the contracting office for the American Air force.

I was in their offices for about twenty minutes, I wanted to check on the service levels for each contract and see what had to be done to correct them if anything was not correct. The officers could not believe that I was not on a plane already and laughed at the fact that I had gone to check on the contracts. One of them, a Sargeant who I knew quite well, we shared some laughs but also some serious words. He said some real nice things to me and said, "Man it is great to see you alive, we were all praying for you man but you look a bit rough Gary, hey you been on the beer I think?" I replied, "Yes Sir, that I have been, it was my birthday on Thursday the 8th of April, so had to celebrate." He came back, "Yes you are right, Gary. I thank you and respect you for coming in and your men have been great I have to say, you and Paul have formed a great team for sure, now get your ass home man." One last handshake, papers signed, copies taken with me, happy days that my lads had been keeping on top of things and the business had not suffered, at least I have managed to influence them the right way.

Now over to the laundry to see Ram. When we arrived, he would not leave me alone. We had tears and then tears on tears, he had so much anger and sorrow, it was ok and I understood it from Ram. A Nepali with a heart of gold who appreciated the good things he had been offered in his life and for some reason he believes still to this day that he owes me something, but not at all. A quick tour of the laundry facility, that was all I needed to do. Ram had done me proud; it was time to say goodbye and this time I knew I would definitely not be coming back. I got them all together, said how proud I was of all of them and that I hoped they would have work in the laundry for many years to come. Abu Haider's son came to me as I walked out and stopped me and said, "Boss can I please speak to you?" I replied, "Yes sure you can, tell me my friend?" He said, "My father he told me not speak to many words for you because your normal man and don't expect anything from us but I want to say thank you to a great man I meet. I think the best man I could know is my father and I love him but you Mr. Gerry, you make us all men in here, we feel smart now. We are sad again that you are leaving us but we understand you cannot stay. This morning my father give me message for you, he said to say you are the number one man in his life ever and for me." I just nodded and smiled, I had to get out of there, too heavy for me, one last speech, "Ok my lads, goodbye and keep safe."

With that I turned, walked away and joined Tommy in the Land Rover and said, "Tommy, pull away please, let's go." Tommy said, "Where to now?" I replied, "Tommy I'm now in your hands, I'm all done, thank you so much for your help this morning, I would not have been able to do it without you, top man you are." Tommy made his way back over towards the Italian military camp, this was close to the location where the Chinook would land to pick us up. When we arrived Major Sarah Anderson and her colleagues were standing there as they were coming back with me. It was nice weather, so standing out in the sun was fine by me, so we all just stood around smoking, drinking bottle after bottle of water. My headache had more or less gone and I was not too thirsty anymore.

I was given some ear plugs to put in before the Chinook arrived because of the noise when it comes into land. As I was opening the packet, I could see a Ford Expedition driving towards me with a Kuwait number plate on it, I'm sure that is one of QIT rentals. The car pulled up and Bassim stepped out of the car with Ali, so I told Major Sarah that I would be only ten minutes. She was fine about it as we had time.

I opened, "Hey guys what are you doing?" Ali replied, "We wanted to say goodbye man, you know is right thing to do, plus Paul asked us to make sure we see you and then call him when we are with you, so can we call him Gary?" I said, "Yes sure why not but you will have to be quick because my lift is flying in soon, I'm flying out in a helicopter to Basra." Ali dialled out to Paul and he picked up, Ali passed me the phone and I said, "Hey, what the fuck happened?" He came back, "Hey mate, what you up to? Damn its fucking good to hear your voice mate, fuck it really is. I don't know what to say to you man other than I love you buddy and thank God you got out of that shit. I'm on my way to Iraq, I know you cannot wait but I will catch up and visit you in Qatar when I can. You know I was warned and asked not to return to Iraq whilst all this was going on and I just did not know what to do, everybody said that I needed to keep emotion out of it because many knew that I would be out looking for you and putting myself at risk, plus I might piss some people off. Gary, fuck you, I knew man you would get out of this shit and I just don't know what to say to you, I'm lost for words but just so happy. I got drunk as fuck last night when I heard you was out, so come on tell me?" I said, "Mate listen, I can't talk for long now because I'm being flown to Basra by the British Army in next thirty minutes, so let us try and Skype when I'm back in UK, it is great to hear from you and I'm good mate and all your contracts are ok, the lads done good for you, speak soon, laters mate."

The call was closed and I stood talking to Ali and Bassim for about five minutes. I thanked them both for all their hard work and loyalty and gave my best wishes to them. I felt that I needed to close the talks and allow them to go and that I can move on. We hugged and said our goodbyes. I remember the time back in the villa when I came down heavy on the guys, Ali and Bassim included. I could not help but think and wonder if Ali or one of the others had me set up. Yeah, sure it sounds bad to say or think it but in Iraq you just don't know and I thought the best way was not to think of all the conspiracy theories here, it would be a waste of time because there are thousands of candidates, just forget and move on.

We had been standing there for just over thirty minutes and in the distance, I could see the big bird in the sky with twin blades heading in our direction, it was my taxi. I was asked to turn my back as it came in because of the power of the blades kicking all the nearby shit up into the air. As it came in the swirl of the sand and gush of the wind was something else; my military style sunglasses were worth their weight in gold and the ear plugs seemed to do the job. The back door of the Chinook came fully down and I was met by two medics who guided me onto the Chinook and seated me in between them. I buckled up for the ride and within minutes we were up in the air and heading for Basra, the noise inside this machine was unreal, I could not hear myself talking, crazy. The back doors remained slightly open with a soldier laying down on the floor in front of it, he had his finger on the trigger of a heavy machine gun that was perched on a tripod, the same setup was also on the side of the Chinook. I was hoping that they were not expecting company and it was just formality but I suppose they always had to expect the unexpected. Was I afraid? Funny thing, I wasn't. Why should I be as I'm in good hands and if it happens then I'm not going to be able to change anything, I have gone through the worst part, so stay the course mate.

We seemed to be banking and sweeping all over the place, I'm sure that this was normal practice but the booze in my stomach was starting to move with the motions and I was hoping that it did not want to come up and out of me. The journey was coming to an end and I was given the nod that we would be landing shortly. I could see out of the Chinook and the ground was telling me that the open desert was now filling up with buildings. We swept down to the ground and then we were down safely. I was unbuckled and quickly guided out of the back doors by the two medics. I found myself trying to slow them down a little because my knee would still not move that quickly but we managed to get off smoothly and to safety away from the aircraft.

26 ARRIVING AT SHAIBAH BASE BASRA

After a couple of hundred meters, I was met and greeted by a man whose name was Mike. He was in the Royal Air Force and he explained to me that he had been assigned to look after my welfare whilst I was at Basra. He gave me some papers and said, "Gary, these are the latest newspapers and what they are saying has happened to you. I would like to say that I'm happy to see you safe and I will be looking after you whilst you are here." We carried on walking at a slow pace, still outside, but walking towards a massive sea of canvas tents. As we approached one of the entrances, I could see a wheelchair, I guessed that it was for me and it was welcomed as the knee was cursing me a little. I sat down on the wheelchair and we began the journey to wherever I was going, I'm guessing the hospital.

As we were going through corridors, I could not believe how big these canvas tents were, I'm not joking, I could not see the end of the building, it was outrageous the size of this place. I started to look at some of the papers that Mike had given to me. I looked at Mike and said, "Oh really, wow, they are saying it was a daring SAS raid to free me, really? Where was I when that happened?" I have the utmost respect for any man that pulls on a uniform but that just did not happen but if they were on the ground and had something to do with my release, fair play and all due respect to them and thank you so much. We came to a stop and Mike explained that we had to wait there, we were in a small ward of the Hospital which is where I was going to be staying. I turned to Mike and said, "Mike, are you trying to tell me that this whole area I have seen is a hospital?" Mike replied, "Yes." He also advised that I had not seen all of it yet. What I had seen I could not believe; it was even bigger than anything the Americans have. Wow, that's cool.

A young nurse came over to me and asked me some questions, I was then taken into a room where I was joined by Doctor Steve. Steve was great with me, he was more than up for a laugh so he was right up my street, little did he know that I enjoyed a wind up and piss take. Steve had let it slip that he had a soft spot for one of the nurses on the ward but she was due to be moved to another ward and he was really pissed off about it. He did not want to come out and let it be known he liked her. Well, that was a silly move Steve to give me that sort of information; not that I said anything directly to her but I played on it with Steve and it created a bit of banter. After the checks I was given a full clean bill of health and Steve suggested that I should seek expert advice when I got back with my knee, the shoulder was just down to severe muscle tissue damage and it was just a case of time to let it heal, same as the Italian consultant said. Steve handed me over to the nurses and like most nurses they were very nice and helpful. They helped me bring in my belongings and made me feel at ease in the ward.

My bed was one of about twenty in the room. All my roommates were British soldiers who were in there for various reasons, all of them up and about on their feet, watching television or playing cards to pass the time. Next to me was a young lad called Dean who was twenty-two years of age and was in for severe chest pains. He explained that he had been in Iraq in 2003 for the invasion and then left for Canada, only to return back to Iraq once more. He had his own scary stories to tell, some of them very sad and as he was talking you could see the sadness on his face, so young but so brave. These men and women who serve all over the world, whose work is never unrecognised by me, thank you so much.

Mike came to the ward and asked me if I wanted to have some lunch, plus we had some other tasks to go through, one of which was a debrief come interview. I was not looking forward to it but had to go through with it. We came out of the 'super tent' and made our way over to the eating house, on the way there was a smoking place, so I took the opportunity to have a cigarette. I still had my Ishtar so good news on that front. I had reduced myself down to about eighty a day now based upon how many I had smoked since the early hours of this morning but that is factoring in the case that I had been busy working and I was also in areas that I could not smoke, so things were looking good.

We walked into the canteen, the place was massive, tables and people everywhere. Mike moved over to the area where we could take a tray and cutlery before walking to the service area. I spread my eyes on the food before me, it looked mouthwatering and I was ready to try and eat as much as I could. Mike could see me over thinking about what to choose, he said,

"Gary, you can eat what you want, choose as much as you want." I chose a good decent bowl full of salad, a full plate for main course which looked more like an English 'Sunday Roast' which I heaped with Yorkshire Puddings. Hopefully, I could squeeze in some ice cream and apple pie later.

I sensed that I had eyes on me, and it was not because I was in civilian clothes as there were others also in civvy clothes and not just people in battle dress uniform. I wonder if they know who I am? I wonder if they are thinking, yeah great we don't even want to be here and he comes here to pick up big bucks and lives in the population and creates havoc for us, nut case! Not a lot I can do about it now, what is done is done. Mike chose our table, I placed my tray on the table and as I went to sit down all those around me stood up and started to clap in my direction, it did not need to be explained to me, it was a nice gesture by them and made me feel at home with my own.

I surprised myself with the amount of food I ate. I chose not to eat all the salad bowl and focus on that roast dinner; it was truly awesome! It was not like my Mums but was still lovely. I managed to sneak some homemade apple pie down with ice cream. It was unreal to be having this food, a dream. We came out and Mike knew I would want to smoke, so we headed for the smoking area. When we arrived there, I lit up and Mike said, "Gary, I'm going to see Major Sarah Anderson and make her aware that she can see you shortly, so when you are ready come to my office and then I will take you to her." I replied, "Sure Mike, I will see you in a bit." He went off and I stayed smoking for about twenty minutes, I was not looking forward to the debrief and I hoped they would not push me too far. I just want to chill out and relax.

I arrived at Mike's office and was introduced to a military press officer. He asked me if I was willing to do a short interview for him, it would take about five minutes; I agreed. After the interview he asked me if I wanted any media to be available when I arrived back in the UK. I said under no circumstances did I want any media and if possible, to notify my family not to be there either. He told me that I would be flown back to the UK and would arrive at RAF Brize Norton. I was ok with that but I did not want anyone to be there, I just wanted someone to drive me home. He told me that the media were pushing him on where and when I would be arriving but he had not disclosed that information to anybody. Ok cool. Major Sarah then came to the office and she said she had arranged a room for us to sit and talk about the last seven days and to also talk about what would happen when I got back into the UK. They needed to understand if I wanted any specialist help, like a quack or something.

Major Sarah and I walked out of Mike's office and made our way to this quiet room that they had arranged. On entering I saw the same two men who were with Major Sarah when they visited my hospital bedside, so it was them three and me. I was told that I was not allowed to smoke in the room, so a great start this was. I thought "Fuck this!" I don't see why I should have to put up with that demand and it was definitely not going to be possible if this 'chat' was going to take too long. So, I simply said that if I felt that I wanted to smoke I would stop the interview and go outside, end of.

Two hours passed and I was stressed to fuck, so I stood up and said I was leaving the room for a cigarette or two. As I left the room, I walked as quick as I could. I was infuriated on how I had been questioned. I was answering questions, twice over, it was borderline interrogation and I did not like it. I was blowing up at times; what kind of fucking brief is this shit? The descriptions of everything were spot on, locations, personal descriptions and remembering all the details whilst going through all this bollocks. My language was not pretty and some of the looks were interesting to say the least but at the same time I was not getting a 'Fuck you as well Gary' vibe back. I sat outside smoking and thought, I know this is your job, you do this all the time but I don't see why I should be like a fucking parrot, they were driving me mad. When I returned, I made it clear that I knew what they were up to then made it clear from my side that if they wanted to play this game then I would start playing the game with them, I also had some background to these interview techniques. Game on!

Well, what little that speech did. They continued with the same line of questioning for another two hours and we are only halfway through it. Fag break again and this time I will take longer, fuck 'em. I was shattered with all this bullshit, my head was on fire and I was angry with them, fuck this crap, I have had enough!

Back in the room, it was relentless, the questions changed to statements. It was just frustration now, perhaps I was in the wrong and should have been keeping my cool. They asked a question in one way and the very next question was the same but said in a different tense. How many times did they have to keep telling me that this information is vital and could go towards invaluable information for others in the future? Yeah, ok I get that but not to the degree where it is just repetition, you are wasting my time and also you are restricting my smoking time.

One thing I knew for sure and so did they, my descriptions of all of the locations were more or less spot on, I think they could not understand how good my information was when you consider the stress I was under. Another two hours had surpassed us, so I just got up from the chair to go outside and Major Sarah said, "You may as well stay here for now as we are nearly finished." I was having none of it and said, "I am sorry but I need the toilet urgently." I did go to the toilet but then went out for a break again, how can they not understand how dependent I have been on nicotine, it has been my best friend for the past eight days and I'm sure it will continue to play its part for a few more days to come.

The debrief continued, the nearly finished quote was another ninety minutes. Good job I chose to go to the toilet earlier as my planned stomach change was happening and I don't have the luxury of many clothes now and any sudden bowel movements would be scary. Done! Finally finished. My quiz masters thanked me for my time and explained that I had done well and that my anger was understandable in the circumstances and that my behaviour was reasonable. I felt a little better about the situation as no one can say that they enjoy telling people to fuck off but it was explained that they had been there before with even more intense replies… noted.

I was able to leave the room and once outside and lit up a cigarette and sat drinking an ice-cold bottle of water, Major Sarah had phoned Mike to let him know I was finished. Mike informed me that he had arranged for me to have a haircut and also to have my teeth seen to, nice one Mike. Haircut was first on the list, not too difficult to do, the same boring style I have had for the past twenty years but I have to say it was cut to perfection. Kudos to the stylist. Now it was the teeth and I hate the dentist chair. I must have been in the chair for about forty minutes. Electronic brushes, drills and all sorts of gear to clean my teeth up; I had never had this treatment before. The majority of the time Mr. Dentist and his assistant were having a good laugh on my behalf, unfortunately I had no choice but to join in which is easier said than done. Laughing at the same time of having your mouth wide open and pools of water in your mouth was awkward but good fun. Oh, my goodness, when he had finished, I could not believe the job he had done, a top-drawer job! I was very happy with his work but when I took a glass of water to rinse my mouth, haha, what the fuck! My teeth were ultra-sensitive and of course the laugh was on me again. The feel of my teeth was so smooth but I think I needed room temperature water from now on.

The time had really kicked on, Mike and I went over to the canteen, once more I had a lovely feed for just over half an hour. I could see that Mike looked a little tired and I felt it was best to say something to him that would probably suit him and me. I said, "Please don't take this the wrong way but I feel you need to sleep soon and I have some things I need to sort out, plus I want a little time by myself, it has been a testing day for me with Major

Sarah Anderson, I need some space mate." Mike said, "No problems Gary, yes, I think it is a good idea and I will see you at 0800 hrs tomorrow, I shall come over here to your ward." I replied, "That will be great, I shall either be in the ward or out here smoking, sleep well and a big thank you for all your support and guidance today." We shook hands, I thought it would be best to go and get a nice mug of tea and just sit around outside. I was anticipating a sleepless night due to the time I would be spending in the toilet but I hoped I was wrong.

I pretty much just chilled out over the next few hours, smoking and drinking tea. It was nice to taste a good strong brew. Where I was sat, was only twenty meters away from the toilets and as I thought I was starting to be more regular than I wanted to be, but luckily for now, I had no pains. It had been nice to sit alone, look up at the stars and think about how I would be changing, the way I will think and behave will change, I believe for the better. I got back to the ward, grabbed the wash bag, brushed my teeth, had a shower but resisted to shave as I needed to rest my skin for forty-eight hours, I'm still a bit sore from hacking it off last night. The fresh fruit and veg was working its wonders, it is definitely flushing me out, diarrhoea had set in.

I woke up at 0700 hrs, the night was not too bad. I was a little busy in the toilet and each visit I was lighting up a cigarette but I think I was able to sleep for just over four hours, the good thing is that I was not feeling that tired but the diarrhoea was going to be a worry. So, into the bathroom for a lovely shower. I never thought in life that I would get super excited with the feel of water on my body but I did, hopefully I was not causing a problem to the base for running out of water.

I made sure I was ready for when Mike arrived and to my surprise Mike brought me a lovely cup of coffee. Considering I'm not a coffee drinker, kudos once more to him, simple things but made me feel extra special. During the coffee talk he explained that the day could work out to be boring for me. He had to complete some paperwork, catch up on some other work and make sure everything was in place for my journey tonight, I was going back to the UK on a military flight. He was extremely brief with regards to the journey but made it clear that I would leave the military base by car and would fly out of Basra International Airport. The base I was on, its real name is Shaibah Air Base, opened in the early 1900's by the British and was then handed over to the Iraqi Air Force in 1956 and in the 2003 invasion the British forces took it back, the place was massive. I was scheduled to fly out of Basra International at 2330 hrs, so it was going to be a long day, most of it alone. No problems, I can try and have a think on what I had to plan for in the coming few weeks. Time to get a pen and pad of paper.

I was wondering how far the journey would be to the airport. What kind of escort was I going to have? Am I ready for this trip and do I have to make it? I was hoping that it would go quickly and then the flight home, it would be nice to think I could sleep a little. I'm sure I will find out later when I arrive in the UK at Brize Norton. Who will be driving me back home to Northamptonshire?

After Mike left, I went over to the canteen to have breakfast. I was caught in two minds what to do, what should I eat? I kept it simple, boiled eggs, fried egg on toast and scrambled eggs, if it can slow up the shits then all is good, rice was also on the menu. Then back to the smoking area. The weather was nice today, not too hot, nice to chill out in. I had shade where I was sat. A few mugs of tea and some conversations with some soldiers passed a couple of hours for me and took me towards lunchtime. The clock ticked along quite nicely.

My head was in a good place for now. I was excited to be going home and more or less knew how long I wanted to be back. I was going to be leaving again to return to the Middle East, I knew I would return quite quickly. I had considered the early stages when returning home, there will be a few buckets of tears to get through. I had to respect those that wanted that time to hug me to death and get there worries off their chest but there is a fine line also. For me it is about moving on with my life as soon as possible, I cannot afford to walk the wire with my emotions, pointless feeling sorry for myself and I will deal with any forms of stress as time goes by. Do I need experts to sit me down and say, "Hi Gary, how do you feel and what do you think about this and that?" Not for me thank you, I will self-analyse for the years to come.

I needed another pack of Ishtar so I went back to the ward. As I walked in, Doctor Steve was on duty. We stood and talked for a while and exchanged some piss taking about a certain nurse. Steve had some free time on his hands so he took me for a free tour of the tent. Basically, the base I was on was the hospital base and the particular tent I was in was massive, it was like a little city. It is extremely hard to explain and was just as hard to come to terms with the size of the damn thing. What it did make me realise is that our boys do not do things on a small scale, it was just corridor after corridor and so many rooms. Steve eventually went back to work and I went back to working on the art of chilling for the rest of the day, plus lunch was coming. I wonder if the 'Sunday Roast' will be on again? I was just in the mood for Yorkshire Pudding again.

Lunchtime! Be smart Gazza and try to eat foods that soak up fluids! I really hope that I will not be spending too much time in the toilet when I'm on the aeroplane, that would be very embarrassing for me. I had been given medicine for my stomach but it was only helping me slightly, today the bathroom was calling me every twenty to thirty minutes. After a sensible lunch where I was joined by Mike, we went back to his office and had to run through my timetable, so that broke up my day. He finished off a few things and he allowed me to use a computer so I could check my emails.

Just after 1600 hrs Mike was ready to sit me down and go through the plans for me. He started, "Ok my mate, we are going to be leaving here at 1800 hrs, so you have two hours to prepare, you don't have any packing so you can just shower and chill. Now the journey by car is no more than forty minutes, I will be travelling with you to the airport and will stay with you until you take off. We will travel in a 4x4 car and will have other cars in front and behind us, our security are all British boys, so you are in very good hands my mate, let me say, the best you can get. How do you feel about travelling by car, are you nervous about it or are you a hardened expert now?" Mike gave me a small grin and a tap to the arm. I replied, "I'm ok about it mate, I am sure I will be fine, as you said I have the best men with me and it is only forty minutes, no issues." He replied, "Good stuff mate, I knew you would be up for it, as you said we have the best tools, so I will see you fifteen minutes before we leave, let us meet at your office, the smoking point."

So, I went back to the ward and got my stuff together after a shower and shave. Yes, skin seems to be handling the blade today. I got dressed and Doctor Steve handed me my papers and signed me out, good man. Back outside in my office I was waiting for Mike, well on time and continuing to enjoy the weather, which had been kind for me today and made me enjoy a chilled time. No humidity and a gentle breeze. In my head I was thinking of boredom and stress but it was the opposite, the power of the mind was blocking things out but I knew that I would have to come out and play very soon. Mike was on time, he pulled up with a driver, I chucked my stuff in the back of the car and then we made our way to the main car park, where we would meet up with the others. We arrived at the other car park, Mike got out of the car and went for a walkabout; I just stepped out for a while, grabbed a bottle of water from my bag and stood around. Mike came back after ten minutes, as he approached me, he said, "The lads are coming around with the other vehicles now, they will be making some last-minute checks and adjustments, then we will be on our way mate." Five minutes later three other 4x4's arrived and out jumped my protection team; it looked like the car I was travelling in was one of three cars. I would be in the middle car and one either side of us, I could count fifteen bodies, all looked to be fully armed, I felt good.

Mike signalled for me to get in the car, as I got in Mike joined me on my right side and a big lump to my left, plus four other weapon carriers in with us. I was happy to know that these fifteen lads had the tools and I was telling my mind that Basra was not the same as Baghdad. I always heard of more issues in Baghdad than Basra but that is not to say that our lads had it easy, not at all, I guess it was my way of diluting the chances of anything kicking off and challenging my final leg to safety. The cars pulled out of the base and once they had they confirmed good radio comms back with the base and between each other. On coming out of the base, within minutes I realised that we had a helicopter flying high above us, eyes above us just in case we were coming towards any potential issues, nice one lads, now I do feel extra cool about it.

As Mike said, true to his word, the journey was completed just after thirty minutes and the lads were the business; radios were always in action making sure our travel went like clockwork and no hitches.

We came into the parking area of the airport, the drivers parked up in a controlled area and there was quite a big presence of security around us, good to see and the walk to the entrance was just a casual walk with no thoughts of experiencing a last-minute fatality. I followed Mike out of the car, one of the lads grabbed my luggage and Mike led the way to the entrance of the airport which was only about one hundred meters away. As we got inside Mike made his way to a desk to provide them with some papers for me, I had to have special clearance papers made. I was getting on a military aircraft, a big transporter and also there was the added issue that I had no passport, that and all my other means of identification were taken from me by my babysitters! I just stood around as Mike was going through the tight system. He had given me the heads up that it could take half an hour, no issues, they allowed you to sit, stand, smoke and have a coffee. Everywhere as the eye could see were massive sandbags, the type they use at all military installations and quite strange to see inside an airport. I guarantee that on the other side of here I'm not going to be able to walk around too much and for sure the Duty-Free shop won't be open and there will be no food court.

We were good to go. As we walked through the system, every few meters were an armed guard and I was getting some weird stares as I walked through with my West Ham shirt and tracksuit on. I was amongst military uniforms and others who looked like they had been on safari; but weird looks were better than the looks I was receiving this time last week. Last Tuesday I was in the middle of a battle, how times change. We walked up some stairs and then walked into an area that is used by the military press, we had walked into a very comfortable area, a little VIP compared to the other parts. I noticed the many sofas in the room and it was quiet also, so at the moment it looks like I could have the chance of lounging about if I needed it. Mike went off to an area out of sight, then appeared with a large mug in his hand and a brown paper bag in the other and said, "Here you go mate, a nice large coffee and a packed lunch, I'm afraid there is no food service on the aeroplane but you can eat this nice packed lunch. Now if you leave that there and come with me, I can show you the smoking area and toilets." Mike walked me to the area to smoke, the toilet was close by and with that he returned back upstairs. I went to the toilet and found myself up and down the stairs for a few hours, not good. From 1930 hrs till 2230 hrs, I was hardly off the toilet. Very bad timing, to get so bad and the flight was going to last for seven hours, without being able to smoke was a challenge but it could be a benefit in disguise. I was really hoping that I would be able to sleep on the plane but of course I did not realise that the reality of being able to sleep on this transporter was nearly impossible. It would be a lovely thought that I could fall asleep, then the next thing I would hear is, "Gary can you sit up and fasten your seat belt as we are landing", I can only dream.

Mike managed to get two minutes with me, "Gary we now have to get you downstairs, hand over your luggage and then you can get on the plane." We went through a security check area; Mike said his goodbye to me and then he was on his way back to the base. I thanked him for all his advice and support, all the time Mike was never pushy and he let me have my space, nice man who knew how to deal with me, his last words were to suggest I never return to Iraq... noted!

I was led across the tarmac with my other travelling friends, some needing the aid of crutches to walk and a couple on stretchers who had survived their own personal experiences. As I got to the back of the aircraft, the true reality of the size of it was unreal, it was huge and I'm sure if you could lift a terraced house up from the ground you could fit one in here, no problems. I walked up the ramp and walked towards a seating area. A polite man came over to me and said, "Hi there, is your name Gary please?" I said, "Yes I'm Gary." I was shown to my seat and I chose to sit down once I had asked him where the toilet was. I was told that once the seat belt sign had been switched off, he was going to give me a sleeping bag so I could go to sleep on the floor if I wanted to. I just sat in my seat watching these brave men and ladies go through their routines before taking off. I have so much admiration for these people and I'm getting a live show watching them perform, thank you so much for what you do. The floor of the aeroplane was a bare metal floor, sleeping bag or not, the planned sleep was not going to be a comfortable ride I'm sure but let us try. Moments later this big bird started up its engines and then we were taxiing along the runway... take off! We were on the way to 'Blighty'... now it had sunk in; how lucky was I to be on this journey back home.

The flight was a good one in terms of timing and smoothness, I don't recall any turbulence but sleep was not easy, the hard metal floor was not going down too well with my condition and I was in and out of the toilet. My bowel movements really kicked in during the early afternoon and had got worse as the day went on. My mind was telling me two factors; the extra food I was now eating and the quality of it was flushing all the bad stuff out. I am sure I don't have any major issues as that would have been picked up in the two field hospitals.

This big old bird touched down at Brize Norton just after 0430 hrs and I was not feeling too bad and to be honest I was not thinking too much at this stage. I knew that somebody was going to be waiting for me as Mike had told me so and arrangements had been made to take me home. That is all I was interested in; I had already asked my support team to notify family that I did not want any form of a home coming and definitely no media. After collecting my luggage, I was escorted to a building where I was met by a man from the British & Commonwealth Office. Please excuse me for not remembering his name but let us presume his name was Peter. Peter was extremely professional from the moment I met him and as we came through quite a simple system, he led me to a very luxurious room. I was very taken back by the elegance of the room and it even had a bar, fully stocked too and even though it was 0500 hrs I was open to a drink if it was offered and even more so after what he was about to tell me.

We sat down on a sofa and Peter asked me generally how I was feeling? He had mentioned that he had been in daily contact with my Mum and also that Mr. Jack Straw had also phoned my Mum a couple of times. He then said to me, "Gary, as you know when you were in Basra you had requested that you did not want any media attention just now and no family to be here on your arrival?" I replied, "Yes that is one hundred percent correct, why do you ask?" He replied, "Well there is no media but your Mum insisted that she should be here, what can I say Gary, I think it is better that she was here, she came with your wife Lisa, your mother and father-in-law, what's your thoughts?" I sighed, "I wanted to leave this for as long as possible and deal with it when I got home, baby steps but now I have to deal with it. Ok Peter this is how it has to be and if you explain it this way to my Mum, she will listen I think, she knows me. I'm going to ask you to say to her now, if

196

anyone does not respect my wishes then I will just walk away, simple. You tell all of them they can sit there on that sofa and I will be over here, we are just a few meters apart, they can see me and talk to me. I'm sure there are things you want to say to us all as a group but I'm asking you to keep as much emotion out of this as possible. Last, you must tell them all that I will control the number of hugs and kisses, let me go to them, not for them to come to me, especially my Mum Peter, she will not like it one bit and that is why you need to be strong with my Mum and make it clear that I will walk out of the room if it goes too far." Peter nodded, smiled at me and explained that he understood my requests, his reactions told me that he did not necessarily agree with me but he was going to pass on my words.

Before he left the room, he asked me if I wanted a drink. I looked at the brandy bottle and said, "I will have a large brandy and ice thank you, I will need it now for what is about to happen." Peter poured me an extra-large Brandy, good man. He then opened a connecting door to another room where my family were sitting, they were only next door and if he wasn't quick, I was sure my Mum was going to knock the door down. Peter came back to see me, sat down with a smile/half grin on his face and said, "Ok Gary, everyone is ok with what you are asking, I'm grinning because your Mum did not seem exactly too happy about it but she has agreed to follow your request, so I will go out and get them now and sit them down here." I replied, "Just give me another ten minutes please, let me have a cigarette and finish this Brandy before you let them in. Was my Mum crying when you were talking to them just now or is, she ok?" He replied, "No tears Gary but she is nervous of course, I have got to know your Mum quite well during this week, she has not had it easy at all." Peter allowed me to smoke in the room and finish my brandy. I went to the toilet to make myself comfortable and when I came out, I sat down and waited for Peter to show them through.

He was gone for two minutes, then the door opened; Lisa, my Mum and Lisa's parents walked in, Peter guided them to the sofa. I looked up and gave an ordinary smile and perfected a nod of the head to say I was ok and it was good to be home, I knew what everyone was thinking. We all sat and just looked across the table that divided the two sofas and Peter asked me if I wanted to start proceedings, so I agreed. I did not waffle on in detail, I just said that generally I was ok, I mentioned that I had the shits, I have pain in my knee and shoulders, I was smoking a lot and getting my appetite back. I made it clear that I didn't want too many questions about the events, and that they just give me some space and I would gradually open up about it if I felt like it. I didn't want to be treated any differently than I was treated in normal life, yes sure we have all had a shit week but now is time to move on. We had to think of the positives and be happy for what we have, for me it was simple, I was alive and breathing. It could have been a lot worse.

My Mum's first words were, "West Ham drew on Saturday with Derby and lost yesterday to Crystal Palace one nil." I just nodded and said, "You see some things never change Mum. Nice bit of humour." We all kind of sat there looking like we had never met before but that was fine by me. Peter spoke and touched upon some points about how he could continue supporting the family and some other general information. I didn't want to drag this out anymore and suggested that I was ready to leave, so as we all stood to our feet, I took the plunge and embraced everyone. Mum's tears came as I knew they would but she was as good as gold to be honest. Peter led us outside and we walked to the car park where the car was to go home. I was told I was going to the house of Lisa's parents because my Mum's house was besieged by the media, they did not know where Lisa's parents lived.

27 A NEW LIFE

We arrived back to Wellingborough in good time, nothing heavy on the roads and we only had to stop once so I could use the bathroom. We arrived at the house, I decided it would be best to have a shower and then just chill for the day, to do nothing in particular, I knew there would be many people who wanted to visit me. Lunchtime was coming and my Dad phoned to make sure it was ok to come over, he had taken the day off from work; my sister Helen and her Husband Steve came, plus Lisa's close family.

My Dad was cool when he first saw me, usual stuff, handshake, a hug but nothing heavy, he knew the crack and focused on the positives. He knew how to deal with it, he just started to talk about West Ham, the two games on the long weekend and my mates in Irchester who all were asking about me. From the time I had been taken, my Dad could not go to work, he wouldn't go to the local Irchester Sports Club, which was a regular haunt of his, mine also when I was back in the UK. He explained how the lads of the Sports Club had been comforting and supporting him, very touching to hear but did not surprise me. Welby and Alan Abrahams, good friends of mine visited him at home, solid lads, plus so many others who helped him in his hour of need. The media outlets found out that Irchester Sports Club was close to my heart, so they paid a visit to the club to try and get any gossip about me but were very quickly given the cold shoulder and a selective choice of words by my mates. I knew it was going to be hectic with friends phoning me, wanting to visit me or meet up. I was fine with it but always made it clear that I should not be treated any differently than before, just say simple things and don't ask me to go into so much detail.

From the time the media found out I had been taken they had been camped outside my Mum's house and from what I knew, they were being a pain in the rear to her, to the extreme where she could not leave the house without someone following her. She explained that she found herself in a completely different world, she was centre of attention as the media tried to extract any information about me from her and all around her. My Mum's best mate Sylvie had travelled from London to be with her whilst all of this was going on. Sylvie, what a diamond of a lady you are, I cannot express my love enough for you, thank you. The Foreign and Commonwealth Office had stated to Mum that it was important not to give any information about my past, especially since I had a previous career in the Police Service, that kind of information in the wrong hands could be dangerous for me, some may put two and two together and get five.

I had been on and off the phone for most of the morning and I wanted to take a rest from it. Lisa's Mum house was quite full throughout the day, my Mum didn't want to leave too early, she wanted to make the most of the time with me. It was just after 1100 hrs, my Mum's phone rang, she passed it to me and I said, "Who is it?" Mum replied, "He will not say, he has only said you know him and for sure you would want to talk to him." Mum smiled and I took the phone from her. On taking the phone I said, "Hello how can I help you please?" A voice sparked up on the other end, "Good morning, is this Gary I'm speaking to please?" I said, "Yes Gary here, how can I help you please?" "Hi Gary, its Alan Pardew, can you speak for a minute?" I was motionless as I turned my head to my Mum and said, "Sorry did you just say you are Alan Pardew, are you serious?" My face lit up and so did my Mum's and everyone else in the room. Alan replied, "Gary I promise you I'm Alan Pardew and if it is ok, I just want to talk to you for only two minutes, is that ok with you?" I'm thinking, "Is the Pope a Catholic?" It was a jaw dropping question, West Ham's Manager is phoning me up and asking if he can talk to me, this is not happening! I said, "Yes sure go ahead I'm free, how are you, Alan?" Alan replied, "Listen mate I just had to phone you, I can't believe what I heard on Sunday just after you had been released. For someone who has been through that and to ask how West Ham got on does not make sense to me but it tells me many things about you mate. I got home the other night after the Palace game and as you know we lost one nil and I was trying to put things in perspective here about what is and isn't important at the moment and you have inspired me mate. Gary as you know we are playing Coventry on Saturday and I want you to be my guest of honour. I want you to be here, you cannot say no to me. After we finish this call, I will have a lady phone you, her name is Angela and she will tell you everything for the plan on Saturday. I truly think and believe this could be an inspirational thing for us at the moment as it puts so many things in perspective as I said and we need the points Saturday." I just said, "I'm shell shocked for sure Alan, it's not

200

every day of the week that West Ham's Manager phones you up and asks you to come to a game, I would love to be there, can I bring a couple of people with me please?" Alan replied, "Gary no problems, I think you can bring a couple with you, of course you can, as I said Angela will call you soon and she will arrange it all for you. I will leave you in peace now as I know you will have so much to do and I will see you Saturday, come on you Irons Gary." I could not believe what I had just done, I turned to my Mum and said, "How on earth did all that happen?" Mum replied, "He phoned me yesterday, he had got my details through a friend in the media, so I said that he could phone you as a surprise and I would not say anything to you at all, how good is that?"

Before my Mum left, she gave me four pages of A4 paper and on it were the notes and details of different media outlets, television, radio and newspapers. Mum had told me that they had all given their details and asked me to give them all to you and you can contact them when you wish. I was in shock, four full pages listing the big shots in the UK and also media from Italy, China, Japan and the USA.

I made the decision of going to the town centre of Wellingborough, buying a new telephone, sim card and getting to work on the phone. I planned to do various interviews on television, radio but made a caveat with them to only start after the coming weekend, I wanted to enjoy my day at West Ham with no drama. I spoke to various newspapers and agreed to sit with a journalist from the Sunday Mirror on Friday, we would go to a quiet location in Northampton and I would open up on the events that had taken place on my one week's 'holiday' in Iraq, courtesy of Muqtada Al Sadr and the Mehdi Army.

On Wednesday the 13th and Thursday 14th of April, I more or less stayed inside the house of my in-laws as I thought it was better to allow others to come to me rather than me to them, to go to places like my Mum or Dad's house would not be good and also places like Irchester Sports Club; so, I kept a low profile.

What I did have to do was work out how I was going to get brand new ID documents, such as my passport, driving licence and birth certificate; I had none of these items, and I knew it would be a headache. My captors had taken everything from me. Have you ever tried getting any ID documents when you don't actually have any form of ID to prove who you are? Sounds crazy to say but I was a nobody and also had no fixed permanent address in the UK, mission impossible nearly. I had to go down to London to get my birth certificate, from there I could get my passport and driving licence. I had arranged all three with in twelve days so they were ready and available so I could be on an aeroplane on the 25th of April. Yes, I was flying back out to the Middle East on the 25th of April. What started off as a headache, worked out ok in the end, it just involved some travel to London and Peterborough, job done. I booked flights for myself, Lisa and Christian, we would fly out on the 25th of April to Qatar as I had to get on with my next project. As I said, I'm not going to dwell on the past, move on. When I told my Mum that I was going back so early, I could tell she was not happy, she wanted more time with me and deep down, I know she was hoping that the bad experience would make me stay in the UK all the time, afraid to leave the safe shores of the UK... not for me.

Angela phoned me from West Ham United Football Club, she had arranged for three tickets and asked me if I could arrive at twelve lunchtime. Kick off was at 3pm, the day all arranged.

The Friday arrived and I was scheduled to meet Rupert from the Sunday Mirror in a pre–arranged location in Northampton, a really lovely five-star location. Family, friends came along to enjoy the luxury of the pool, amazing food and grounds, whilst I had the pleasure of being interviewed once more, reliving the events of the previous week. I had agreed to do the article and I knew when I made the agreement what I was letting myself in for and to be honest, Rupert was brilliant with me. I broke down a few times, difficult not to, the memories being so vivid. It took just over three hours, I was emotionally drained whilst everybody else had been chilling and making the most of the five-star treatment, no problems though because I was going to have the ultimate day tomorrow when I'm with 30,000 of my mates at West Ham.

Friday evening was a low-key event, I was in bed early but I was like a kid with candy and just so excited about what was happening tomorrow... so surreal. One minute you have four guns held to your head and the following week Alan Pardew has asked you if you want a VIP day at Upton Park.

I woke up around 0600 hrs, crept down the stairs so no one could hear me to make a cup of tea and have a cigarette. It was a nice fresh April morning, good enough to sit outside in the back garden, few cups of tea and a few fags before I was going to treat myself to a mega portion of bacon sandwiches. Six slices of brown bread and I decided to use twelve rashes of bacon, three fried eggs that had a crispy base but a soft yolk and some HP sauce, life is good! Yes, I have gone from one extreme to the other here and over the course of one hour I had munched my way through it all, just in case I could not have lunch or had to choose between eating or something claret and blue orientated. I had decided that I was going to wear a white Polo Shirt, black dress trousers and a pair of black oxford shoes, smart but casual. The two guests I had invited were my sister's husband and my Dad. Dad being a Charlton Athletic supporter and my brother–in–law a supporter of a team that plays in red that David Beckham used to play for… let me leave it there.

On the subject of David Beckham, ironically for me I did not make the front page of the Sunday Mirror on Sunday 18th of April, that was taken by David Beckham as he had decided he wanted to play the field with Rebecca Loos. If it had not been for 'golden balls' I would have made front page, I ended up as the middle page spread. My ex-partner Sharon did a typical 'kiss and tell' on me; for some reason she chose to go to town on me and created stories that would have seen Pinocchio's nose grow!

I would be driving for the day, so I would pick my Dad and Steve up at my Dads house in Irchester. I had a quiet word in Dad's ear and asked him to make sure he dressed suitably for the day, so when I pulled up outside his house and tooted the horn of the car, he was sat by the front window, he was ready. He walked out in a beige coloured suit, wow Dad! I was about to say he made me feel happy but then he exposed the red shirt he had on! He could not resist it, a bit of banter for wearing the red of Charlton, yeah ok you get away with that one.

28 COME ON YOU IRONS

We set off nice and early as I just wanted to be chilled for the whole day, if I arrive a bit early then so be it, plus I wanted to get a good parking space near the ground. I knew my Dad wanted to go to the Boleyn Pub. My Dad was born in the Northeast near Sunderland but my grandparents moved to London when Dad was five years old, they moved to Greenwich, next door to Charlton, so he became a Charlton fan but when Charlton were away, he would go West Ham.

I managed to get a good parking space, about quarter of a mile away, perfect in many ways, getting some fresh air, savouring the walk and when we come out, a good place to exit quickly. As we were walking down the street West Ham fans were stopping me, "Hello mate, sorry but are you Gary Teeley, and best of luck to you mate, good to see you got home." It was a little funny because my Dad was gagging for a beer and he was bitching a little that people were stopping me; to be honest I was very surprised that so many did. Surely, I can't be such big news but obviously I am. I know it had been mentioned on the news; the first thing I asked when I was released, was, "How did West Ham get on?" and also the fact that I was televised in Iraq with my West Ham gear on.

We walked in The Boleyn on the corner of Green Street at 1100 and Dad was allowed to have a pint. I had decided to drive because that way it would force me not to drink and I could remember every minute also having no alcohol would make sure that I was not going to be emotional. We left the Boleyn just before twelve, Dad didn't want to leave but once he was walking, he was ok. He loves a beer at the best of times and he was now back in his old stomping ground. We had to go to the main entrance of the stadium, go to the reception and ask for Angela, she would be our host for the rest of the day. We walked through the double doors of the main entrance; I gave my name to a lady and she asked me to wait. I was just soaking it all up, I was buzzing inside but at the same time could not stop thinking how surreal it was, very lucky to be here and even extra lucky standing here now.

A lady with blonde hair walked towards us, she said, "Hello I'm Angela, pleased to meet you all, I hope you are ok Gary, I trust you had a good journey, if you can come this way so we can get things started, big day ahead." Angela was absolutely stunning, what a beautiful looking lady, truly drop dead gorgeous, making my day even more perfect. We followed Angela up some stairs, then through a series of corridors, she walked us into a lounge where there were light drinks available and a selection of sandwiches. Angela said, "If I can ask you to help yourselves to a cup of tea or coffee, I will be right back once I have tracked down Alan, he wants to see you before the game Gary." Angela left us to fend for ourselves, so it was cups of tea times three please Dad. He had not made me a cup of tea for years, "Dad, do the right thing, Steve and I will have tea, ta now." He replied, "Why should I put the kettle on?" Steve and I just laughed, "Dad there is no kettle it is a machine duh, tea bag in the cup and hot water in, touch of milk."

We sat for about ten minutes; we were allowed to smoke so I lit up a cigarette. I had some Ishtar left and Dad was not too impressed with the smell, he thought they were made from camels' stuff, I explained to him that the damn things were my best friend for a while, he just laughed. Angela came back, sat with me and said, "Alan will see you in five minutes, after that he will take you to meet the players in the changing rooms, ok?" What could I say other than, "Oh thank you Angela, that will be great." She stood up and said, "So see you in five minutes?" What a result, this is just unreal, I never ever thought in my lifetime I would be doing this but here I am living the dream, I really can't believe it is me here, I really can't.

Angela came back in and said, "Gary let's go, Alan is kind of ready I think, lots going on and I'm sorry for making you wait." I replied, "Making me wait is fine." Shit me I was waiting all last week; this is a doddle. We had only been walking for about a minute through some corridors and then Angela stopped, knocked on a door, she opened it and said, "Come on Gary in you come." I walked in, followed by my Dad and Steve and there in front of me was Alan Pardew the West Ham United Manager and Peter Grant the Assistant Manager.

We shook hands and I introduced Dad and Steve to Peter; when I introduced Peter back to them, I explained to Dad and Steve who he was, just in case they did not know but for sure they knew Pards. Alan started off the conversation to clear the air, "Gary, I wanted you down here today because I cannot start to understand what you have been through and then on your release the first thing you say is how did West Ham get on, I truly could not grasp that. We could not win against Palace for you after drawing at home to Derby and after the Palace game I was at home and it came on the news, it kind of knocked me for six but then thought, I want you here. To be honest with you, one I think you deserve it mate and two I think you could also help us by meeting the players today and letting them understand the reality of how much your club means to you, especially now as we are chasing that play off place, for me you are an inspiration, Gary." We were in his office for about twenty minutes talking in general about the push for the play offs and what he has planned over the next few years. Alan asked Dad and Steve who they followed, so Dad had his moment talking about Charlton as Pards had played for Charlton; fair play Dad, enjoy the day. Alan and Peter had both been changing for the game and they were ready to leave the room. Alan came over to me, sat down, placed his hand on my shoulder and said, "Gary we are going down to see the players now, I have spoken to Christian Daily and he should be sorting them out a little, I hope."

Peter led the way out of the office and through the corridors, schoolboy stuff or what, I seriously had to keep pinching myself, am I really here? We came to a door that read 'HOME TEAM'. Alan opened the door and that was me in the West Ham changing room, match day at Upton Park and I started to get a lump in my throat. Alan called Christian Daily over and introduced me to him, we shook hands and then he started to take me around the dressing room to meet the players, Michael Carrick, Steve Lomas, Hayden Mullins, Bobby Zamora, Marlon Harewood, Don Hutchinson to name a few! What a buzz! It seemed that there were four of five different ghetto blasters going at the same time, it was crazy and noisy. Alan and Christian were trying to get some kind of order going with them all. Alan got me to sit down on the edge of the treatment table and got all the players gathered around for group photos. It was sheer madness as they were all jumping all over each other, singing, "Ere we go! Ere we go! Ere we go!" and "Irons! Irons! Irons!"

Alan and Christian took me to one side and asked me if I would just say a few words to them, so I said I would try but I'm very emotional, but I can try. They called some order amongst the team, as best as possible and I kept what I said very simple, "Lads it is not easy for me today, thank you so much for this but most of all, please win for me today, this means so much to me and many others. As a minimum, put a shift in and make me proud of you all. I believe I lived because of this moment now. I have set the scene for you all, take it to them today and remember that shirt you are wearing means more to me than you know." That was me done and Christian could see what it meant to me. I had some tears and it was all a bit too much, just so surreal, a dreamland.

Don Hutchinson came over to me and said a lot of nice words, he was a class act, taking a brand-new West Ham shirt around to get the players to sign it for me. I got a freebie signed shirt, which was class. I said a final thank you and goodbye to the players but they were in their own worlds and I know they were focusing on the game, time to go for me. Angela met us outside the changing rooms with Alan and he said to me, "The lads have said they are not going to let us down today, thank you for doing this for me it means a lot, just enjoy the rest of the day mate. I have to get on now, lots of things to do, great to see you Gary, Angela will now spoil you, enjoy." Handshakes all around and then he was off jogging back into the changing room before going to make some interviews I believe.

Angela said, "Gary, I will take you upstairs so you can all sit down and eat your lunch, we have a great menu today for you." She led the way and we followed on and into the 'White Horse Lounge', famously named after the FA Cup Final of 1923, when a white horse came onto the pitch. There were vast numbers in the stadium that day, 126,047 (official), but 300,000 (estimated) fans had turned out to watch Bolton Wanderers vs West Ham. The name of the horse was, "Billie" and Bolton ran out two nil winners in the first ever FA Cup Final at Wembley. The West Ham team that day included, no other than the legendary Vic Watson who is the clubs leading goal scorer, scoring 326 goals for West ham, which included 13 hattricks and coincidentally he joined West Ham from Wellingborough Town; small world.

As we walked in Dad gave me a quick nudge and winked, I knew what he was trying to tell me. What a touch, he was most impressed. Angela showed us to a table and positioned in the centre of the table was a menu and my name was on the top of it. As Angela left us Dad said, "Bloody hell mate you got your own table with your name on it, come on then, let's go and get you fed blue and have few drinks." A buffet to choose from, good for me but Dad was struggling on what to choose. Steve and I made three visits, taking the opportunity to have a little of everything, Dad made up for his lack of food by his visits to the bar, typical. I was happily stuffed to say the least, sat with a soft drink and having a few Ishtar to help it digest. The clock was telling us that kick off was only fifteen minutes away, Angela came in the lounge and said, "Hi Gary, I trust you enjoyed the food?" I replied, "It was amazing Angela, spoilt for choice and we all enjoyed it, thank you." She said, "Gary I would like to take you and your Dad to your seats, Steve will sit with me in the press section, if that is ok?" Steve just nodded and seemed happy about what Angela had said, who wouldn't be, having the chance to sit with her, a lovely lady as I said and was amazing the whole day, a star.

She took us up into the stadium, it was an unbelievable feeling as the 'Theatre of Dreams' appeared once more before my eyes, very emotional, sounds silly to say but so surreal as I keep saying. Angela had arranged our seats in the Directors Box area, Dad was sat to the left of me, it was a brilliant view but I could not stop thinking that I wanted to be in the Bobby Moore Lower with the lads, that was real home for me. The players finally came out to the National Anthem of Upton Park, "I'm Forever Blowing Bubbles", being sung by 26,000 fans. What a sound and feeling, this is home for sure, what an amazing buzz.

West Ham deserved a one nil lead at half time, courtesy of Bobby Zamora scoring just after Coventry failed to clear from a corner, cool finish. I was up out of my seat but had to remember where I was, I couldn't be jumping up and down and singing for my life; not the 'done' thing up here. Dad was sure that there would be more goals in the second half, "Come On you Irons!" Just as the whistle went for half time Angela was on my shoulder and she said to me, "Gary the half time draw is going to be made by you, Alan would like you to do it please, if you can all come down with me, I can sort it from there." I looked at her and said, "You want me to go out on the pitch, and do it?" She replied, "Yes Gary, centre circle is where it is done and you will be announced onto the pitch." I said, "Angela I don't think I can do it, I think it will be too much for me to handle, if that makes any sense to you?" She looked at me, seemed to understand what I was saying and then Dad said, "Angela just give me one minute with him?" She nodded and Dad took me to one side and said, "Listen to me for once, you don't send this one back mate, get out on that pitch now. I will be down there with you, go and make me proud, let me see my boy on that turf, it will be like you're playing mate." He knew the buttons to push with me, "Ok Angela, lead the way."

We were back down near the changing rooms and as we walked past, I could see the steps leading out up onto the pitch. She walked us up and forward and I stood on the huge West Ham badge near the touchline, looking at the words in front of me, "Academy Of Football", looking all around the stadium. What a view.

It was time. The man with the microphone in the centre circle stepped up and said, "Now to make the halftime draw our very own Gary Teeley who was released last week from being held hostage in Iraq, let's give him a big round of applause and welcome him onto the pitch?" I stepped onto the pitch, tried to focus on making my steps as quick as possible and also making a point of looking around me. I could hear all the seats going back as the crowd stood up and next, I heard, "Gazza's coming home, is coming, Gazza's coming home." That was it, I was gone, that stone in my throat appeared, the emotion running through me was unreal, what a feeling, this time last week I was being told hundreds of militias were looking for me so they could sell me on and now I'm in my real home.

As I reached him in the centre circle he said, "Gary, tell us how you are feeling right now?" I was truly speechless, I managed to compose myself enough to say, "I'm ok but it is a bit hot in here, it's all a bit too much if I'm honest but I'm here." He replied, "I'm sure it must be Gary, so can I ask you to pick a number for me please?" I put my hand in the large drum, pulled out a number and hopefully the winner will remember me for many years to come knowing that I pulled it out. He then said, "Gary thank you so much for coming out here today and we all hope that you enjoy the rest of your day, once again, welcome home." We shook hands and I made my way back to the touchline. As I was walking, I turned to all sides of the ground and applauded them. What a feeling, one I will cherish for the rest of my life.

Angela was stood waiting for me, along with Steve but no sign of Dad, she suggested we should go back to the White Horse Lounge to meet up with Dad, where else could he be? We walked into the lounge and he was nowhere to be seen. Oh great, that's all I need, having to make an announcement that a Dad is missing, along the lines of, "If you find a man who answers to the name of Mick then please take him to reception!" Angela suggested that I go back to my seat and she would look for him, so we returned to the Directors Box and there he was sat in his seat. When I sat down, I said, "Where the bloody hell have you been? I came off the pitch and you were gone, we then went to the lounge to look for you but you were not there, so where you been?" Dad replied, "I left the side of the pitch to go and have a swift half in the lounge but then found myself in another kind of lounge bar but not the original one we had the food." I said, "Only you could come out with a story like that!" I can't take him anywhere.

The second half got under away and the Hammers came out flying. They dominated the game but I was nervous as I felt we needed another goal to seal it and it came in the way of a penalty, taken and scored by David Connolly; not as prolific at West Ham as he was at Wimbledon but that will do for me if we can close it out. The final whistle went and we were back in the playoff spots again. What a result, perfect ending to the game.

During the second half my phone rang, it was Rupert from the Sunday Mirror. He asked me if I was willing to make do interview for ITN News after the game, so I agreed I would do it. They had permission from West Ham that it would be done pitch side, so I had to make my way back to the White Horse Lounge where I would meet Rupert and the ITN crew. Dad, Steve and I went down to the pitch again with security and the ITN new team. They wanted to film me in the stadium, talking about the events in Iraq. Part of that meant me running up the steps from inside and out onto the area where the big West Ham badge is displayed. They made me run up the steps at least ten times and my knee was not very happy about it. I could hear my Dad say, "Hey, he hasn't come here today for a trial you know, hey Gary I think it's your medical?" He did get a laugh from a few.

The interviewer was Romilly Weeks, she was very good with me and did not press me too much. The interview was my first on television in the UK. Luckily, I was kept away from the press and media for most of the day and did not make any comments. I completed my interview with ITN News, then it was time to depart the stadium, it was all over. Angela walked me to the front entrance and I was left kind of speechless on what to say to her, it had been quite an extraordinary day to say the least. Dad and Steve both enjoyed the day, it was not about who supports who, it was about enjoying such a memorable day. A day when I was invited by Alan Pardew the West Ham Manager, I was his VIP guest, had my name included in the match day program, received a signed West Ham shirt and had every man and his dog wanting to shake my hand.

We came out onto Green Street, Steve and I walked to the car and Dad waited outside the front of the ground, how good of him. We came back to pick him up, made our way through the traffic and we got lost a little due to some road changes but it was not too much out the way, I made good progress and the journey flew by. The three of us continued talking about the events of the day. I know Steve enjoyed it because he likes football in general but for my Dad, West Ham was close to his heart, his second team. When I dropped him off at home he said, "Now that blue was a day, glad you chose me to come with you boy, one of the best days of my life, didn't we just have a day?" In my mind I said back, "That we did Dad that we did." Thank you, Alan Pardew for making a dream for me and Dad, awesome!

29 LIFE IS GOOD

On Sunday the 18th of April the Sunday Mirror was being sold as usual and included my exclusive interview for reading. If you had bought the Mail on Sunday on the same day you could read my ex-partners 'kiss and tell'; such is life.

From Monday 19th April until Saturday 24th of April I was flat out with television and radio Interviews. These interviews would go on until 2009, as after 2004 I was deemed to be an expert on hostage taking, so five years after my experience, the media continued. I think the interviews ended up helping me get things off my chest, not always easy, depending on how far I went into the very bad times, it was something that was not easy to relive.

I was taken by my captors on Monday 5th of April 2004 at 1155 hrs, I was released on Sunday 11th of April 2004 at 1500 hrs and was returned back to the UK on Wednesday 14th April at 0430 hrs. I was now back on an aeroplane to Qatar on Sunday 25th April. Many could not understand how I was able to do this but it depends how you look at it. What am I supposed to do, curl up in a ball and feel sorry for myself? That will not be the case for me, no way will they get the better of me. I get it that they felt the relative safety of the UK shores but it does not mean to say that all of the Middle East is like Iraq. I was going back to Qatar and I had no issues with Qatar whatsoever.

So many people have asked me, what was it like to have four guns held to your head? What was it like when they first ran by the windows and were coming in the villa to get you? It is nearly impossible to explain it, unless you actually reenact it and to do that, the person would have to agree to go through the pain barrier and I don't think any normal person would agree to take that.

After 2004 I travelled quite a lot to Lebanon, Syria to do consultancy work and I was never fazed by being there. I remember back in 2006 when I was in Syria, we were in the car and all of a sudden, I saw a roadside sign and it said, 'Baghdad 248KMS' and at the same time my good friend Nadal looked at me and we laughed at each other and he said, "Are you ok you feel nervous?"

On Tuesday 9th of January 2007, I was in Qatar and my phone rang. I looked at the screen and the country code of Iraq came up. I took the call and on answering I was given the news that an aircraft flying from Turkey to Iraq had crash landed and only one person had survived. Paul was on the flight and died on landing. Moments after receiving the call I had to phone his Dad in America to give him the news, not easy to do but I had to do it.

Paul Johnson was an American man who I had a lot of respect for, a great genuine and caring man. We had some great laughs and times over the three years I knew him and Paul helped me so much at a time in my life where I was not sure where it was going. As the story says, we went to Iraq together, I left and he stayed, only for me to return in the March to relieve him of his work so he could go home and see his newborn, Donald. That's how much I thought of Paul, I felt like I had to repay him, I went back to the lion's den for him.

Just after Paul's death I sat one day and was thinking it should have been him and not me who was taken but if it had been Paul, many say he would not have come out alive. Paul carried a lot of guilt around with him because of what happened to me. He always said that it should have been him, not me and that he was so sorry about it all. I could always see it in his eyes and hear it in his tone. Paul, it was never your fault mate, just bad luck on my part. Thank you for helping me when I needed help and I am sorry that I could not be there for you to catch you. You will never be forgotten in my life… cheers mate.

History cannot be re-written. I was the first official civilian hostage taken on the 5th of April 2004. After me they fell like dominoes over the coming weeks and months of 2004. I never knowingly had any nightmares or bad days, until September 2004. I was contacted by various media outlets when Mr. Ken Bigley and two Americans had been taken and I knew which group had taken them. The media were pushing me to be interviewed and make comments of these sorts of experiences, what they were going through and what could be the outcome? From memory, it is the only time that I had turned down an interview as I felt very uncomfortable about this. What gives me the right to gloat about my survival when I knew deep down Ken was never going to survive his ordeal. The group who had Ken, he had no chance. Rest in peace Ken.

One of the most frightening things is, to this day, I find it hard to recognise fear. How can I be in fear when I have experienced something as strange as that? Of course, I see it and feel it but it does not bother me, after all what could be worse? I know I don't like anyone to control me, take my freedom of space or choice away, for me it brings back the memories of having that freedom taken from me and being taken hostage in a hostile country with militia as my babysitters.

Since 2004, I cannot count the number of times I have stepped in, defused many fights and arguments, suggested to people that it is better to shake hands and move on. Life is so short if we think about it, make the most of it.

So, what happened leading up to the 5th of April 2004, was there any warning for the week ahead? The 31st of March saw the American military step up its power in the City of Fallujah in the North of Iraq after an incident where five private security operatives from American company Black Water were ambushed, burned and butchered before being hung from a bridge over the Euphrates River. It was reported that Abu Musab Al-Zarqawi was behind it all. Zarqawi of course had his fate sealed June 2006 with two 500lb bombs being dropped on a meeting he had attended. Al-Zarqawi and his followers had taken Ken. It later came out that Ahmad Hashim Abd Al–Isawi was responsible for the slaughter and butchery. The 4th of April saw the American Marine Commanders hit Fallujah with around 2,000 troops.

So came the time of the spring uprising. The first was the rise of a conservative Shiite cleric called Muqtada Al Sadr and his militia, the Mehdi Army, in the south of the country. Muqtada al-Sadr also had great influence in the Sadr City section of Baghdad (Sadr City, which was Saddam City, was renamed after the invasion, in honour of Sadr's father, Grand Ayatollah Mohammad Mohammad Sadeq al-Sadr). With the fall of Saddam Hussein, Muqtada al-Sadr emerged as a Shia leader by rejecting the US-led occupation of Iraq. Al-Sadr created the Mehdi Army in June 2003. Muqtada Al Sadr opposed the Americans coalition forces being in Iraq and he ordered his Mehdi Army to take hostages, go on the offensive where they could. Al Sadr's father was a religious leader and politician and he was opposed to Saddam Hussein; his grandfather apparently murdered by Saddam Hussein's government. Tuesday the 6th of April, the battle that raged for eleven hours or so, between the Italians and the Mehdi Army, it was one of many battles that was kicking off all over Iraq.

When I look back, do I have anything against those that took me? I thought about this long and hard and asked myself, how would I feel if I had a foreign force in my country? Would I like the chance of a reunion with them? Haha, no chance! Not even to ask them how they feel about it now, I know the answers and at the end of the day I got out alive.

To this day people ask me how I got released and I don't know the real answers. I was told so many different things, from a daring SAS raid to the local Sheikhs coming through and speaking to Mr. Al Sadr for me. Whoever it was, thank you and I owe you my life.

For Mr. A and Mr. H during this story I did not use their real names, why? When I was back in the UK, I had a phone call from Scotland Yard and they wanted to visit me. I could have said no but I was willing to give up my time, free of charge so they could ask me some questions. My Mum was polite enough to allow them to come to her house and talk to me, face to face. I answered all their questions honestly and truthfully to the best of my knowledge but there was no way on this earth that I was going to give the full details of Mr. A and Mr. H.

Mr. A, well his name was Adel and Mr. H was Hashem and at a later date I was able to speak to them on the telephone when I was in Qatar. I found out that they actually worked for an organisation, and it was an organisation that worked on hostage release and prisoner release... now it made sense. I owe Hashem and Adel my life but how do I repay them? How can you repay someone who saves your life? So, was I going to shit on them in an interview, absolutely not, not ever! Just for the record, those who came to my Mum's house from Scotland Yard had to be shown the door as they kind of messed up the hard and soft guy pitch. Oh well. Thank you, Hashem and Adel.

My Dad passed away in October 2008 and I know that April 2004 with Alan Pardew, left a long and lasting impression with him. He would always speak of that day when he got the chance in front of others for bragging rights. Fair play to you Dad, as you said when I dropped you off, "Didn't we have a day boy?" I'm so happy that I chose Dad to come with me that day. Good call Gazza.

My Mum passed away in July 2018. Without going into too much detail of her death, right or wrong, I contribute part of her death from what happened to me in Iraq and therefore blame myself for part of her demise in health. We all deal with things differently in life; I moved on immediately but my Mum could never forget. Whether it is right or wrong, many times she would bring it up in conversation and yes, she used to get some weird, bizarre looks and comments but as I said, each to their own. My Mum could never come to terms with what they did to me, not that I never told her everything, she had so much anger in her and emotion about it. Who suffered the most from my experience, I believe it was my Mum and I knew it when I was being held. I was trying to shut myself off from thinking about it but deep down, I knew and the guilt was killing me. I'm so sorry Mum for what happened, I did not see it coming. I thought I was safe until the Americans turned the heat up and the locals responded, what else they could do?

Eighteen years on and I'm still in the Middle East, back in Qatar who are hosting the Football World Cup 2022. Did April 2004 really happen? Now it is just a faded memory. Did the events finally catch up with me and change me? It many ways it did catch up with me and I have to live with it.

But I survived and I am doing just fine.

Printed in Great Britain
by Amazon

27702466R00126